Rise to the Challenge

RISE
TO THE
CHALLENGE

A Memoir of Politics, Leadership, and Love

*To Susan —
with thanks for all
your support for Peter —*

MARLENE M. JOHNSON

Marlene

University of Minnesota Press
Minneapolis
London

Published by the University of Minnesota Press
111 Third Avenue South, Suite 290
Minneapolis, MN 55401-2520
http://www.upress.umn.edu

ISBN 978-1-5179-1761-6 (hc)
ISBN 978-1-5179-1801-9 (pb)

A Cataloging-in-Publication record for this book is available
from the Library of Congress.

Printed in the United States of America on acid-free paper

The University of Minnesota is an equal-opportunity educator and employer.

32 31 30 29 28 27 26 25 24   10 9 8 7 6 5 4 3 2 1

For my parents, Helen and Beauford, my first guides
For Peter, whose love and enthusiasm changed my world

Contents

Prologue

January 4, 1983, was a chilly Minnesota day. As usual, I woke up early, but that would be the only usual aspect of the day. Today I was to be sworn in as Minnesota's first woman lieutenant governor—and at thirty-seven years of age perhaps one of the youngest as well. I recalled the final words that Sigurd Olson typed before he set out on what would be his final cross-country ski trip: "A New Adventure is coming up and I'm sure it will be a good one." Aspects of this day already signaled the many new experiences I would face during the subsequent eight years. But at that moment, I was focused on the immediate requirements of my swearing-in.

As my excited staff and I prepared to walk to the Rotunda of the State Capitol for the ceremony, we were interrupted by my friend Vivian Jenkins Nelsen, who stopped by with a gardenia in her hand. She pinned it to my lapel, commenting that "no lieutenant governor should be without a flower." Her gesture touched my heart and helped me walk taller as I headed out the door to take the oath of office. The memory of this moment has often reminded me how small acts of kindness can have large and unexpected impacts.

The Braham, Minnesota, primary school's choir opened the swearing-in ceremony. The choir director, Paul Wrege, had been my high school choir director. Now, listening to the music program, I deeply appreciated his initiative in bringing the choir to the Capitol that day. The children performed on the upper level of the Rotunda, overlooking the space below where the audience was assembled.

My sisters and brothers, aunts and uncles, and many friends were present, and I was particularly moved to see longtime friends I hadn't expected. Among those were Muriel and Mark Wexler, smiling broadly as we caught each other's eyes. I recalled fondly the two summers I had spent as an au pair in their home. We had stayed in touch, although we hadn't seen each other for a few years. Having them with me as I began this new journey was a special gift.

My mother held the Bible on which I placed my hand, and my long-time Macalester friend Municipal Judge Harriet Lansing, a judicial appointee of Governor Rudy Perpich in his first term, administered the oath of office. In my brief inaugural speech, I noted the historic nature of my election, acknowledged my mother for her guidance and support, and expressed my sadness that my father was not there to share this moment. I applauded Governor Perpich's vision for expanding opportunity for women and people of diverse ethnicities, and spoke to the administration's agenda for tourism as an economic driver in the state's economy. I concluded by saying, "When one of us does something that hasn't been done before, it changes things for all of us." This phrase guided many of my initiatives throughout the years.

My inauguration was a breakthrough for women in state government and a step on the journey to a public service career that I had envisioned for myself, yet it had happened so fast it was hard to believe. I felt ready for a new challenge, while at the same time I was aware that I had much to learn and that my long-held professional and personal insecurities lingered. I was excited to get started and determined to do all I could to do a good job and help create more opportunities for women and minorities in state government.

I doubt that my family was that surprised about this moment. Among my siblings, I had been the one engaged in advocacy and politics, following in our dad's leadership footsteps. My siblings had often teased me about always being in charge and starting new things, and periodically suggested I would run for office someday. It was my family who had instilled in me the values of public responsibility and service.

At the time of my election along with Governor Perpich, the women's political movement was in its second decade, yet in most U.S. states the number of women who held elective office at any level was in the single digits. In his earlier term in office, Governor Perpich had established his personal commitment to increasing the role of women in government with his 1978 appointment of Rosalie Wahl as the first woman to serve as a justice on the Minnesota Supreme Court. He had also created the Open Appointments Commission to advise him on candidates for seats on state boards and commissions. His choice of me as his running mate was further evidence of his ongoing commitment to expanding opportunities for women and people of color.

For me, serving as lieutenant governor was a chance to learn about state government and gubernatorial leadership as I assumed primary responsibility for the areas Governor Perpich had assigned to me in the administration: leading the open appointments process, with the goal of expanding opportunities for women and people of color, and establishing tourism as key to Minnesota's economic development. Once in the role, I also came to understand how persuasion and influence could be used to open doors. I came to recognize the opportunities offered by leadership in a broader frame, a perspective that would expand my understanding of the diverse positions from which one can lead. These experiences served me well throughout the professional roles I would later play in the private and public sectors and in my volunteer leadership roles in nonprofit organizations.

My eight years of public service were an extraordinary experience, despite the particular challenges and disappointments of the final year. Early in our first term I met Peter Frankel, the Swedish businessman who would become my husband and chief supporter, helping me recognize my professional capacity and strengthening my self-confidence. Later, during the period of transition from public to private life, then finding a new career path, Peter's support strengthened my resolve to move forward and gave me the confidence to accept an exciting new challenge. Our transatlantic life and my international education leadership work felt like the perfect continuation of my public role in Minnesota. The rhythm of my life was a rich mix of public policy, management, public affairs, higher education strategies to expand international education, personal and professional travel, and family engagement in Minnesota, Sweden, and Washington.

With the encouragement of Peter and many friends, I had long considered writing a memoir, but the demands of my professional and management responsibilities left me neither the time nor the inclination to tackle such a project. Then in August 2010 Peter fell down a flight of stairs, suffering a permanent brain injury. I mourned the loss of my vibrant husband and the relationship we had forged. Now Peter's care and engagement with him at whatever level was possible became my new normal. At the time of his injury, I was the CEO of an international education nonprofit organization, a role I thoroughly enjoyed. My leadership was well received there and produced considerable success for the organization, but at a personal level, I felt deep sadness and loneliness. Yet despite my personal crisis in managing Peter's care I found strength and capabilities I did not know I had.

In the following years with Peter, every day I faced the reality that he was not the person I married. While physically present and aware of a few things, he could not give me the feedback, encouragement, and warmth I had come to count on. Being with him, observing him, reflecting on and figuring out what his needs were at any moment, I recalled the perspectives and ideas he had shared over the years, and I was reminded of how profound each person's gifts of love and guidance to others can be.

‖‖‖

Writing this memoir has helped me understand that my capacity for leadership, support, and collaboration has been the thread connecting the elements of what anthropologist Mary Catherine Bateson has described as "composing a life." From organizing my first small service "club" of girlfriends in primary school to responding to my parents' encouragement to propose to our local school board that foreign-language instruction be added to the curriculum in my high school, I learned early not to blindly accept the status quo and to work with others toward making change.

While attending Macalester College, I found myself in the heart of local government when I organized my fellow students to participate in St. Paul politics. Then, as a young entrepreneur with no previous business experience, I quickly learned about the power of the support of other women entrepreneurs, which contributed significantly to my success and well-being. As we organized to create a network of like-minded entrepreneurial women for moral support and technical guidance, we soon experienced the impact we could have collectively in the larger community. Organizing political women and serving on several community boards expanded my understanding of the community and where the opportunities for influence were greatest. When public leadership came calling and I was elected Minnesota's first woman lieutenant governor, I had the chance to define a role and demonstrate leadership in a broader environment.

By the time I served as CEO of a major nonprofit organization, the patchwork of my life experience had given me a rich base from which to work. The values of my family and community—working for change, supporting each other, and considering our impacts on others—were common threads. From each platform (organizing students to engage in local politics, encouraging women entrepreneurs to band together for personal and professional support, and organizing women to become candidates and actively support each other), collaboration and mutual support became the essential aspects of my leadership.

Peter's personal encouragement and generous professional guidance enhanced my skills and strengthened my confidence in ways that would have been unimaginable earlier in my life, and for this I am eternally grateful. I have relearned the value of listening, of seeking alternative ideas in search of a desired outcome; I know now that it is often possible to create change and solve problems from outside the expected framework, and that engaging a diverse group of individuals to address a problem will inevitably produce exciting and unexpected results.

I have also learned that it is essential to pay attention to the quality and talent of the individuals I choose as partners, and that my leadership responsibilities include supporting each member of the team by setting parameters, nurturing individual members, showing kindness and generosity, encouraging collaboration, and overcoming unhelpful distance among various individuals and teams within the organization. Further, I have come to understand that leading by example—in the way we treat others, in our choice of language, and in how we respond to crisis—affects our capacity for leadership and ultimately determines how others learn to assume leadership as well. Recalling Vivian Jenkins Nelsen's kindness to me on the day of my swearing-in ceremony, I have been more intentional about the details of leadership, from sharing lunch with staff to inviting less likely individuals to lead staff discussions, choosing staff holiday gifts to honor historic moments, and writing personal notes to celebrate individual achievements or acknowledge personal challenges.

This memoir is an exploration of my private and public leadership journey, and the special role that Peter played, both in our first twenty years together, when his support was active and enthusiastic, and later, when his early voice of support stayed with me as I learned how to lead from the role of a spouse advocating for the visibility and needs of one who could not speak for himself.

I

.,\\\\\\\\|||||||////,

Minnesota's First Woman Lieutenant Governor

Looking around at those gathered for my swearing-in ceremony, I knew that the historic nature of this moment was on everyone's mind. This day was the first postelection opportunity to celebrate my election and the official start of a woman's role at this level in state government. The Rotunda of the Minnesota State Capitol quickly filled with family and friends, state government staff, and others from all walks of life. The audience included many parents bringing their daughters to witness this historic event that represented another crack in the glass ceiling. My mother was so proud, and we both quietly acknowledged to each other how proud my dad would have been. As nervous as I was, it was reassuring to have Judge Harriet Lansing, my longtime friend from college, administer the oath of office.

I'd written my inaugural speech over New Year's weekend at a burger joint in Helena, Montana, where I had spent a few days cross-country skiing with my Macalester College roommate, Montana rancher Cathy Campbell. In the speech, I applauded Governor Rudy Perpich's vision for expanding opportunities for women and people of diverse ethnicities in his earlier service as governor in 1976–78, noted the historic nature of my election in 1982, and spoke to the Perpich–Johnson administration's commitment to focusing on tourism as a key component of Minnesota's economic development and further expanding the participation of women and people of color in state government. The concluding sentence of my speech summarized the view that has guided my work throughout the years: "When one of us does something that hasn't been done before, it changes things for all of us."

We had initially assumed that Governor Perpich and I would be sworn in at a common ceremony in the State Capitol. In a private meeting during the transition, however, the governor shared with me that his swearing-in ceremony would be held at the Hibbing High School, with Justice Rosalie Wahl officiating. He wanted his inauguration to reinforce the importance of his Iron Range roots and the community of friends who had played a significant role in his election, as well as his commitment to education as the "passport out of poverty." Governor Perpich told me that he also felt that having my own swearing-in ceremony would give greater visibility to the historic aspect of my election as the first woman lieutenant governor. This conversation would be one among many during the course of our two terms in which the governor's privately shared guidance encouraged me to recognize an opportunity.

The governor's decision put the responsibility for planning my inauguration in the hands of my team. We decided on a ceremony in the Capitol Rotunda, a break from the tradition of holding such events in the legislative chambers. There would be limited seating and standing room for the two hundred to three hundred people in attendance for the fifteen-minute ceremony. Paul Wrege, my high school choir director and now director of the primary school music program in my hometown of Braham, Minnesota, offered to bring the primary school choir to perform and share this historic moment in Braham's history as well. We accepted this lovely offer immediately.

Following the swearing-in ceremony, at the invitation of the governor, my family and a few friends joined me for a luncheon at the Governor's Residence, where we enjoyed a lovely private extension of the inaugural celebration. As we shared stories and reflected on the events of the day, we recalled my first public advocacy experience, when, as a teenager, I urged our local school board to add two years of foreign-language instruction to the high school curriculum.

My petition to the school board was indirectly prompted by Minnesota's attorney general, Walter Mondale (who would later serve as our U.S. senator and as U.S. vice president under President Jimmy Carter), who had recommended that I apply to Macalester College. As executive director of Minnesota's first electric cooperative, my father made regular day trips to the Twin Cities, and in early 1962 I accompanied him on one such trip, during which we met with Mondale. Dad told the attorney general that I was starting to research colleges to attend and asked if he had a recommendation. When Mondale learned of my interest in politics and law, he suggested that I consider Macalester. He had attended the school himself for a couple of years, and he had married the daughter of Macalester's chaplain. Mondale shared stories about a favorite political science professor, G. Theodore Mitau, and I was hooked! I wrote to the college for information and started planning.

The first thing I learned was that Macalester required incoming students to have had two years of high school foreign-language study. I was dismayed, as Braham's high school did not offer any foreign-language instruction. My parents urged me to petition the school board to add two years of foreign-language instruction to the curriculum. I built a case and presented a proposal to the school board. The board's consideration of my proposal was not without conflict—even the parents of one of my friends felt that it was inappropriate for a student to advocate in this way and were upset that my parents had encouraged me.

Fortunately, there was considerable support for the change in curriculum, including from the high school's faculty. One of the athletic coaches had minored in Spanish in college and saw this as an opportunity to expand his teaching portfolio. So I was able to take Spanish during my junior and senior years, which allowed me to apply to Macalester College. Foreign-language learning was always challenging for me, but the experience of advocating to the school board piqued my interest in public activism.

At the time of my inauguration in 1983, my family and most of my friends did not know that for the previous couple of years I had discussed the idea of running for office with a small group of confidants. An entrepreneur friend had commented that she believed my passion was public service and social change rather than business. As she saw it, I had pursued having my own business primarily because it enabled me to make a living while establishing visibility in the community. She advised me to embrace my interest in public leadership and start actively thinking about how to do it.

Although I had thought about running for governor, my life as an entrepreneur didn't offer a clear view of how that could happen from a base other than the legislature. A legislative vacancy that I might fill in the State Senate or in the House district where I lived seemed unlikely. Then my state senator, Nicholas Coleman, announced his retirement in 1980. I briefly considered running for that State Senate seat until County Commissioner Diane Ahrens announced her candidacy. She had been a strong supporter of mine, including recommending me for appointment to the board of Landmark Center in St. Paul. I would not run against her. I also felt more suited to the executive branch. Governor Perpich's invitation to join him on the ticket in 1982 was consistent with what I had already been thinking about.

Running for lieutenant governor felt like the natural outcome of my range of experiences over the past fifteen years. One of the less recognized advantages of growing up in a small town is that one inherently develops an awareness of society beyond the town in the course of one's everyday life. During my childhood, school athletic and music competitions required bus travel to other towns virtually every week, so I gained a sense of the larger state; in contrast, those who grow up in a big city might rarely travel beyond the borders of that city. My parents were active in our community, and my father founded and led the state's first electric co-op, which gave him a strong sense of being part of the national strategy for bringing electricity to rural America. Our family discussed political issues on a daily basis and had contact with political leaders such as then U.S. senator Hubert Humphrey, Congressman John Blatnik, and Minnesota governor Orville Freeman.

An interest in other societies and cultures was also central to our family. We made many excursions into the Twin Cities for entertainment, to see films such as *Around the World in 80 Days* or to enjoy the Ice Capades or dinner at Fuji Ya Japanese restaurant. Summer vacations were cross-country road trips, visiting national parks and historic sites and learning about the vast cultural complexity of our country. At home we celebrated United Nations Day and supported UNICEF as we learned about other cultures. Our family hosted my half sisters' international student friends from St. Cloud Teachers' College, some of whom became longtime family friends. And we were the host family to New Zealander Graham Collins, Braham's third American Field Service student.

A second thread in my development was my business career. I cofounded a marketing and communications business in 1970, which provided financial independence and gave me a leadership position from which I could participate in the community. Women's entrepreneurship was emerging in the 1970s, so those of us leading our own firms had more visibility than might otherwise have been the case. As community organizations began to feel the need to include women among their leadership ranks, entrepreneurial women were tapped for these opportunities simply because we were CEOs, albeit of our own small firms. Generally, chambers of commerce represented the interests of larger businesses, and there were no women in leadership at the Fortune 500 companies in the Twin Cities in the 1970s. Few of the women entrepreneurs I knew felt welcome at their local chambers of commerce. Then one day the *St. Paul Pioneer Press* featured a story about Susan Sands, an entrepreneur with a new business. I phoned her immediately. Soon we were in her attic office getting acquainted. It was a relief to have someone to talk to about the travails of day-to-day life as an entrepreneur. A few years later, we shared an office space, and then we worked together to create the Minnesota Chapter of the National Association of Women Business Owners (NAWBO).

Third, my engagement in community and political activities broadened my perspective and expanded my network of friends and resources, increased my confidence, and improved my sense of well-being. Not having grown up in St. Paul, I lacked a natural network there. A common anecdote among St. Paul residents was that no one ever moved more than one zip code away or beyond the Catholic parish they had grown up in. Being a single woman added to my challenges, as invitations to social business events were generally extended to couples. Thankfully, my service on community boards introduced me to business and community leaders I would not have met otherwise and helped me understand the range of needs and resources in the community. Initially, I was invited to serve on the board of Working Women, a local nonprofit devoted to helping women who were transitioning from managing households and family care to jobs in the commercial sector. I soon learned that I was recruited to help address an ongoing management crisis. I was disappointed that the organization's leaders had not been forthcoming about the situation when they invited me to serve, but through my work with them I gained new confidence in my ability to play a constructive role in addressing such problems. And, importantly, I learned much about the emerging need in the community to support women entering the workforce.

Fourth, I had played leadership roles in fostering women's participation in politics. When Jeannette Wagner and I founded our business Split Infinitive in 1970, we announced in our initial statement about the firm that our work holidays would be on the birthdays of Elizabeth Cady Stanton and Shirley Chisholm rather than those of Abraham Lincoln and George Washington. In 1972 I was an early supporter of Chisholm's candidacy for president of the United States, and I was determined to support women in politics. The opportunity to do that came that same year, when Linda Berglin, one of Split Infinitive's freelance graphic designers, decided to run for a seat in the state legislature. Her south Minneapolis district was a short drive from our office. Door-to-door candidate and volunteer visits throughout her legislative district were an essential aspect of her campaign, and I committed to be Linda's door-knocking partner.

It was a marathon strategy and required consistently high energy. I accompanied Linda five days a week, each of us knocking on doors on one side of the street. At the end of each block we touched base to share information and keep each other motivated. Linda was the first woman to run in this district, and there were those even in the Democratic–Farmer–Labor (DFL) Party who felt the district was not ready for a woman. Following a couple of hours of door knocking, we would join other campaign workers for a burger at the local pub. At times I was also Linda's advocate in private meetings with party leaders who took issue with various things she was doing; their complaints often seemed to reflect their discomfort with having a woman candidate. As I learned more about campaigning, I came to appreciate my instincts for the strategies and day-to-day decision making required in a grassroots campaign.

2

.\\\\\\\\\\|||||||||//////.

From Private Citizen to Public Servant

The June 9, 1982, announcement of my candidacy marked the begin-ning of a balancing act, as I strove to keep my business operating while actively campaigning for the office of lieutenant governor. It was a turbulent time for the business, organizationally and financially. Our election victory required a permanent shift of focus for me and an operational solution for the business.

This was also an emotional and uncertain time for Split Infinitive's whole team. Having my mother in the office as the bookkeeper and my aunt as administrative assistant helped considerably. They understood the business and gave me honest assessments and recommended action as necessary. My mother and aunt thoroughly enjoyed working together and with me, and they had long supported the business in countless ways. We had built the business for twelve years, and the agency had provided a platform from which to serve our clients while allowing me to assume a range of leadership roles in the community. Now, the end of that chapter evoked feelings of loss and sadness along with the excitement of new challenges—a powerful lesson in adapting to change!

A fellow NAWBO member from Chicago agreed to buy the business and manage it day to day. Ultimately, she closed it a year later, but that year provided valuable transition time for staff and clients.

The transition period between the election and the inauguration was a time of intense learning. During the campaign, the governor had repeatedly articulated his vision for the lieutenant governor to take on two specific roles: leader of the state's tourism agenda and cochair of the Open Appointments Commission. Now we needed to put specific strategies in place to fulfill that vision.

The Perpich transition team was established immediately after our victory in the primary election, as it was widely assumed that we would win the general election. Terry Montgomery, the governor's chief of staff in his 1976–78 term, led the team and would serve as chief of staff in the administration. Immediately following the general election in November, the transition team moved to offices in the Capitol designated for the governor's staff; an office was also designated for the lieutenant governor's team, although we did not have a paid transition staff. George Perpich, the governor's brother, and George's wife, Connie, served as my advisers on transition matters.

In a private meeting soon after the election, the governor counseled me on three points. First, he gave me an open invitation to attend any meetings on his schedule unless specifically told otherwise. This meant, he said, that I could look at his schedule and determine if I wanted to attend particular meetings and then just walk in. He would inform Terry Montgomery, chief of staff, and Lynn Olson, deputy chief of staff, of his invitation and expectation. The governor shared with me that during his years as lieutenant governor with Governor Wendell Anderson, he had never participated in a meeting with or had a private meeting with the governor. He was clear that he wanted a working arrangement with me that was in direct contrast to his earlier personal experience as lieutenant governor.

Second, he encouraged me to hold a meeting during the transition period involving all of the stakeholders I envisioned to be part of our tourism strategy. This would give me a chance to articulate my vision, give the parties an opportunity to start reflecting on how it could work, and create visibility for our intention to strengthen the tourism promotion strategy.

Finally, the governor recommended that I resist the legislative pressure to give up the separate lieutenant governor's office to share office space with the governor's team. He felt that I would be more independent and effective with my own office and staff.

From that point on, I was on my own during the transition, to staff my office and begin to frame the agendas that I would lead. My vision was to build a tourism industry that would have an increased impact on Minnesota's economy. I proposed creating an advisory committee to analyze the industry sectors and the economic impact of each, and to identify strategic promotions and ways to finance them with public and private sources. The approach was new, but interest grew as the discussion evolved. The tourism staff recognized that this expanded focus was an exciting step and created potential to grow the tourism marketing program significantly.

Early in the transition, I invited representatives of the hospitality industry, performing arts organizations, government leaders, and professional sports organizations to a meeting in the Capitol. Among the participants was John Myers, retired chairman of Waldorf Paper and chairman of the Saint Paul Chamber Orchestra board of directors. He was enthusiastic about this strategy. He and I had become friends when the Saint Paul Chamber Orchestra was a client of Split Infinitive, and he understood that his public profile added credibility to my effort to build this unlikely coalition. Attendees also included the director of state parks, the director of the Minnesota Historical Society, and senior staff from the Minnesota Twins. All of the attendees were meeting new people and were uncertain about how this strategy would work, but they were curious, and ultimately there was considerable enthusiasm for the potential of the strategy.

Today this approach is common practice, but in 1982 the public policy conversation about tourism as an economic driver was focused solely on the hospitality industry. "Destinations" such as performing arts venues, professional sports arenas, parks and trails, and historic sites were not widely recognized as valuable pieces of the tourism economic development strategy. Our early work paved the way.

Over time, I came to appreciate how important this initial meeting was for my personal understanding of the possibilities and opportunities of public leadership. In the years to follow, I observed time and again how people tend to give priority attention to invitations from public officials, and also how gathering people from disparate perspectives can enrich discussions and outcomes. I used this approach many times during our two terms in office, both in the ongoing expansion of the tourism program and in advancing the set of policy goals that came to be known as the Children's Agenda. Engaging diverse perspectives became a core element of my leadership strategy throughout my career.

Establishing a lieutenant governor's office was uncharted territory for me and for the Perpich–Johnson administration. No previous Minnesota lieutenant governor had ever been charged with specific policy responsibilities. I needed a staff capable of creating and advancing this new role. Although I had hired staff for my business, the requirements this time were different: I needed individuals who understood the historic nature of this new lieutenant governor's office and were comfortable with women's leadership, who believed in government service, and who wanted to help create the lieutenant governor's leadership role in the areas of tourism and the open appointments process.

There were no political operatives standing in line to work for the lieutenant governor. The position was not viewed as one from which important policy work would get done. Further, the experience of women leaders in the 1970s, and my experience in business, was that few men applied for jobs with women-owned firms unless they were responding to blind advertisements that did not mention the names of the businesses. The position of lieutenant governor had no power, and as the first woman in the position, I was not seen as a potential future governor. Working in my office was not considered to be a viable path to success for an aspiring political operative. While the governor had been explicit during both the campaign and the transition about the leadership role I would be taking in the appointments process and the advancement of tourism, those directives were not widely recognized or understood.

Dorothy Dahlenburg agreed to serve as my chief of staff. She had been around politics and understood the dynamics even though she had not been a traditional "operative." She had a strong, quiet personality and critical inner strength. I had known her for years and trusted her. We wanted our staff to reflect the diversity that the administration was committed to creating throughout state government. Our initial team comprised one white man, one Black woman, and three white women: working alongside me were a scheduler who had previously worked in local government, a receptionist, a speechwriter, and a caseworker. We were young, with modest political and government experience. We shared an excitement about the historic nature of the work ahead, re-defining the lieutenant governor's role to encompass specific respon-sibilities for the administration's efforts to increase inclusivity in state government and to establish tourism as a recognized part of the Minne-sota economy.

While creating the office and hiring staff, I was also facing further adjustments as I moved from the position of private citizen and small business owner to that of public official, and the strain on my comfort zone was beyond anything I could have anticipated. While I had been in leadership roles at each stage of my life, I had not understood how introverted I was. I was comfortable on my own and at home. To the extent that I wanted a social life, I created it. Now, my daily schedule in-cluded public events requiring me to "perform" and engage. Even going to the grocery store or the gas station, I often encountered spontaneous comments from people I didn't know. One of my coping habits, once I'd returned to the safety of my team's offices, was to ignore people or cut them off, to keep a distance. On one particular day, I behaved that way, and the impact on my staff was harsh, but I did not notice. Dorothy Dahlenburg then followed me into my private office, closed the door, sat down, looked me straight in the eye, and said, "That is the last time you will treat anyone that way."

The quiet, forceful tone she used was like water splashed on my face. I was stunned, embarrassed, and filled with regret. She reminded me that I had to be intentional in my daily interactions. My public role must be thoughtful and consistent, and my personal insecurities must be ad-dressed privately. Dorothy's feedback was a huge gift and has stayed in my ear since.

Soon after we had staffed the office, we invited the archivist for the Minnesota Historical Society to advise us on record-keeping protocols. Because of my position as Minnesota's first woman lieutenant gover-nor, we wanted our records to accurately reflect the historic and sub-stantive role of the office.

A few years earlier, Nina Archabal had become deputy director of the Minnesota Historical Society, and she recognized that the society's archives were lacking in their coverage of the contributions of women to Minnesota's economy, cultural life, and social services. She initiated a project to address this gap, and I was one of the beneficiaries of her vision. The society's archivist staff worked with the staff of my small business, Split Infinitive, to organize our records, which we then donated to the archives. Now I wanted to ensure that at this historic moment, the best protocols were put in place to preserve the records of the office of Minnesota's first woman lieutenant governor.

3

.\\\.

Becoming an Entrepreneur

Since high school I had harbored the idea of going to law school. Yet during the summer after I graduated from Macalester, having spent several weeks working on Eugene McCarthy's presidential campaign, I lacked a sense of what came next for me. I took the Law School Admission Test and applied to William Mitchell College of Law in St. Paul. My heart wasn't in it, so when my application was rejected because of my poor LSAT scores, I felt certain that I wasn't smart enough for law school. An attorney friend offered to help me appeal the decision, but the rejection letter brought back all sorts of academic insecurities from my years at Macalester. In my first two years at Mac I had struggled academically. When I received an F in French at the end of my sophomore year, my poor academic standing resulted in my expulsion. I successfully negotiated a return with specific academic performance requirements, met them, and graduated with my class. But the whole experience was exhausting and had seriously compromised my self-confidence. I wanted to leave academics behind.

I had no clear career goals beyond wanting to work in some area concerning human rights or the reduction of poverty. President Lyndon Johnson's "war on poverty" was an initiative I believed in and wanted to be part of. To pay the rent while looking for a permanent position, I took jobs through a temp agency—my first direct exposure to the world of blue-collar employment. In one position I constructed packing boxes, and later I folded and packaged laundered clothes for a firm that served janitorial businesses. In both cases, the strict routines, short, controlled break times and lunch periods, discouragement of socializing among the workers, and limited interaction with supervisory staff felt stifling. The work was tedious and potentially unsafe, and no safety training was provided. My exposure to this aspect of factory work raised my awareness of the value of union representation, an insight that remained with me when I participated in state policy discussions years later. Even now when I read an account of worker safety issues or the problem of repetitive stress injuries at Tyson plants, Amazon warehouses, and other work settings, those brief personal experiences clarify for me the challenges and injustices still often faced by today's workers.

In November 1968, I proposed to the director of St. Paul's antipoverty agency an entrepreneurial experience for young people that included establishing a Christmas tree selling location in their neighborhood. The director was a risk-taking, creative person who decided to give it a try. The project achieved modest success, but it required too much oversight to scale to similar projects. In this first professional job, I experienced how motivational it is to have a boss who is willing to take a chance on the ideas of an enthusiastic young person who might have limited experience. This was my introduction to a learning organization. Subsequently, I worked as director of the agency's inner-city youth programs, before running the summer youth program at the St. Paul YMCA, serving as the first woman program director at the St. Paul Y.

The summer youth program provided local young people with a day on a houseboat on the St. Croix River, with swimming, nature, and food. In addition to directing that program, I was responsible for working with neighborhood organizations to recruit youth to participate. The Y hired a communications freelancer, Jeannette Wagner, to help us promote the program. I enjoyed working with Jeannette—she was creative and had practical advice to offer, and I found it comforting to have a female colleague. Most important, I learned the difference between running a program and promoting one. It soon became clear to me that building a new program was a full-time job, and promoting it another job entirely. Trying to do both risked doing neither well. I wasn't successful in communicating that conundrum to my boss at the time, but I have remembered it as I've worked in a variety of management roles since then.

By the end of the summer, Jeannette and I had started talking about establishing our own business, doing communications/marketing for nonprofit organizations. This was 1970; I was two years out of college, with limited experience to bring to such an endeavor. Jeannette had worked at an advertising agency previously, so she knew the basics of the business. We considered my limited experience in nonprofits as our other "expertise"!

Jeannette's husband would support her while we started this endeavor. I was on my own, and the Y agreed to keep me employed on a part-time basis for a year, ensuring I'd be able to pay my rent and eat while we got started. Our office was in the basement of Jeannette's home on East Franklin in Southeast Minneapolis, our desk a door across two two-drawer file cabinets. We pooled our cash resources (two hundred dollars each) to buy a rebuilt Selectric typewriter. Split Infinitive—Advertising, Public Relations, and General Brilliance was our name and our intended image. Our business plan: Jeannette would write the copy, I would manage the day-to-day work, and we would both meet with prospective client organizations in the nonprofit sector. We would hire freelance graphic designers for each project. Among the first of these designers was Linda Berglin, who was elected to the Minnesota State House of Representatives in 1972, and later served in the Minnesota State Senate.

To generate business, Jeannette and I wrote a short letter to *Minneapolis Tribune* columnist Robert T. Smith, describing our enterprise. We introduced Split Infinitive as "a new woman-owned business, planning to do things differently. Our holidays will be the birthdays of Shirley Chisholm and Eleanor Roosevelt, rather than Washington and Lincoln. We will focus on 'general brilliance.'" The day our letter arrived on Smith's desk, he called, and hours later he was in our office visiting; his next column featured a story about our business.

An immediate response to the column came from Chuck Desnick, owner of Friday's Deli in Lowertown St. Paul. Chuck wanted a direct mail piece to market his catering business. We had our first client. Linda Berglin accepted the design assignment, and we were off and running. Within weeks, we produced a direct mail brochure, inserted in an envelope with bold, raspberry-red Helvetica type on the left side reading:

SOME PEOPLE SPEND
ALL WEEK THINKING
ABOUT FRIDAYS

The brochure produced new business for Chuck and for us. Those first years were both exciting and terrifying. I was learning much, and also worrying a lot. Everything was new—this was my introduction to trying things, adjusting, and trying again. Later I would come to understand that this was "Experiential Learning 101," and even later, I realized that as we gathered perspectives from others, we were practicing "action learning."

We were grateful to receive advice periodically from Nick Coleman and Bob Goff, owners of an established local advertising agency. Nick was a friend and my state senator, and he was enthusiastic about offering guidance and encouragement. I consulted him before we accepted two accounts in particular: the campaign of Councilwoman Rosalie Butler for mayor of St. Paul and the business communities' campaign in support of the I-35E route along the West Seventh Street corridor. Both campaigns were opposed by the DFL Party, so I was concerned about the effect that taking on these clients might have on our future opportunities. Nick encouraged us to take the accounts, believing that the experience would outweigh the risks. He thought we would benefit from working with Butler, the first woman to run for mayor of St. Paul. I admired her tenacity and strength as she conducted her campaign amid considerable negativity, even as she faced a kidney transplant. (On a personal note, she was the first woman politician to wear a pantsuit in city hall!) Butler lost the mayor's race, and the I-35E corridor became the only stretch of the interstate system with a reduced speed limit. Nick and Bob were right: we gained valuable experience and visibility by taking on those two campaigns.

In 1973, Jeannette left Minnesota, and I needed to decide whether I would close Split Infinitive or stay the course on my own. I was enjoying the independence of having my own business, in part for the personal platform it gave me, which I would not have had from a position in a larger organization. I elected to keep going and established a new office in Lowertown St. Paul, a former manufacturing area of the city that was in its first stage of redevelopment into office buildings, retail spaces, and apartment homes, anchored around Sibley Park. It was an exciting time in the city, and this emerging area felt like a perfect fit for the business.

The first woman-owned law firm in Minnesota—headed by my friend Harriet Lansing, later to become city attorney, then a municipal judge and an appellate court judge—was located down the hall in the building I chose for Split Infinitive. The first studio of Minnesota Public Radio, where the early episodes of *A Prairie Home Companion* were recorded, was upstairs. A chocolate factory framed the front of the building at ground level, welcoming tenants and customers with a glorious aroma and allowing pedestrians to watch the hand-dipped chocolates being made through its large windows. Fiorello's Restaurant, on one corner of the ground level, became a regular spot for lunches and after-work gatherings. Several artisans occupied the lower level, reinforcing the independent, entrepreneurial activity in the building.

The first challenge of running the business on my own was having no one to answer the phone when I was meeting with a client or prospective client. I mentioned this predicament in a phone conversation with my favorite aunt, Ruthie Nelson, and she gave me the solution: call forwarding, the telephone innovation of the time. She suggested, "How about forwarding your calls to me while you're away from the office?" It was a great idea and a generous offer, which I accepted immediately. For the next several months, I forwarded the agency's calls to Ruthie's phone; she answered with "Split Infinitive" and took messages. She found the work interesting and loved helping me out. It was a terrific short-term solution and strengthened an already special bond between Ruthie and me. Later, she joined our staff and was with the firm until it closed. Until she died in November 2023, Ruthie was my "clipping service," sending me news stories and obituaries she knew would be of interest.

Being a sole proprietor forced me to acknowledge how much I needed to learn to run a successful firm. I could no longer rely on someone else to handle those tasks I was unfamiliar with. I knew of few resources that I could draw upon, but I did know about the Metropolitan Economic Development Association, an organization devoted to building entrepreneurial capacity in minority-owned businesses. I had met Elizabeth (Liz) Pegues, director of training at MEDA, through mutual friends and had learned about the association's Business Leadership Program. I reached out to Liz to see if I might enroll. She thought that I would benefit from the program and could be an asset to the group. My one employee, Jewell Lewis, and I were accepted in the next cohort for the program's four-month seminar.

The course was based on the research of Harvard professor David McClelland. Liz and Jeff Howard, a student of McClelland's and founder of the Efficacy Institute in Boston, were the trainers. For one weekend a month for four months, our cohort of fifteen to twenty participants lived and worked together at the Spring Hill Conference Center. The experience was transformational for me—helping me understand my motivations as well as how to differentiate among achievement, power, and affiliation decisions. Jewell and I now had a common language we could use to discuss many issues and move the business forward. The course gave me an intellectual framework for leadership decisions and increased my comfort with seeking help as needed—tools that have been invaluable throughout my life.

Split Infinitive's founding business strategy had been to serve non-profit organizations, but we pivoted to service businesses in order to expand our opportunities. Community banking was our first target, as Minnesota is a strong community banking state. In the early 1970s, many large banks began offering a range of gifts to encourage potential customers to open accounts. Community banks could not compete with that approach. Their competitive edge was their ability to offer personal service and commitment to their neighborhoods. Over several years we developed an expertise in community banking, working with several different banks throughout the region.

Some business opportunities came through referrals or from the visibility we gained from previous work. An example was our work for Karen Desnick, who phoned one day and introduced herself as Chuck Desnick's sister-in-law. She and her husband, Leslie, had been living in New York, working in advertising, when Chuck sent her the brochure we produced for Friday's Deli. She was impressed and noted how successful the direct mail strategy had been for Chuck's business. Now she and Leslie had returned to Minnesota to take over her parents' picture-framing business. She wanted to discuss working with us, so we agreed to meet at the frame shop in Hopkins on Saturday just before closing, and then go for dinner at a nearby restaurant.

A referral from a previous satisfied client is always a great way to start a relationship with a new prospective client. Arriving at the store on Saturday afternoon, I was able to observe Karen and Leslie's interactions with their customers. This was also my introduction to the framing business, and it resulted in a lifelong interest in the framing of art and other treasures. By the end of our dinner, Split Infinitive had a new client—and I had made a new friend with whom I would share personal joys and challenges, organize entrepreneurs, create the Minnesota Women's Campaign Fund, and work to engage more women in public service during the Perpich–Johnson administration.

4

Organizing for Political and Community Change

My earliest memory of organizing was in primary school. I gathered three of my friends to form the Helping Hand Club. Our plan was to visit elderly women we knew. Later in primary school and then in high school, 4-H was my main extracurricular activity, providing me with important lessons in leadership. The 4-H pledge—"I pledge my head to clearer thinking, my heart to greater loyalty, my hands to larger service, and my health to better living, for my club, my community, my country, and my world"—became my worldview. 4-H members gave "demonstrations" at each meeting, after which we responded to questions and feedback from our peers. We exhibited and presented demonstrations at county fair competitions, and those who won blue ribbons presented at the Minnesota State Fair. For my State Fair presentation, I demonstrated how to make bread.

Although my family did not engage in partisan political activities, political and social justice issues were regular topics of conversation in our home. We were Democrats, but as general manager of the electric co-op, my dad worked with politicians of both major Minnesota parties to ensure continued support of the Rural Electric movement. He felt it was inappropriate for him and his family to be engaged publicly in partisan campaigns. As a result, we never posted partisan candidate signs in our yard or bumper stickers on our car.

In the summer of 1963 I was nominated by the local American Legion Auxiliary for the first cohort of Minnesota Girls State. It was exciting and inspiring to be among a couple hundred girls assuming roles as members of the Minnesota House of Representatives and Minnesota State Senate, as well as governor, passing legislation in our mock government. By the end of the weeklong event, I was inspired and motived to be more involved in politics going forward.

While my academic experiences at Macalester College were generally traumatic and left me feeling pretty insecure, my leadership of the Young DFL organization on campus was energizing and rewarding. Throughout the year I successfully recruited speakers from Joan Mondale to party chair Warren Spannaus to speak at our meetings, and in the winter of 1966 we organized precinct caucus attendees in support of Lieutenant Governor Sandy Keith's challenge to Governor Karl Rolvaag for the DFL Party endorsement. This was my first foray into party politics. At that time, by state law, precinct caucus participants and voters had to be twenty-one years of age. Most of us students were not yet twenty-one, but we organized and recruited neighborhood residents to attend along with those students who met the age requirement.

We had worked hard and had anticipated how many votes we needed, so we were not surprised that Sandy Keith prevailed in our precinct. However, we hadn't known that the precinct was home to Doug Kelm, a key adviser to Governor Rolvaag and a longtime DFL operative. He did not take the defeat lightly, and immediately filed a lawsuit challenging the outcome, maintaining that students could not participate in the precinct where they attended college.

Three St. Paul attorneys, Ray Faricy, John Sullivan, and Jonathan Morgan, represented us pro bono, but we had to raise three hundred dollars for the court costs. On the spot I had my first political fundraising experience—selling VOTERS (Voluntary Organization to Encourage Registration of Students) buttons for one dollar each. We prevailed in court. Keith won the DFL Party endorsement but lost the primary election to Governor Rolvaag.

As a result of this political challenge to student participation, in the next session of the state legislature State Senator Nick Coleman introduced and helped to pass legislation giving Minnesota college students the right to vote where they attended college. Within one year we had tested the existing political participation system, defended our position in court, and achieved legislation to codify the full participation of students. I was learning how to organize, count votes, create political strategies, and change the law.

Community internships during my years at Macalester were transformational. In my first internship I saw up close how to take action to address racial bias, poverty, and lack of opportunity. Paralee Milligan was my guide. As director of the employment program of the Ramsey County Citizens Committee for Economic Opportunity, created in response to President Johnson's antipoverty program, she led by example in every aspect of her role. She was brilliant, wise, kind, and strong.

Mrs. Milligan had graduated from college years earlier, but directing this employment program was her first professional position. Racial bias had prevented her from being hired for anything other than factory work. During her years at a piecework factory, she slowed her pace and took long breaks to avoid producing too much, which might have offended the supervisor or put undue pressure on other workers who were not able to work at her pace. Now, she was directing an employment program, recruiting employers to commit to opening opportunities for Black workers, and preparing Black job seekers to be ready for these new opportunities and to feel safe applying for them.

My intern assignment was to identify potential employers and determine the appropriate person in each firm for Mrs. Milligan to work with. I met many of the agency's clients and had hours of conversations with Mrs. Milligan during these months. She encouraged and guided her clients in preparing for interviews and learning new skills. With me, she generously shared insights and responded to my questions. She had a remarkable capacity for engaging with all people without bias or intimidation, a great sense of humor, and enormous patience. As I witnessed her kindness and clarity with clients, listening to them and creating opportunities for them to go beyond the parameters of their past experience, I learned leadership lessons that I have sought to embrace throughout my life. Paralee Milligan was my first mentor.

After working on Linda Berglin's campaign, I was motivated to become more involved in women's political action, so I attended the next annual meeting of the bipartisan Minnesota Women's Political Caucus. I knew few others who were involved in the MWPC and had no specific plans other than to find a way to be engaged. Hours later, I had been elected chair of the statewide organization! In retrospect, the ease with which I was recruited might have given me pause, as I eventually learned that no one else was willing to take on the role of chair. But I was anxious to be involved and naive about the emergence of partisan feminist organizations.

I had not been involved in DFL Party politics since my time at Macalester, so I had limited knowledge about the establishment of the DFL Feminist Caucus. Specifically, I did not understand that the DFL Feminists expected—or hoped—that the bipartisan MWPC would die a natural death when partisan feminist organizations were created. Without that historical knowledge, and because I believed strongly that a bipartisan feminist political strategy was critical to the change we sought, it felt like a perfect time to serve as chair of the MWPC. We made plans to become a statewide organization with several local chapters. Soon I was driving around the state making a case for a bipartisan strategy, establishing local chapters of the MWPC, and encouraging women to run for office.

In 1972 there were still some pro-choice Republicans in the Minnesota State Legislature. I believed that a bipartisan strategy to recruit and support women candidates could leverage both parties to see the promotion of women candidates as politically advantageous. I had observed that the DFL Party had been slow to recruit women candidates for DFL-majority or even swing districts. My perspective was that the liberal male candidates who had been waiting their turn to run did not want the competition. The GOP seemed to recognize that a woman candidate could be a winning strategy in a swing district.

The tension between the DFL Feminist Caucus and the bipartisan Minnesota Women's Political Caucus continued. Many DFL Feminists could not tolerate the idea of a feminist organization supporting Republican women and blamed me for keeping the bipartisan organization alive. I didn't mind the blame, as I believed in the strategic value of the bipartisan strategy. Although my leadership role in the MWPC was an accident of timing, the more I observed the political parties' attitudes toward women candidates, the more committed I became to a bipartisan approach to recruiting women candidates at all levels of government.

As chair of the MWPC, I represented Minnesota on the board of the National Women's Political Caucus. There I also met the founders of the Women's Campaign Fund, a bipartisan organization raising funds to support pro-choice women running for Congress and the U.S. Senate. It was a compelling idea, and I soon envisioned a strategy to establish a similar organization in Minnesota to support women candidates. I felt that Minnesota needed a statewide bipartisan women's campaign fund committed to electing women to local and statewide offices. The idea was germinating, but with so much to do in building the MWPC, I didn't discuss the idea with anyone for a year or two.

Then, late in 1981, Kathleen Ridder and I were among a group of women traveling by train to Duluth for a meeting. Kathleen was an active Republican feminist and a leading supporter of women's athletics at the University of Minnesota. Her husband was part of the Knight Ridder newspaper organization, and their network was broad and deep. I shared with Kathleen my idea for the Minnesota Women's Campaign Fund, patterned after the bipartisan Women's Campaign Fund in Washington, D.C., which supported pro-choice women candidates of both parties in their campaigns for seats in the U.S. House of Representatives and the U.S. Senate.

Kathleen was enthusiastic about the idea, and we spent the remainder of the three-hour train trip brainstorming about how we might create such an organization in Minnesota. We envisioned a bipartisan, statewide fund that would support women running for office at the local, state, and national levels. We shared the view that success would require an up-front commitment to both urban and rural parts of the state and a diversity of leadership. We further believed that by making the fund bipartisan we would be able to leverage financial support across party lines.

A key element of our philosophy was that the founding members would be a mix of women with wealth and women who were entrepreneurs. Our formula for the founding board was 50 percent Democrats and 50 percent Republicans, 50 percent women of wealth and 50 percent entrepreneurs, and at least 30 percent from outside metropolitan areas. We jointly developed the prospect list and created a "business plan" that called for each founding board member to invest one thousand dollars to cover the initial administrative requirements of the organization.

Around this same time, the leadership of the Minnesota Chapter of the National Association of Women Business Owners, including Karen Desnick, Susan Sands, and Roxanne Givens, held a planning meeting to develop strategies for increasing NAWBO's impact on women's businesses and their communities. One of the goals the group established was to raise one hundred thousand dollars toward electing women to office in Minnesota. Karen Desnick, chair of the Minnesota Chapter, supported the goal, but she looked at me with the question "How will we accomplish this?" It was a perfect case of serendipity. The concept that Kathleen and I had been discussing needed just this kind of energy and commitment. We were on our way.

Each person on the founding board of the Minnesota Women's Campaign Fund told us that she had never before personally written a check for one thousand dollars for a political cause. Some women had been co-donors with their husbands at that level, but they had not written the checks. The husband of one of the founding board members (a CEO of a Minneapolis Fortune 500 company) told me privately that he had wanted to write the first check, so he could share in the "credit." He said it was a big adjustment for him, but he came to understand the importance of the strategy and acknowledged that a new day was coming. I admired him for recognizing his reluctance, and for becoming an enthusiastic supporter of the MWCF.

The organizing meeting of the Minnesota Women's Campaign Fund was held in early June 1982 at the Minneapolis Club. That morning, the *Minneapolis Tribune* published a column on the editorial page about the founding of the MWCF, quoting Kathleen Ridder and me. Two days later, my candidacy for lieutenant governor on the Perpich ticket was announced.

Serving on the board of Landmark Center was my introduction to several key business, philanthropic, and government leaders in St. Paul; as a board member I also learned about public–private partnerships and about the role of the arts in building community and contributing to the economy. Ramsey County Commissioner Diane Ahrens nominated me to one of the community leader positions on the board. Diane was the first woman on the County Board of Commissioners and a highly regarded leader. Landmark Center, the restored former Federal Courts Building, had been renovated and repurposed as an arts center. The Landmark Center board was chaired by St. Paul philanthropist and activist Betty Musser, and members included John Myers, the retired chairman of Waldorf Paper Company; Tom Swain, an insurance executive and former chief of staff to Governor Elmer L. Andersen; and Ken Rothchild, a highly regarded local business executive. Serving on the board with these leaders introduced me to a wide range of perspectives and networks that have enriched my life for years.

I also served on the board of Face to Face Health and Counseling Center on St. Paul's east side, a position that stretched my understanding of the social needs of our community in profound ways. Led by Nan Skelton, the center worked to identify signs of abuse in adolescents and supported young people facing early pregnancies and other medical crises. Guided by the seminal research on adolescent abuse by Dr. Michael Baizerman and Dr. Ira Loures, Face to Face trained educators, social workers, and first responders to identify signs of abuse in adolescents and also developed methods of working with abused youth to help them heal. This was my introduction to how research can inform policy and the development of training for frontline social workers, teachers, and police officers. I have often reflected on the value of this community experience for my later role of advancing policy changes as lieutenant governor.

As the interest in women-owned firms expanded, so did the interest in Split Infinitive and in me as a business leader. One outcome was that I was selected as one of the Ten Outstanding Young Minnesotans in 1980. I was nominated for this honor by Ken Rothchild, with whom I had served on the Landmark Center board. There were three women among the TOYM awardees that year, the first in which women were included—a recognition of women's increasing role in public life. Historically, the male honorees had attended the awards ceremony with their wives, so the women honorees of 1980 were told that we should be escorted by our spouses. I was the only single person receiving the award, and I struggled briefly with how I should manage the situation. I decided to invite Ken Rothchild to escort me that evening, and he graciously accepted.

5

Campaigning at the Local, State, and National Levels

In 1968, during my final year at Macalester, I organized for Senator Eugene McCarthy's campaign for president at the precinct caucus level. I was at such a meeting when we got the news that President Johnson would not seek reelection. The political dynamics changed immediately. Macalester's Young DFLers were already supporting Senator McCarthy for president, so we started looking for opportunities to work on the national campaign. By April several of us were assigned to work on the Indiana campaign. Doing so meant leaving school a week before the end of my final semester. Macalester accommodated our request to leave early on the condition that we turn in our final papers prior to leaving campus and that we accept that our final grades would be based on earlier exams.

Our college experience officially behind us, Larry Fredrickson, Tim Heaney, and I piled into a car and drove to Indianapolis; from there we were dispersed to local communities throughout the state. I was assigned to open a McCarthy for President office in Shelbyville. The local Farmers' Union communications director and his wife were my hosts, providing bed and breakfast, indispensable guidance, and endless conversation night after night. I found a vacant storefront to serve as an office and set up the space. Word got around quickly, and people dropped by to say hello before I was even settled. The first visitor welcomed me to Shelbyville and offered to provide whatever assistance I might need.

I didn't see him again, but I learned later that he was the local leader of the Ku Klux Klan!

Indiana was a tough environment for McCarthy's campaign, and the small rural communities particularly so. Those of us who were sent to such towns—mostly recent college graduates or members of Vietnam Veterans Against the War—were enthusiastic and energetic but inexperienced, with limited appreciation for how resistant the communities would be. We identified supporters and put on small local events to share Senator McCarthy's views, and we interacted with those who stopped in at our storefront offices.

On the night of the primary election, the Shelbyville campaign workers joined local people to watch as the voting results were posted on a blackboard at the courthouse. It was a long evening, so a few of us from the McCarthy campaign walked to a nearby bar for a break. There were no vacant tables, so we headed for the bar, only to have several men get up and offer us their table as they moved to the bar. I felt embarrassed, but they insisted. When the bartender took our order, he informed us that in Indiana it was illegal for women to sit at the bar. The men's gesture of giving us their table was standard practice. I would later share this story while working in international education, as a reminder that one needs to live in another culture to understand its nuances and traditions.

Senator McCarthy lost the Indiana primary to Senator Robert F. Kennedy and Governor Roger Branigin. The next day, I emptied the storefront, turned in the keys, and headed back to Indianapolis for a new assignment for the next group of primary elections the following month. I was sent to Sioux Falls, South Dakota, where I was assigned to open the McCarthy office in Mitchell, George McGovern's hometown.

The essential McCarthy supporters in Mitchell were the local Catholic priests and the Averys, a Unitarian farming couple, who provided my B&B accommodation and stimulating late-night conversations. The priests delivered furniture for the storefront headquarters, and within a day we were up and running. I now felt experienced, if somewhat surprised to have active support from the priests. In my hometown, clergy rarely got involved in political campaigns beyond giving sermons the Sunday before the election, as the minister in our family's Evangelical

Covenant Church had done when he urged parishioners not to vote for John Kennedy—a message not well received in our family!

On election day, the priests were out of town at a three-day retreat, so I delivered their absentee ballots to the election judge in Mitchell. No one suggested that such a service invited voter fraud; rather, it was understood as a way of ensuring that everyone who wanted to vote could vote. Now, reflecting on the election-day restrictions that South Dakota and other states have put in place, it is difficult to imagine where those fears come from. Election night in Mitchell was quiet, and after a late-evening visit with my hosts, I went to bed tired but satisfied that we had done our job well. Hours later we awoke to the news of Senator Robert Kennedy's murder in California. Closing down the campaign office that day was a slow-motion exercise as we processed the consequences of yet another political assassination.

I headed back to Minnesota, feeling numb and uncertain about further engagement in the 1968 presidential race. Senator Humphrey would be the nominee, and having put my stake in McCarthy's candidacy, I saw no further role for me to play in the campaign.

Shirley Chisholm was the next presidential candidate I was inspired to support, when she ran for the Democratic Party nomination in 1972. This was a significant and historic moment. Chisholm was the first woman and the first African American candidate for U.S. president, and I supported her for her courage in articulating historic truths, expressing a vision for a different future, and putting a marker in the political landscape. Her candidacy forever changed the possibilities for women and for what this country could become. Hers was a short-lived effort, but it resonates even today. As I was writing this chapter in 2023, Congressman Hakeem Jeffries of New York was accepting the position of leader of the House Democratic Caucus; speaking on Shirley Chisholm's birthday, he noted that she previously represented the district he now serves.

In the spring of 1972, Linda Berglin announced her candidacy for the Minnesota State Legislature. I enthusiastically signed up to be Linda's door-knocking partner, and for several months Linda and I walked the streets of her district five days a week, going from house to house to meet the residents. I thoroughly enjoyed getting to know the neighborhoods of her district and the people who lived and worked there. The excitement of knocking on the doors of strangers to tell them about Linda and her vision for serving was invigorating. Most people were friendly in response to our canvassing, and many were curious about this young woman candidate. A few were hostile and shut the door in our faces. I was learning about grassroots politics, and as the weeks passed, I understood that electing Linda and other women candidates would be a huge change for this south Minneapolis district and our state. Upon reflection I have come to realize that this experience grounded me in the importance of grassroots engagement and the subtleties of gender bias within the DFL Party as well as among constituents.

Linda was one of six DFL women elected to the legislature in 1972, and she went on to serve several terms in the State House and later in the State Senate, where she chaired the Health and Human Services Committee. Linda's leadership was instrumental in virtually every expansion of the state human services budget for more than thirty years, for child-care and children's health programs and much more.

Early in 1976, a telephone call from Gloria Griffin put me on a path that combined my entrepreneurial and political interests and capabilities. Gloria shared her intention to run for Congress as the DFL candidate for the Second District, against Congressman Tom Hagedorn. The district was a Republican stronghold, so she understood that her candidacy was a long shot, but she saw it as an opportunity for a woman candidate and volunteers to be recognized. She did not expect to encounter serious competition for the DFL endorsement. Nevertheless, the endorsement would have to be earned, as Tom Kelm, DFL establishment power broker, lived in the district. Gloria assumed that he would not support a liberal, feminist candidate.

Gloria asked me to serve as her campaign manager, with the understanding that I would continue to run my business as well. She wanted the campaign office to be located in St. Peter, which meant that she and I would both have to drive back and forth daily. I had not managed a campaign previously, nor did I know any DFL Party leaders in the district. A rational assessment of my responsibilities to my business in addition to the demands of this new role would have suggested that I turn down the offer, but I didn't do a serious assessment. Instead, I just started figuring out how I would manage it all. Gloria committed a modest sum to register the campaign committee and open a bank account, and I signed up for a campaign manager's workshop led by Mike Berman, a former member of Walter Mondale's staff and a Democratic Party operative.

Party leader Ray Hemenway was an early and enthusiastic supporter of Gloria's candidacy. The glint in his eyes as we discussed strategy reflected his love of politics and his commitment to changing the status quo. Ray knew everyone and was respected by all wings of the party. He loved the idea of a woman candidate and was a constant source of advice and perspective. Mankato State University political science professor Carolyn Shrewsbury, a longtime DFL activist, signed on as well. And so it went.

By the time of the endorsing convention, we knew where our support was by name and precinct. There was another candidate—possibly running as part of a scheme by some to keep Gloria from being endorsed on the first ballot. On the second ballot we were a few votes shy of the two-thirds majority required for the endorsement. I went to Tom Kelm and asked if he would produce the needed votes on the third ballot. "How many do you need?" he replied. Understanding that he knew the answer, I gave him the exact number we needed. If I was wrong, Gloria's campaign would be over before we got started. On the third ballot, Tom delivered the number I asked for, giving Gloria Griffin the endorsement as the DFL Party's candidate against Tom Hagedorn. It was my first experience in counting votes when the stakes were high. "Details matter" is a lesson I've carried with me ever since.

The campaign was exhilarating and exhausting. Keeping up with the day-to-day organizing—recruiting local leaders, producing literature and signs, raising funds, and creating a calendar of media events and interviews to increase Gloria's visibility—was a monumental task.

Early in the campaign, Gloria and I went to Washington, D.C., to introduce her to the Democratic Congressional Campaign Committee, the National Committee for an Effective Congress, and anyone else who would give us a meeting. The reception was lukewarm. Tom Hagedorn was considered unbeatable, and Gloria was not the DCCC's idea of a good fit for this rural district. We returned to Minnesota with no financial support from the Democratic establishment, but now they knew who Gloria was and what she stood for.

The daily routines of the campaign were normal. We had modest financial resources and limited experience, but we were aware that this campaign was a terrific opportunity for women to be involved in a congressional race. There had not been a woman running for Congress from Minnesota since Coya Knutson was elected in 1954. This year we had the added election-cycle excitement of the Carter–Mondale ticket. A campaign favorite was a T-shirt with a silk-screened graphic designed by Esther Malabel, with the slogan "Grits, Fritz & Gloria" above an American flag.

While our Washington trip did not produce DCCC support, my friend Congressman Gerry Sikorski successfully recruited Senator Joe Biden of Delaware as a guest for a fundraiser for Gloria's campaign. Biden's involvement added credibility and generated financial contributions from individuals who had not donated previously. His support for Gloria's candidacy despite her lack of establishment endorsement was my first experience with an elected official being willing to act outside the usual boundaries. Biden's actions reinforced for me that long-term political success requires grassroots political work on an ongoing basis, not just when victory is assured. The example that Biden set—of personal integrity, empathy, kindness, and commitment to grassroots work—is one that I have tried always to remember.

Throughout the campaign, there was tension between Gloria and me regarding lines of responsibility. By late September, she insisted on taking control over operational matters that would usually be left to the campaign manager. Initially, I tried to accommodate her choices. I was inexperienced, and I sometimes doubted my own decisions. I also lacked a confidant with whom I could share my challenges, someone who could help me gain perspective and advise me on shaping a different approach. The friends I normally would have confided in were all people I had recruited to support Gloria's campaign, so it didn't feel appropriate for me to share my frustrations and concerns with them.

By early October, disagreements between Gloria and me were coming to a head. I saw no way to change the situation, so I decided I should resign from the campaign. I spoke to Ray Hemenway about what I was planning, and, to my surprise, he understood immediately. He had observed situations that concerned me further, and he supported my decision to resign prior to the end of the campaign. He agreed with me that a private resignation would be appropriate; Gloria would then inform the staff of the management change.

I was deeply sad, but I knew the decision was the right one. Upon reflection, I have come to see this campaign management experience, including my decision to resign, as an important lesson in how our values are reflected in the way we treat people and how people's interactions can have significant impacts on the effectiveness of an organization. This lesson has been reinforced for me repeatedly throughout my career, but this experience gave me my first insight into the critical management strategies of openness to others' views, consideration of others' needs, and willingness to share decision making.

On election night, I stopped by the campaign gathering to greet Gloria and the campaign workers and supporters. Gloria and I remained colleagues and supporters of each other in our various roles over the years. We never spoke further about this experience after the election. To my knowledge, neither of us discussed the situation with anyone other than Ray Hemenway.

6

\\\\\\\\\\\\\\\\\////,

Engaging with Entrepreneurs

A story in the *St. Paul Pioneer Press* about entrepreneur Susan Sands was all the motivation I needed to give Susan a call. The possibility of connecting with another woman facing many of the same challenges I was experiencing was exactly what I longed for. Within days, we were visiting in her home office as though we had known each other for years. It was a relief to find that we had so many interests and challenges in common.

We would become good friends, share office space for a time, and ultimately work together on a larger strategy. In late 1973, a news story mentioned an upcoming conference of the National Association of Women Business Owners in Washington, D.C. Susan and I decided to attend, and off we went. There we met founding NAWBO leaders Susan Hager, Denise Cavenaugh, and Dona O'Bannon, who were surprised to learn that we wanted to organize a Minnesota chapter of NAWBO. They understood our desire to have a local organization of women entrepreneurs, but the NAWBO bylaws made no provisions for chapters. We asked them to change the bylaws because we wanted to be part of a national movement and were confident there would be interest in other parts of the country as well. That was not what they had expected, but they agreed to look into it.

Back in Minnesota, Susan and I got to work identifying women-owned firms, scheduling initial introductions, and gathering a few women at a time to discuss the idea of forming a state chapter of NAWBO. Most of us were in our twenties and thirties, enthusiastic about building a network of women that would offer support and guidance about running a business. I believed that a diverse founding group was essential to ensuring that the organization reflected the diversity of Minnesota. Our initial organizing team agreed that the founding group should include a variety of business types owned by women of different ages and racial and ethnic backgrounds, as well as women from all areas of the state.

Our commitment to diversity required intentionality, as we realized that most of us primarily knew people like ourselves. We took the time necessary to build a prospect list that included African Americans, recent immigrants, more experienced entrepreneurs, and owners of many types of businesses. Among the founding group were Roxanne Givens, an African American who headed a firm providing elderly housing, and May Yue, a Chinese American investment adviser.

Most of the founding members owned small businesses and had limited financial capacity to fund the organization. Recognizing that we needed the support of more experienced businesswomen, we reached out to a few recognized and successful entrepreneurial women. That list included Leeann Chin, founder of the Leeann Chin restaurant chain; Ebba Hoffman, CEO of Smead Manufacturing; Reiko Weston, founder/owner of Fuji Ya restaurant; Louise Saunders, owner of Charlie's Cafe Exceptionale; and Constance Bakken, CEO of Citizens Independent Bank in St. Louis Park. We met with each of these women in person to make the case that women entrepreneurs needed an organization like the National Association of Women Business Owners, and that the Minnesota Chapter of NAWBO needed the credibility and support of highly respected women like them in our membership. Ultimately, all of these women became supporters and mentors as well as financial backers of the chapter. Charlie's Cafe Exceptionale in downtown Minneapolis became one of the chapter's favorite venues for meetings.

By the time of our organizational meeting, the NAWBO bylaws had been changed, and the Minnesota Chapter became the association's first chapter outside Washington. NAWBO became and remains very important for many women entrepreneurs. For those of us in the Minnesota Chapter, our monthly NAWBO meetings became a priority. Membership provided a safe space to discuss challenges unique to women in business, as well as to share expertise and services, find business opportunities among members, and gain access to resources, from bankers to accountants to marketing experts. Many of the founding group's members developed extraordinary lifelong friendships.

Meanwhile, five women were newly elected to the Minnesota State Legislature in 1972, joining Helen McMillan, the only woman who had been serving previously. An unanticipated outcome of this election was that the membership of the St. Paul Athletic Club was about to change. Historically, the club had limited its membership to white men, but the previous year it had admitted its first member of color, Urban League executive Bill White. Then, in January 1973, as was customary at the beginning of every legislative session, each Minnesota legislator received a letter from the club president offering a complimentary membership during the legislative session. It was a form letter, and it soon became obvious that the club leadership had not known that there were now six women serving in the legislature.

Upon receiving her letter, Representative Linda Berglin decided to take advantage of the offer. She made a plan to have lunch at the informal Buffet Cafe, the one restaurant in the club where women were not allowed to dine, even as guests of a member. She informed *St. Paul Pioneer Press* journalist Mary Ann Grossman of her intentions, and at noon on the appointed day, Linda came through the line at the Buffet Cafe. The workers, all women, refused to serve her, per the rules of the restaurant. The next day, the *Pioneer Press* reported on the refusal to serve Representative Berglin, and the media coverage created an opportunity that ultimately led to the club's decision to admit women as members. The club's leadership had been discussing the issue of admitting women internally for months, without taking action. Now those board members who had been advocating for the change built on the momentum created by the press report, and within weeks, the St. Paul Athletic Club began accepting women members.

In response to this historic change, Susan Sands, Harriet Lansing, and I, among other women, joined the St. Paul Athletic Club. For the next several years, my days began with a 6:30 a.m. run on the club's indoor track or a workout in the gym, then breakfast at the third-floor restaurant. The club's rooftop restaurant became a regular spot for business lunches. My membership enhanced my ability to grow my network among the St. Paul business community—a concrete reminder of how systemic and historic biases have denied similar opportunities to so many women and people of color.

By the time President Carter hosted the first White House Conference on Small Business in 1980, the National Association of Women Business Owners, including the Minnesota Chapter, was well positioned to ensure that women entrepreneurs participated. In 1979, the president appointed a commission to oversee preparations for the conference, and each state was expected to hold its own conference to engage business owners in building an agenda leading up to the White House Conference.

Unexpectedly, I played a personal, unofficial role in relation to that commission. Late on a Saturday night, my friend Louise Saunders, owner of Charlie's Cafe Exceptionale, called me. Vice President Walter Mondale had called to tell her that President Carter wanted to appoint her to the White House Commission on Small Business. Arthur Levitt, chairman of the American Stock Exchange, would chair the commission. William Norris, CEO of Control Data in Minnesota, a corporate leader widely recognized for his proposals for small business development strategies, would also be appointed to the commission.

The vice president and Louise had been partners in a Minneapolis law firm prior to his service as Minnesota attorney general. Louise was not happy about her appointment to the commission. She told Mondale that she knew nothing about small business development and was not interested in being involved in politics at any level. The vice president insisted, so Louise gave in, on the condition that "Marlene agrees to assist me, including traveling with me to meetings." The vice president knew me and felt pretty sure I would agree to help Louise, so he accepted her condition. A few minutes later, Louise called me and excitedly relayed the vice president's request and her demand that I help her fulfill this obligation. I assured her that I would enjoy helping, but being away would be a strain on my business, and I could not justify the expense of traveling around the country to several meetings. "No problem," Louise assured me, "I'll cover those costs."

For the next several months I accompanied Louise to commission meetings across the country, hearing testimony from entrepreneurs and listening to the commissioners' deliberations. I also joined Louise, William Norris, and Arthur Levitt for late-evening meals and other informal meetings. While it was challenging to be away from my business, the opportunity to hear such rich conversations among the commissioners, and to have so much personal time with Norris and Levitt, among others, was exciting and inspirational.

The Minnesota Chapter of NAWBO, led by Karen Desnick, ensured the participation of Minnesota women entrepreneurs in the White House Conference on Small Business. NAWBO had considerable credibility, but it was an adjustment for the U.S. Chamber of Commerce to share the platform. Meanwhile, the NAWBO national office was working with the White House on a proposal for a White House office devoted to women-owned businesses. The proposal was controversial, and including it as one of the final ten recommendations of the White House Conference—a framework that the White House had established—would have required dropping one of the other top priorities developed by the state conferences. The White House's solution: in his opening speech to the conference, President Carter announced the creation of a White House office on women's entrepreneurship. This eliminated the need to include a proposal for such an office among the ten recommendations submitted to the president at the conclusion of the conference.

It was an important win for NAWBO, and the first time I had participated in the creation of such a "workaround" solution. Later that year, I was among the NAWBO leaders invited to the White House for the signing of the executive order establishing the Office of Women's Business Ownership.

7

\\\\\\\\\\\\\\\\\\\\\\\\\\\\\\\.

The Potential of New Opportunities

In the early months of 1977, the Minnesota State Legislature established the Small Business Committee to develop legislative proposals to
strengthen small business development. Half the members were to be
owners of small businesses appointed by the governor, and the others
would be legislators appointed by the Senate and House. State Senator
Collin Peterson, author of the bill that created the committee, encouraged me to seek a governor's appointment.

This seemed like a terrific opportunity to learn more about state
government, work directly with policymakers, and create a space for
NAWBO to be involved in public policy. I called the governor's office
to request a meeting with Governor Perpich. I did not know Governor
Perpich at the time, and I had not had any previous contact with the
governor's office. Mark Dayton, the governor's scheduler, returned my
call. Knowing that I was a leader in NAWBO, Mark assumed I wanted the
Small Business Committee appointment, and he suggested that I could
get it without meeting with the governor. I told him that I would not
accept the appointment without speaking to the governor first, because
I wanted to share my vision for how I would approach the work. Mark
relented and gave me a ten-minute appointment.

When we met, the governor expressed his interested in NAWBO and
in the general increase in numbers of women starting businesses. He
supported the idea that the committee should focus on recommending specific legislative action and not on tax cuts. He agreed to appoint
me to the Small Business Committee and assured me that he would

consider the committee's recommendations. We spoke for half an hour, and I left feeling enthusiastic about the governor's leadership, having observed how comfortable he was meeting new people, hearing new ideas, and approaching things differently.

Governor Perpich's 1977 appointment of Rosalie Wahl as the first woman to serve on the Minnesota Supreme Court galvanized women in supporting his reelection. I concluded that this moment was also an opportunity to engage more women in political fundraising. I called the Perpich reelection campaign office and offered to host a women's fundraiser aimed at reminding voters of the governor's appointment of Justice Wahl and other women judges. We asked each invitee to make a donation of twenty-five dollars—most had not previously supported any campaign at that level.

The event raised more than one thousand dollars, an impressive sum in 1977. Both Rudy Perpich and his wife, Lola, were excited by the turnout, the recognition, and the financial success. Fundraising was then and continued to be the governor's least favorite aspect of campaigning. As it turned out, this was the only fundraiser of the Perpich campaign for which the host did all of the work of inviting donors, providing refreshments, and hosting. This was my inaugural fundraiser— one of dozens I would host over the years as I became comfortable with the role and committed to increasing the participation of women in this aspect of political action.

Having enjoyed the experience of planning and hosting this fundraiser, I quickly recognized that I would want to do it again. I decided to create a personal system to make the planning of such events easier and to control the costs, leaving more of the funds raised for the campaign. I learned that buying disposable plastic wine glasses for two events cost as much as buying reusable restaurant-supply glasses, so I immediately purchased two cases of wine glasses (seventy-two glasses) from a restaurant-supply shop. The practical side of hosting was in place as well as a prospect list, which grew from the list of those invited to that first Perpich fundraiser. I was embracing the political work of helping people "part with their cash" for ideas and people they believed in.

Later that fall, the director of the World Press Institute at Macalester College asked me to arrange for the twelve WPI journalists to interview Governor Perpich. The director hoped that as a board member of WPI with access to the governor, I could break the stalemate that he had reached with the governor's staff. Because the WPI journalists were foreigners and were not reporting for a Minnesota audience, the staff would not prioritize an interview during the campaign period.

I spoke to governor's staff on behalf of the WPI and was initially turned down, but I persisted. I knew the governor would enjoy visiting with the journalists. Eventually, a half-hour appointment was confirmed, and I joined them for the meeting. The governor engaged with the journalists enthusiastically, responding to their questions and asking them questions as well. After about forty-five minutes, the governor stood up and asked me to accompany him to his private office for a minute. There he told me that right after our meeting he would be flying to Wadena, Minnesota (an hour and a half away), for an evening campaign event. He said there were four seats available on the plane, and he offered to take along three of the journalists if I would be the fourth and serve as their host and guide at the event. Of course I agreed, so we returned to the group and he shared his proposal. The journalists were excited, and among them determined which three would go. The flight on a King Air plane was a first for the journalists, as was the event in Wadena—a classic, small-town campaign gathering at the VFW Hall, with speeches, polka music, and burgers, potato salad, and beer. The governor enjoyed such events, and for the journalists, it was a perfect introduction to grassroots campaigning in the United States.

Governor Perpich and most of the DFL ticket lost the 1978 election in large part because of the public's anger at Governor Wendell Anderson for appointing himself to the U.S. Senate to succeed Walter Mondale when Mondale became vice president. But in a year and a half I had established a bond with the governor: I had been appointed to the Small Business Committee, hosted a women's fundraising event for his campaign, and arranged for the WPI journalists to interview him. I knew that I wanted to find a way to stay in contact with Governor Perpich as he moved into the private sector.

The following year, as I was planning one of my regular trips to Washington for a meeting of the board of the National Association of Women Business Owners, I read a short news article that mentioned that Rudy Perpich was living in New York City while preparing for his European work on behalf of Control Data. I decided to try to meet with him at the conclusion of my time in D.C., so I asked his brother George for his phone number. The governor was pleased to hear from me and suggested that I join him and Lola for dinner the following week in New York. Over dinner, he inquired about my work with NAWBO and shared his excitement about living in Europe and helping to establish business opportunities for Control Data. He also said he relished this period as a private citizen. That was the last time we spoke until June 1982, when, on the day of the organization meeting of the Minnesota Women's Campaign Fund, I had a sense that my life was about to change.

Earlier that week, newspaper headlines had speculated about whether Rudy Perpich would run for governor again. He had left his job working for Control Data in Europe and was encouraging the speculation, while also suggesting that he would select a woman as his running mate. One article reported that he had met with Secretary of State Joan Growe, and other women mentioned as possible running mates included legislators Linda Berglin and Phyllis Kahn.

I had read the articles and the names being suggested and had written in my journal, "If he wants to win he'll ask me to run with him." Later on the day of the MWCF founding meeting, attorney Bruce Quackenbush called to ask if I would be open to a conversation with the governor.

"Yes, of course," I replied, "and I'll know if you tell him that I'm willing to talk, because he'll call me."

"You're kidding, right?" Bruce responded.

When I returned to my office after the MWCF meeting, my mother handed me a telephone message slip that read "Call Governor Perpich." The look on her face told me that she understood that much was about to change.

I called the governor, and he asked me to meet him at the Brothers Deli in Edina. I was excited but not surprised by the governor's call. In retrospect, I realized that each time I had met with him, he was observing and responding to my capacity for leadership. He had always been open to new people and ideas, and spontaneous meetings with him often yielded exciting and innovative results. I learned later that I was one of the few Minnesota colleagues who had reached out to him during his time in New York after he left office.

On this day, his choice of a meeting place was classic Rudy Perpich "doing things on his terms." He made the appointment with me himself, taking no chance that someone else would share the information. The deli where we met was off the beaten track. It was not staked out by political reporters seeking a scoop on his choice of a running mate. Many customers recognized him and responded with smiles rather than speculation.

After ordering a piece of chocolate cake for himself and a coffee for me, he laid out his plan. He understood that he would not get the DFL Party endorsement, as Attorney General Warren Spannaus was well liked and had been organizing for a year. At the same time, Perpich had strong support among the DFL Party's grassroots, particularly on the Iron Range. In the election of 1978, Perpich had been the top vote getter among the statewide DFL candidates who lost. He knew many voters were disappointed that he had lost, and he understood that the loss reflected the public's anger with Governor Anderson for appointing himself to the U.S. Senate.

The governor explained to me that he wanted his lieutenant governor to have specific responsibilities: to lead Minnesota's tourism strategy as an economic development tool and to chair an appointments commission to advise him on candidates for all of the state's boards and commissions. His goal was to increase the racial and gender diversity of every board and commission. He intended to articulate these plans during the campaign.

He told me that he believed that if he had not served as lieutenant governor he would not have become the first Catholic and the first non-Scandinavian to be elected governor of Minnesota. He felt the same would be true for the first woman governor, and he wanted his legacy to include creating the opportunity for a woman lieutenant governor to become governor. He said that he intended to resign in the middle of his second term, giving his lieutenant governor the opportunity to run on her own. He planned to work in the private sector for four to six years after his governorship, to build financial security for his family. He saw me as an asset to his ticket because of my background in small business and my experience in organizing women business owners; the fact that I had grown up in rural Minnesota before becoming established in St. Paul was also a plus.

I felt calm, anxious, and interested. I resisted accepting his invitation to join the ticket on the spot, feeling that I should reflect on the consequences for me and my business. I told the governor I wanted a few days to think about it. He shook his head. "You can have a day. There is too much media interest and the decision needs to get settled." I agreed to call him the following day.

Driving back to St. Paul, I thought about my interactions with the governor over the years, most recently in New York. I learned later from his brothers that he had mentioned our New York meeting to them. On a more practical note, it occurred to me that this might be the last time I would drive my Datsun 280Z sports car. I'd had it for a year and a half and was really enjoying it, but I imagined that a foreign-made sports car would not be a suitable vehicle for a Minnesota lieutenant governor candidate in 1982.

When I arrived back at Split Infinitive, my mother followed me into my office, assuming she knew what Governor Perpich had said but wanting it confirmed. I told her the high points, that I had overnight to think about it, and that I intended to meet with a few friends to help me consider my choice further. She was excited and supportive.

A few hours later I was in my living room surrounded by four friends—two attorneys, Jean Heilman and Bruce Quackenbush, and two entrepreneurs, Karen and Leslie Desnick. The attorneys pulled out a legal pad, drew a line down the center, headed the columns "Pro" and "Con," and started articulating all the cons! At which point Karen the entrepreneur interrupted and said, "I think this is the wrong way to spend our time. Haven't you already decided to do this? If so, shouldn't we be discussing how to help you be successful?" It was a beautiful moment for me. I hadn't actually said yes out loud, but Karen was right, I had decided.

The following morning I called the governor and said that I was ready to talk, so he and his brother George came to my apartment. As we sat at my kitchen table, I told the governor I was definitely interested, but there were a few things I needed him to know about me—concerning my business, my family background, my personal relationships, and matters that could create controversy. After I completed my "inventory," he reviewed the items one by one and talked about how he felt about each, with a nod to George for confirmation of his perspective. He concluded that we had a partnership, so we shook hands and agreed that we would announce my candidacy the following day. Between now and then we would not be seen together. We discussed who I would work with on the campaign to get the announcement written and me prepared.

Amazingly, the secret held, despite the fact that one of the most active political communications persons at the time lived in the condominium building next to mine. She knew the governor well, and she and I knew each other. But since my name had not been on the list of women speculated to be under consideration by Governor Perpich, she had not been keeping an eye on my building. While he had been talking about selecting a female running mate, there was general skepticism about whether he would do so since it was acknowledged that Joan Growe and perhaps others had turned him down. There was also evidence that the political establishment was not ready for a female lieutenant governor candidate. The Republican Party gubernatorial candidate had rejected State Senator Nancy Brataas as a running mate, and DFLer Warren Spannaus had rejected Joan Growe as a running mate.

The press was told that Governor Perpich would introduce his running mate at a press conference the next morning. At that press conference he also articulated his intention that the lieutenant governor would lead Minnesota's tourism promotion strategy and chair the governor's Open Appointments Commission. He further stated his commitment to the full participation of women in his administration and to greater diversity of gender and ethnicity on all state boards and commissions, as well as in the judiciary, where the governor has appointing authority. Governor Perpich staked out a historic space in Minnesota politics. For the first time, a woman was running for lieutenant governor, and with its opening message, the campaign committed to inclusion.

It had been less than five years since my first meeting with Governor Perpich. Until now, I had initiated every meeting or other interaction we'd had. We had engaged on policy issues, on creating opportunities for foreign journalists, on political fundraising, and ultimately on simply keeping in touch following his election loss. I could not have anticipated this outcome, but from our first meeting I understood that I was getting to know a unique political leader and learning how to make things happen. The campaign was under way, and my relationship with Governor Perpich had moved to a new place.

8

Traveling with the Governor

In the first weeks of the campaign I learned the basics of campaigning by traveling the state by car, with the governor driving. His vision for job creation and education as the passport out of poverty touched people, and his personal warmth and humor were infectious. He drove from town to town with no staff, meeting volunteers, small business owners, farmers, and workers in cafés, small factories, and other venues. People's affection for him was obvious. Late one afternoon as we were returning to St. Paul on I-35 from northern Minnesota, Rudy stopped to pick up a hitchhiker! My first reaction was disbelief and apprehension. Once settled in the back seat, the young man did a double take and said, "Rudy, is that you?" Rudy nodded in acknowledgment, and our new passenger continued, "I'm really sorry you lost the last election. We didn't want you to lose, we were just mad at Wendy. You've got my vote this time for sure." Rudy smiled and we had a lovely conversation for the remainder of the drive.

I soon learned that the campaign had limited money in the bank, few major donors, and no fundraising strategy. I also had not appreciated how much the governor disliked fundraising. When I handed him my mother's five-hundred-dollar check for the campaign, he was visibly moved and broke out in a huge smile, commenting that it was the largest donation the campaign had received.

In late June, my friend Betsy Griffith was in St. Paul to give a speech. I'd met Betsy at my first board meeting of the National Women's Political Caucus, and over the years we had become good friends. Her Minnesota visit had been scheduled weeks before I was a candidate, and I had invited Betsy to join me for dinner one evening while she was in town. When I mentioned my plans to the governor, he invited himself to join us. We had a lively conversation, and as we left the restaurant, Betsy handed us a check for 250 dollars for our campaign.

Later that summer, former GOP governor Elmer L. Andersen called my office to invite the governor and me to visit the corporate headquarters and distribution facility of his company H. B. Fuller in St. Paul. I'd had cordial interactions with Governor Andersen through St. Paul community work, and as former governors, Perpich and Andersen had known each other for years and shared a deep mutual affection.

Within days, Governor Perpich and I joined Governor Andersen on a walk through the distribution center at H. B. Fuller. The employees shouted greetings to "Rudy" and "Elmer," displaying a warm camaraderie with both men. Later, in a private conversation that included his son Tony, who was CEO of the company, Andersen told Perpich that he thought it was very smart to have me as a running mate; he believed it would be a significant factor in the campaign outcome and that we had an excellent chance of winning the primary and the general election. As we left his office, he handed Governor Perpich a check for five hundred dollars for the campaign. By this time, Perpich had concluded that I was a fundraising asset for the campaign.

During the primary campaign, tensions within the DFL Party were inevitable, and the party's endorsement system resulted in a few challenges. The party-endorsed candidate for governor, Attorney General Warren Spannaus, was a popular officeholder. Spannaus favored abortion rights and gun control, but he had declined to choose Secretary of State Joan Growe as his running mate. The DFL Feminist Caucus was focused on policy issues rather than on electing women, so it enthusiastically supported Spannaus based on his positions on abortion and gun control, on the assumption that his administration would pay particular attention to those issues.

Perpich was antiabortion. He had the support of anti-choice activists, but he told me in our first meeting at the Brothers Deli that he was comfortable with my pro-choice position, that he intended to avoid legislation limiting abortion, and that he was committed to expanding the participation of women and racial minorities in every aspect of state government, including his cabinet. My candidacy was a first step toward making good on that commitment.

A few DFL members of the founding board of the Minnesota Women's Campaign Fund were openly hostile to my decision to join the Perpich ticket. They supported the DFL-endorsed candidate, Spannaus, and felt that I was damaging the women's movement in Minnesota. Yet most DFL entrepreneurs and Republican board members of the MWCF actively supported our campaign.

The governor's Iron Range supporters were not pleased with my being on the ticket either. I was a young, pro-choice female whom they didn't know. They did not understand how I could be an asset to the governor's election.

I quickly recognized that I should not focus on these conflicts. I was the official candidate and needed to engage in the day-to-day work of meeting constituents, making speeches, engaging with voters one-on-one or in small groups, and fundraising. Once I had my own campaign schedule, I was accompanied by a campaign volunteer, often George or Connie Perpich. Both of them had been enthusiastic supporters of the decision to have me on the ticket and did everything they could to support me personally and make the case to their Iron Range friends that I was a major asset to the campaign. They had their own networks throughout the state: George had been chairman of the State Senate Health and Human Services Committee, and Connie was a lobbyist for Planned Parenthood of Minnesota and South Dakota. The statewide network I had built through the Minnesota Women's Political Caucus and the Minnesota Chapter of the National Association of Women Business Owners was also now a campaign asset.

As the day of the primary election approached, I was surprised to learn that the governor would be on the Iron Range on election night. The campaign staff would have a small gathering at a downtown St. Paul hotel, but I decided to invite friends and family to my St. Paul apartment to watch the news coverage of the election returns on my small black-and-white TV. Connie and George Perpich and Tony Perpich were there, as well as Karen and Leslie Desnick, my mother, my sisters Rosalind and Marlys, my niece and nephew Beth and Brent, and Marlys's fiancé, Bob Nesheim; also there were my brothers Warren and

Wayne, who made a surprise visit from his home near Chicago. It was a long evening, with the results remaining close. Eventually, Sandy Keith called from the campaign headquarters to confirm that we had won by twenty-five thousand votes, and to ask me to come down to the hotel event and make a statement. The governor had reportedly gone to bed without waiting for the results!

Sandy had initially felt that my selection as a running mate was a mistake, but over time he became an enthusiastic supporter. He had known me since 1966, when I worked on his primary campaign. He and Rudy had served together in the legislature, and Rudy had supported him in his primary race against Karl Rolvaag. As he watched me campaign and bring new support and energy to the ticket, Sandy became a big fan. George and Connie accompanied me to the campaign's downtown election-night gathering to acknowledge and celebrate the victory of the Perpich–Johnson ticket. We did not communicate with the governor that evening.

The day following the election, the campaign assembled key members of our original organization along with select individuals from the Spannaus campaign. The combined team moved immediately to create a winning strategy for the general election. Emotions were intense, ranging from excitement to annoyance as the Perpich primary team made room for the new crowd. In an informal gathering in an outer room, the governor stood with a few of the original team from the Iron Range. In response to a comment I made, the specifics of which I've long forgotten, Representative Joe Begich objected vehemently, adding, "What did you ever contribute to this win, anyway?" I calmly responded, "Twenty-five thousand votes!" The governor smiled, and the conversation got back on track. I would often recall that exchange as the moment I began to understand the importance of being able to defuse tension with a simple and quiet comment that clarifies the issue and concludes the debate for the moment. On numerous occasions throughout my career, I was well served by my ability to reduce tensions among constituents, colleagues, and friends. My goal was to keep dialogue positive and productive by encouraging civility and mutual respect. I was clear in my appreciation of others' points of view. Most DFL Party operatives knew Perpich well and liked him, and many had worked for him in his previous administration. A Perpich–Johnson win in the general election was widely assumed, so being involved in the campaign was now in their personal and partisan best interests.

Our campaign headquarters staff expanded and established a Minneapolis location, and a few former Perpich administration staff members, including former chief of staff Terry Montgomery, started work immediately to establish a transition team in preparation for governing in 1983. Our campaign appearances were generally coordinated with legislative races throughout the state. Not having been in the legislature, I was meeting new legislative leaders as well as voters, visiting new cities and towns every day. Most of the people I met—even those who planned to vote Republican—viewed Rudy as their friend, someone they trusted and admired. These days of campaigning were intense, and I often arrived home exhausted and not quite sure how to process what was happening.

At one point the governor commented to me privately that he did not understand how I could manage without a husband. Accustomed as I was to the biases against single women, I initially heard his comment as sexist—as an example of the traditional expectations about the roles of women and men. But I came to appreciate that his perspective was more nuanced; he was concerned that I didn't have the kind of support that he found essential to his well-being and his success. He relied on his wife, Lola, to be his sounding board and supporter at every turn.

I had always had several friends who were intimate confidants, and during the campaign I continued to count on them, sharing my new experiences and insights with them and relying on their help in processing all that was going on. That had always been my reality, and I accepted it without question. Whenever I got home early enough in the day, I maintained my habit of an early evening walk—on Summit Avenue with Deborah Howell, around Lake Phalen with Nan Skelton, or around Lake Harriet with Karen Desnick. For years, these walks had been great times to decompress, relax, and process. During the campaign, the time I was able to spend with these friends continued to be a huge help, but often, the campaign day ended too late, and all I could do was collapse in a chair for a few minutes before going to bed. Picking up the phone to arrange a walk or simply to talk out the events of the day was more than I felt up to. The adjustment of becoming a public person and having limited time to share my experiences with trusted friends left me with a sense of loneliness that was quite new to me.

The DFL Party organized the election-night celebration for all statewide candidates in the general election. It took place at a Minneapolis hotel, with all the standard festivities of a DFL event, including music and refreshments, to entertain the activists and volunteers as they watched the returns and waited for the candidates to show up. Governor Perpich spent election night on the Iron Range, where his political base was centered. This annoyed the DFL Party establishment, who felt he should be present at the official election-night celebration.

I spent the early part of the evening with friends and family, gathered in a large suite on an upper floor of the hotel where the DFL celebration was held. My mother and siblings were there, along with extended family members and friends. Photographer Charlie Geer, a friend, documented the evening. It meant a lot to me to have my closest friends and family with me for this historic moment, as I prepared to represent the gubernatorial ticket on a stage with the other statewide DFL officeholders at the official celebration. It was my first time in the role of a DFL elected officeholder, and the experience was both exciting and intimidating.

In less than six months, I had made an unlikely journey without the political base that most candidates bring to a campaign. My family and close friends were all very supportive, but none were political operatives. I had often thought about my dad during these months, feeling his pride but wondering what role he would have played. I wasn't a lawyer, with the backing of a law firm that assumed that some partners would be involved in politics for periods of time and then return to the firm. I had not been a DFL Party activist. I had not had a legislative career or held a local government office. But I had paid close attention to my opportunities to interact with Governor Perpich on a range of issues during the past years, and we had developed a mutual respect and enjoyed working together.

I was a single woman embarking on an adventure no woman before me had attempted, and without a spouse for personal support. I was partnered with a governor who had been a lieutenant governor previously but also was not a DFL political insider. He laid the groundwork for me throughout the campaign by articulating the specific roles and responsibilities the lieutenant governor would have in the administration. His confidential guidance would be invaluable in the early days, and over time I would find my footing as the administration's leader in those areas.

By the time of our reelection campaign in 1986 I was feeling comfortable in the role of lieutenant governor and generally enjoying public speaking and the other day-to-day work of campaigning. Despite Perpich's antiabortion position, we were endorsed by the DFL Party. The governor's policy achievements and his appointments reflected significant long-term change. His appointments of women and people of color to dozens of boards and commissions as well as to positions in the judiciary were record breaking. Governor Perpich established pay equity, and his cabinet reflected Minnesota's diversity. Our administration's record was one the DFL was proud to support.

At the same time, George Latimer's challenge in the primary changed the tenor of the campaign. The governor considered Latimer a friend, and so was angry about his decision to run. He was also upset that Arvonne Fraser, Latimer's running mate, appeared to be managing part of their campaign out of her office at the Hubert H. Humphrey School of Public Affairs at the University of Minnesota. I had known Latimer personally for years and considered him a friend as well. I was disappointed and annoyed that he chose to run for governor, but I never felt that he could mount a serious challenge to Perpich. Having grown up in rural Minnesota, I knew that urban politicians rarely understood the rural half of the state, and I believed that he would not have enough time in his first statewide campaign to solve that problem while running against a governor who was so well known and loved. I had also known Arvonne for years, and at times we had publicly disagreed about the best approach to increasing the number of women officeholders. I knew she would generate support in Hennepin County, but she had no experience statewide. For me the primary campaign was something to get through without overreacting.

In our first term we had successfully advanced all of our priority policy agendas, from school open enrollment and the postsecondary option for public school students to the Children's Agenda, and the governor's appointments reflected the diversity that he had actively sought.

Campaign consultant Ray Strother called our record "the best-kept se-cret." The reelection campaign strategy focused on education and eco-nomic development. In my speeches, media interviews, and outreach throughout the state, I reminded voters about our investments in the Children's Agenda and the Whole Child Initiative, and pointed out how we had opened doors for women and people of color. Regarding economic development, I documented the expansion of Minnesota's tourism program and the resulting increase in tourism revenue enjoyed by many of the state's businesses. I kept a full campaign schedule, fo-cused on reaching two groups: women voters, through an emphasis on the governor's appointments of women to the judiciary and to boards and commissions, as well as his commitment to pay equity, youth ini-tiatives, and the Children's Agenda; and voters in the local communities directly affected by the economic benefits derived from the promotion of historic sites, parks, and performing arts venues.

Our primary victory was strong, and Latimer endorsed our ticket the following day. I maintained a full schedule of campaign activities: parades, local media interviews, county fair visits, door knocking with legislative candidates, and fundraisers. I also spent ten days at the Minnesota State Fair, which was a favorite activity of mine. As a young member of 4-H, I had exhibited at the State Fair and competed in a demonstration project. My family's trips to the State Fair had always in-cluded visits to the DFL booth to meet public officials, along with such treasured traditions as getting milkshakes at the Dairy Building. Now as lieutenant governor, I visited with farmers selling milk at the fair, stopped by the beekeepers' booth to join them in selling honey, com-peted with the state's commissioner of agriculture in the cow-milking contest sponsored by WCCO Radio, attended the 4-H animal auction, and of course made daily stops at the DFL booth to visit with constitu-ents. The State Fair was a terrific conclusion to the summer campaign.

We won the general election by a substantial margin. I was ready for campaign mode to be behind us and was looking forward to returning to the work of governing. I did not yet know that my future held an un-expected assignment to lead the state's budget process. But I did believe that this was the final campaign I would be in with Governor Perpich. I had long nurtured a private goal of running for governor, and I shared this goal with the governor when he asked me to be his running mate. At that time he told me that it was his intention to resign in the middle of our second term. Besides wanting to have additional time in the private sector to strengthen his family's economic security, he wanted to facilitate the election of the first woman governor of Minnesota. Whether or not the governor served a full second term, I would soon need to decide if I would run for governor in four years, because if I was going to run, I would have to establish a campaign organization and a strategy.

9

Defining the Role of Lieutenant Governor

Serving as Minnesota's first woman lieutenant governor and also having responsibilities that had not previously been part of the lieutenant governor's duties weighed on me. I needed a crash course in state government, and I needed to think in new ways to advance our agendas, notice and create new opportunities, and bring new constituents into the process.

The decision to publish the lieutenant governor's daily schedule—something no other lieutenant governor's office had done—was intended to reinforce my role in the administration. The schedule would provide ongoing information about my specific responsibilities, showing my daily activities related to meetings of the Capitol Area Architectural and Planning Board, the tourism marketing strategy, and the ongoing work of the open appointments process. Later, the Children's Agenda would be included among my scheduling priorities.

Chairing the Capitol Area Architectural and Planning Board is the statutory responsibility of the lieutenant governor. The CAAPB ensures that the Capitol building and its precinct are restored and maintained in a manner consistent with the design intentions of Cass Gilbert, architect of the Capitol. The CAAPB executive director sought my active engagement with the building restoration work that was then under way and outlined upcoming issues regarding future building in the Capitol precinct. I had little experience in these areas, but I looked forward to learning. Public and private meetings related to this work would be included on my published calendar, a first step in enhancing public awareness of the work.

The Open Appointments Commission, established by executive order of the governor, was a second priority. It would be advisory to the governor, tasked with helping him to achieve his goal of increasing the racial and gender diversity of all state boards and commissions. The governor appointed retired pharmacist and longtime community activist Sam Grais to cochair the commission with me. My team would staff the commission. Sam had been involved in advising the governor on appointments during his previous term and was enthusiastic to be back doing this work. Members of the commission reflected the diversity we sought in all the appointments on which we advised the governor.

Hank Todd, director of the Office of Tourism, had helped me organize the meeting during the transition that set the stage for expanding the tent of the organizations we wanted to work with us on the tourism agenda. In our first meeting, we agreed to create the permanent Tourism Promotion Council and established a schedule for its first several meetings. The Tourism Office staff looked forward to the energy and opportunity that would result from having my leadership and the governor's support. Hank and I agreed on the various organizations that would be represented on the Tourism Promotion Council and outlined the initial agenda. The organizations had been thinking about the possibilities since we had met with them during the transition, so we felt optimistic about moving forward. The Tourism Promotion Council would review and comment on marketing strategies and advocate to the legislature and the industry for a marketing campaign supported by the state budget and industry contributions.

The budget process got under way soon after we took office. In another first for a Minnesota lieutenant governor, I was asked to attend all meetings with the governor in which department budget proposals were reviewed. I often felt like the one person in those meetings with no previous state budget experience. Consequently, my staff and I began reviewing the advance schedule for each agency's presentation and identifying grassroots advocates with specific knowledge of programs in those departments who could help me prepare. I met with individuals to understand their perspectives on the programs, the questions they felt were most important, and the level of support they were hoping to achieve.

Mary Anderson was one of the people I relied on for this invaluable background support. She was a longtime advocate for people with disabilities and a long-standing Perpich supporter, and she became an indispensable guide and a good friend to me as well. What a force of nature she was! She would arrive at my office, deliver a concise overview of the issues, and give me five-by-seven-inch cards filled with details and questions that I could raise in the budget meetings. I always felt energized and knowledgeable at the conclusion of our meetings and was able to attend budget sessions with confidence about the questions and issues I wanted to pay special attention to.

The budget review was an intense and exciting process. I was learning about state government and how a budget was constructed to reflect priorities; most important, I was learning to identify the ways in which I could influence decisions from a position with no authority. The governor noticed my preparation and understood that I was getting help from outside the bureaucracy. At times I asked questions that produced further discussion and interest from the governor and sometimes improved the bottom line for specific programs.

On occasion, I noticed a budget item that I had not anticipated and that had not been on the agenda for discussion. The line item "fire fighter pension" was such a case. As the discussion of this item was winding down, I asked: "Why does the state budget include a firefighter's pension? I didn't know the state had a firefighting unit." The governor glanced at Finance Commissioner Gus Donhowe and asked, "Do you want to tell her?" That's when I learned that the state funded a pension for local volunteer firefighters based on their hours of service. I asked if this was a secret known only to the volunteer firefighters—I assumed that they knew about the pension, but wondered if their spouses knew. Was this one of those extra sources of income that didn't get noted in family budgets or even in divorce agreements? In 1983 there were no female volunteer firefighters in local jurisdictions, and I suspected that sharing the information about the pension fund could be an excellent tool for encouraging women to become volunteer firefighters. The governor and Gus acknowledged that my observations were likely correct. That was all the encouragement I needed. As we concluded that budget session, I made a suggestion to the governor: "From today I will talk about the firefighters' pension in my speeches to women's organizations throughout the state, and I will start encouraging women to serve as volunteer firefighters." The governor seemed pleased that I had noticed this detail and supported my intention. My grasp of state government responsibilities was growing by leaps and bounds. At the end of each day I was exhausted, exhilarated, and coming to terms with how much I had to learn.

During our first year I worked intentionally with the key staff of the Office of Tourism and the other state agencies with roles in tourism to build synergy among the agencies to sustain a longer-term program. "Explore Minnesota" was introduced as our marketing slogan and later adopted by the Department of Transportation for use on license plates. The increased visibility of historic sites, state parks and trails, and the rapidly expanding bike trail system had a significant economic impact on communities. I often spoke to local chambers of commerce about the value of encouraging development among local businesses that had not yet established connections with Minnesota's natural and historic resources, from bicycle rentals to bed-and-breakfast and other hospitality accommodations.

The annual Lieutenant Governor's Bike Ride was established to showcase the diversity of Minnesota's bicycle trail system and to reinforce the economic value of the system to local economies. Each year we chose a different part of the state for the ride, with routes that included back roads, rail-to-trail bike lanes, and local community streets. The rides were open to all citizens and cosponsored by the communities involved.

The work of the Open Appointments Commission was a continuation of work I had engaged in throughout my career. From leading the Minnesota Women's Political Caucus to founding the Minnesota Chapter of the National Association of Women Business Owners, I had often spoken of the importance of full participation of all citizens. My perspective was that when women and men and people of color were all at the table, discussions were richer, with a more comprehensive range of views expressed; this in turn enabled better decision making. The commission's work, and the governor's commitment, offered the chance to act on those values, which I have continued to emphasize in every position I have held.

Sam Grais was an enthusiastic cochair of the commission. We mapped out a schedule of meetings and identified the universe of boards and commissions requiring gubernatorial appointments, paying particular attention to the boards that currently had no women or people of color among their members. We identified vacancy dates, published the vacancies, and invited applications. We also actively recruited as necessary to create diverse pools of candidates. The commission reviewed the applications, interviewed several candidates for each position, and presented the governor with a diverse slate of candidates for each vacancy. I briefed the governor on the commission's recommendations, which were kept confidential.

Learning that the Board of Medical Examiners had never had an African American member, I set out to identify a prospective candidate. What an exciting search that was! Everyone I consulted recommended Dr. Cassius Ellis of St. Louis Park. He agreed to be considered, and soon Governor Perpich appointed him. Dr. Ellis's presence on the board was an initial shock to that previously closed system, but within a couple of years he was elected chair of the board by his peers.

The governor's appointment of a woman to the Board of Accountancy was another disrupter of the old norms. A few days after the appointment was announced, the executive director of that board visited me. He was accustomed to being consulted by the governor's office, he told me, and he was incredulous about the appointment. I reminded him that the governor had spoken repeatedly about his commitment to diversity of membership on all state boards. I noted further that the appointments process had been published, and he had been free to share his recommendations with the Open Appointments Commission, which was responsible for recommending candidates to the governor. I assured him that the commission had interviewed the appointee, that her clients ranked her of the highest quality, and that her community service was well documented. As he left my office in tears, I encouraged him to make recommendations for future vacancies, and to include women and individuals of color among his recommendations.

At the conclusion of our work in 1990, the governor's goal that all boards and commissions include women and people of color among their memberships had been achieved. When I see that today the Board of Medical Practice (formerly the Board of Medical Examiners) is more than 50 percent women and more than one-third people of color, I feel pride in having played a role in executing Governor Perpich's vision and in knowing that over time such diversity has become the new standard.

Commission cochair Sam Grais, a gifted and committed doodler, presented each commission member with one of the doodles he had drawn during our meetings. The drawings he did not distribute among the members were auctioned at the annual fundraiser for local PBS station KTCA-TV. Mine still hangs in my home.

Early in our first term, the director of the Minnesota Children's Campaign Fund urged me to assume a leadership role in creating a "children's agenda" for the state. She felt that the historically unique position I held was exactly what was needed to advance such an agenda. She also recognized that Governor Perpich was open to the kind of policy proposals that needed attention. She was determined, and her concept was compelling. I appreciated her holistic approach to creating public policies and programs to serve children and their families. But I was skeptical that I could be an effective leader in this area. As a woman without children, I wondered if I would have credibility on child-related issues. In our family, my sister Marlys was the expert in children. She was educated in child and family therapy, and spent much of her professional life training early childhood education staff and parents of young children. Anything I knew about children's needs I had learned from her.

The Children's Campaign Fund director was persistent, so I agreed to consult others in the administration and then visit with her again. Ultimately, I concluded that I could articulate children's issues from a broad public policy perspective, be an active learner, and provide public leadership that had not existed previously.

Before making a final commitment, I talked to the governor to share my interest and seek his support for my being the administration's spokesperson on all things related to children and families. He cautioned that it would mark me with a "woman's issue" label, which might be politically disadvantageous. I knew he supported making big changes for children and families, so I countered that without my leadership, a children's agenda would not get the visibility needed to make significant change. Furthermore, I felt this role would allow me to demonstrate my leadership capacity, because I would not be sharing it with anyone else. Other areas of policy, such as the environment, were already "owned" by various legislators, so it would be unlikely that anything I could add would make a significant difference in those areas. The governor accepted my reasoning and agreed that I would drive the administration's agenda for families, children, and youth.

My initial challenge now was to frame our initiatives for children and youth to produce new insights, expand the network of citizen engagement in the issues, and increase legislative and community support for further investment. State and local agencies devoted to everything from human services to education to natural resources had roles to play, as did nonprofit organizations such as 4-H and community churches.

First, we created the Governor's Youth Council by executive order, to advise the governor, monitor legislation, and serve as a clearinghouse of information on youth services and programs in Minnesota. The council was established on August 16, 1983, with fifteen members appointed, including five young people. Kwame MacDonald was appointed executive director and guided the council's work over the next several years.

Then we created the Whole Child Initiative to engage leaders from education, business, recreation, and social services to document the contributions of youth, identify community resources serving young people, recognize gaps in services, and develop multiyear action plans to strengthen programs and engagement with the youth in participating communities. In the first year, we invited several communities to take part in the initiative.

I supported these strategies through community visits, media interviews and public speeches, and conversations with community leaders from mayors and school board members to volunteer leaders in Scouting, 4-H, and churches. I was continually reminded of the importance of using my role to engage a variety of sectors of society in addressing community needs. The Whole Child Initiative coordinated with the Governor's Youth Council to produce community action plans that guided youth activities for several years. Ultimately, a range of exciting programs succeeded in engaging young people in the work of their

communities. Under the guidance of Nan Skelton, assistant commissioner of education, this became one of the most dynamic public–
private efforts undertaken by our administration.

Finally, the Children's Agenda was elevated within the administration, resulting in improved coordination between the Department of
Human Services and the Department of Education, an increase in the
governor's budget for child care, and the inclusion of child-care centers
for state agencies and state universities in the budget. To bring added
visibility to the policy initiatives, I proposed that I deliver a "State of the
Children" speech, a suggestion the governor enthusiastically supported.
The speech would articulate a longer-term vision for the well-being of
Minnesota's children as well as budget parameters for the Children's
Agenda for the coming two years. I delivered the speech in the Rotunda
of the State Capitol. In addition to the local media attention it received,
both the *Washington Post* and the *Chicago Tribune* recognized it as the
first such speech in the nation.

When the child-care legislation came before the legislative committee, I enlisted Harvey Golub, CEO of IDS, to testify in support of the
program, encouraging him to talk about his company's commitment to
child-care services for employees as well as his personal experiences of
caring for his own young children. Honeywell CEO James Renoir, a single dad, also spoke eloquently in support of public investment in child
care. Working with both of them reminded me of the value of reaching
out to find new sources of support; it seemed that people usually answer the phone when a lieutenant governor calls, and if a request is
within the parameters of what they can contribute, their responses are
usually positive.

Employer-supported child care was gaining attention in the early
1980s, and we wanted to establish a child-care center near the Capitol
for state employees and another at one of our state university campuses
for students and faculty. Privately, I initially wondered if capital expen-
ditures were necessary or whether we could just budget for operational
costs of child care where needed. The governor's advice: "If we build a
child-care center, the operational costs will more likely stay in the operational budget each year." I was learning more about the politics of
public policy budgeting.

We announced plans for a child-care center near the Capitol only to have several DFL legislators resist the proposal. Previous surveys had found a lack of employee interest. I suggested that on the day the question is asked, parents have a child-care solution and they assume that any new child-care center will not be completed in time to meet their needs. Ultimately, the Capitol child-care center was included in our capital budget, and by the time construction was under way, the waiting list was longer than the number of spots available—reinforcing the view that when a child-care center is a reality, parents will use it. This conclusion—"If you build it, they will come"—also served me in later positions; if a project meets a documented need and is well designed and well marketed, people will respond.

The first major initiative I undertook as chair of the CAAPB was a call for an international competition to establish a design framework for the Capitol precinct—the several blocks around the Capitol that are defined in the legislation that created the CAAPB. There would be several significant building projects under review in the coming years that would need clear guidelines from the CAAPB. In addition, the construction of Interstate 94, which divided the Rondo neighborhood of St. Paul irreparably, had also separated the Capitol from downtown St. Paul further east. The challenge of making the Capitol more visible from I-94 was included in the design competition parameters. There was significant pushback on the idea that an international competition was needed, and despite the governor's support, I decided to retreat on that detail in order to move forward in a timely manner. The firm chosen was young and creative, and provided a valuable framework for the next twenty years. The recommendations included bridge entrances, lighting, and railings across I-94 to create a visual focus on the Capitol from the interstate.

The Minnesota State Legislature and Minnesota Supreme Court both needed additional office space, the newly created Court of Appeals needed courtroom and office space, and the Minnesota Historical Society wanted to expand. Understandably, all these entities wanted to remain in the Capitol precinct.

The judiciary wanted to convert the Minnesota Historical Society Building to a judiciary building, keeping the three branches of government in the immediate Capitol precinct. Several members of the CAAPB supported that concept, and the CAAPB would make the final decision about the judiciary building as well as the location of a new building for the Historical Society should it be relocated.

A site/design competition for the new Historical Society building was conducted first, to ensure a public discussion of the merits of the existing location as well as other site options. The presentations were interesting and the debate intense. CAAPB members were evenly divided. After reviewing several architectural proposals, engaging in extensive discussion, reflecting on all I'd learned, and getting a good night's sleep, I cast the deciding vote for the location where the society's new home, the Minnesota History Center, currently stands. Many years later, it is hard to appreciate how controversial the choice of that location was. Those opposed believed that moving the Historical Society three blocks away from the Capitol represented a huge loss of status. Within months, however, the new location had broad support. As the design was presented and construction began, skeptics were won over by the strong sight lines to and from the Capitol. In the end, it was a dynamic and successful process for the CAAPB and a successful relocation for the Historical Society.

The experience of chairing the CAAPB, which included engagement with several architectural firms, involvement in public comment sessions, and participation in internal deliberations, introduced me to the role of public design, the need for planning, and the importance of education about public design decisions. Today I recognize signs of the choices made by the planning board during my tenure as chair and appreciate the many thoughtful decisions that have guided subsequent developments throughout the Capitol precinct. I gained a deep appreciation for the impacts that public design decisions have on our daily lives, as well as an enthusiasm for the many examples of public art that dot our collective landscapes as a result of public policies mandating that a percentage of construction costs be spent on public art.

During my time as chair of the CAAPB, the board was also concerned with beginning the long-term process of restoration and recovery of interior spaces of the Capitol. Projects included the restoration of hand-painted murals that had been painted over during the two world wars, owing to the anti-German bias of the time. Many infrastructure upgrades were also needed, requiring careful oversight. The restoration and renovation process begun during my tenure has been completed in the past couple of years. It is gratifying to have played a role in getting that important work started.

Among life's joys are the unexpected moments that touch one's heart. On a rare quiet morning in the early weeks of our first term, a visit from former governor Elmer Andersen brought me just such a moment. He walked into my office with a light step and a huge smile on his face. I hadn't seen him in person since our campaign visit to the H. B. Fuller headquarters months earlier, when he told Governor Perpich how much he supported his choice of running mate and that he felt we would win the general election. Now he had come to the Capitol to welcome me to my new role personally and to mark the occasion with a gift. He presented me with a wooden plaque, a thirteen-by-thirteen-inch diamond-shaped oak board into which he himself had burned the words:

?

CONSPIRACY

CORNER

!

We visited for half an hour. Pleased and proud, he reminded me that I was making history and assured me that my leadership would make a difference even during those times when others did not want me to succeed. "This sign is my way of reminding you every day how much your leadership matters," he said. That plaque hung in my office for the next eight years, and it has been in my office at each subsequent step on my journey. I treasure it to this day.

Early in 1983 I attended my first meeting of the National Conference of Lieutenant Governors (now the National Lieutenant Governors Association), held in Washington, D.C. For the first time there were four women among the members. The most politically experienced woman among us was former congresswoman Martha Griffiths. Martha was one of the most beloved politicians in Michigan and was nationally recognized for her leadership on the Equal Rights Amendment and a number of other women's issues when she served in Congress. She had retired from Congress a few years earlier and was recruited to run for lieutenant governor of Michigan on the ticket with Jim Blanchard. He often credited Martha with his victory.

Martha and I met in the first hour of the meeting and engaged informally between sessions throughout the day. She invited me to join her for a private dinner that first evening. During our meal, she peppered me with questions about my background, my role in the Perpich administration, and my relationship with the governor. Then she urged me to keep in mind that I was obligated to be ready to become governor every day. Upon learning that I had open access to the governor's decision-making process, she urged me to be intentional about learning from him, to consider actively whether I would make the same decisions he was making. She assured me that there was no need to disagree with the governor once he made his decisions. Rather, my responsibility was to think about how I would approach the same issues if I were the governor. "Take notes," she continued. "Keep them confidential and reflect. Keep an ongoing list of who would be in your cabinet if you became governor tomorrow—who will you keep, who will you replace and with whom." Martha continued to offer me generous guidance over the years, and years later she hosted a reception in my honor at her Detroit condo to introduce me to her political network. With Martha's advice in my ear, my working journal became an even more important tool as I faced each day. Her mentorship remains among my life treasures.

10

Learning to Punt

Colleagues have often commented on how easily I adapt to last-minute adjustments in plans. My years as lieutenant governor gave me considerable practice in becoming comfortable with handling unforeseen events, but one particular childhood experience marks the moment when I first learned to punt in a crisis.

When I was five years old, my parents recognized my need for structure and challenge. No kindergarten was offered in the local schools, so their solution was to sign me up for weekly piano lessons with Mr. Franklin, our town's full-time piano teacher.

The annual piano recital featuring Mr. Franklin's fifty students was a village highlight. The students all dressed up, and I wore a floor-length organza dress that my mother had made for me when I was the flower girl in a recent family wedding. The students gathered with Mr. Franklin in the basement of the Lutheran church, where the recital was held. As his youngest student, I was to play first. Mr. Franklin and I walked hand in hand up the stairs from the basement and down the center aisle to the front of the church. I hadn't memorized my number—"Flight of the Bumblebee" by Nikolai Rimsky-Korsakov—in the few weeks I had been taking lessons, so I carried my sheet music in my left hand.

I didn't anticipate the need to hold up the skirt of my long dress as we climbed the stairs, so my left hand, holding the sheet music, was on the hand rail. Then, in a split second, I stepped on the hem of the dress, and the stitching at the waist tore open in the front! Embarrassed and not wanting to interrupt our walk up the stairs, I dropped my hand from the railing and grabbed the upper part of the skirt, still hanging on to my sheet music and holding it in front of me as Mr. Franklin and I proceeded up the aisle to our seats in the front row.

When it was time for me to perform, I carefully stood up from my seat and walked slowly to the stage. Hiding the damaged waist of the dress behind the sheet music, I announced my number; I then sat down at the piano, carefully arranged my dress, and played "Flight of the Bumble Bee." When I finished, I stood to take a bow and returned to my seat, again holding the sheet music to cover the torn dress. When I arrived home with my parents, I broke down crying. They had no idea what had happened. Hearing my story, they gave me a hug and told me, "You performed really well, and you handled this small crisis just fine." The dress could be repaired, and I had found a way to complete the performance. This first memory of "carrying on" in the face of the unexpected gave me some early understanding that I could adjust to such situations successfully.

The piano recital incident has been a terrific story to tell over the years. I have often thought about that experience as the moment when I started to learn to adapt quickly. Whenever I am asked how I learned to handle all the last-minute adjustments required in my position as lieutenant governor, the piano recital "crisis" comes to mind. From that moment, I began to realize that, yes, I was comfortable with the unexpected and could adapt as required in any given situation. Years later, when I was serving as CEO of NAFSA: Association of International Educators, the opening speaker for our conference's plenary session, Robert Gates, former U.S. secretary of defense, was several hours late because of an airplane malfunction. While he changed planes and got a police escort to deliver him to the conference hall forty-five minutes later than the session had been scheduled to begin, I joined our board chair, Meredith McQuaid, in "working the line," shaking hands and sharing stories with the attendees who were waiting, creating new stories that added to the lore of the conference and keeping attendees energized and willing to wait.

During my eight years as lieutenant governor, being able to punt, and being comfortable doing so, made many days more fun, introduced me to significant new professional challenges, and changed the course of my life. Two unexpected events in particular remain memorable because of the situations and the decisions I made to embrace the opportunities. Both events were part of my political daily work. One, which began as a scheduling adjustment to accommodate the governor, resulted in my meeting Peter Frankel, the person I would later marry. The other elevated my role in the administration and allowed me to design a new approach to budgeting and advocating for the Children's Agenda.

I could not have imagined a personal life-changing outcome when, early in our first term, I agreed to represent the governor in a meeting with a representative of Britt Mogård, governor of Sweden's Kronoberg County. Governor Mogård and Governor Perpich had met earlier and discussed establishing a formal relationship between Kronoberg and Minnesota. Since I would be in Sweden the following month to open the Minnesota Trade Office, this meeting would also help me prepare for that trip. I agreed to take the meeting, and my previous plans were rescheduled.

At the meeting, Swedish banker Johnny Andersson presented a letter from Governor Mogård proposing a "sister state" relationship between Kronoberg and Minnesota. Andersson and his adviser, Peter Frankel, were on a ten-day business development trip in the United States. The Minnesota visit was the first stop on their schedule. In our meeting, Peter took the chair farthest from me, as he was accompanying Andersson rather than representing Governor Mogård. He participated minimally in the conversation.

The hour-long visit was friendly and casual, covering topics from Swedish culture in Minnesota to opportunities for business between Sweden and Minnesota. I learned that our visitors were staying in Minnesota through the weekend. I casually inquired whether they liked classical music, and when they said yes, I asked if they would like to attend a Saint Paul Chamber Orchestra concert with me on Saturday, to which they also said yes. For years my friends the Desnicks and I had been SPCO season ticket holders. I asked if they would be willing to give up one of their tickets and for one of them to cohost the Swedish guests. Karen had already decided that she did not want to go to the concert, and her husband, Leslie, was happy to participate.

The following day, the governor's office asked me to cohost, with the governor, a dinner for the Swedes at the Governor's Residence on Saturday. The First Lady was out of town, but the governor wanted to meet the Swedes and talk further about the sister state relationship. The Trade Office team would also attend. Since I had invited the Swedes to the SPCO concert, the dinner would need to be an early one, which suited the governor well.

At the Governor's Residence, the governor raised a glass for a welcome toast. With a smile in his eyes, he caught my eye at the opposite end of the table and said to the group, "My goal is to get her married!" I don't recall ever being more angry with the governor than at that moment. I was speechless and met his look with a glare, prompting him to comment, "I'm going to pay for that for a long time." He immediately changed the subject and engaged the group in a wide-ranging conversation, and I pushed this moment of "Perpich humor" out of my mind. By now I had considerable practice moving right along when the unexpected happened. His comment was beyond unexpected, but despite my anger, no appropriate response came to me. I would recall his comment years later.

The SPCO concert was a hit with the group. There was little time for conversation, but I felt an emerging positive tension between Peter and me. After the concert, we went for a drink at the historic Hotel Saint Paul in downtown St. Paul. I was happy to show the Swedish visitors this lovely urban square flanked by historic buildings. Later, as we said goodbye, Peter and I nervously made tentative plans to meet in Stockholm the next month, while I was there to open the Minnesota Trade Office.

Following our 1986 reelection, another event reinforced for me the importance of my ability to punt. Speaking before an audience in a school auditorium, the governor outlined his vision for our second term; I was there, along with his cabinet and senior staff. I recall only one detail of that speech: the governor announced that the lieutenant governor would be overseeing the budget process. Terry Montgomery, the governor's chief of staff, looked at me with the hint of a smile, knowing that I was hearing this for the first time. I can't say I ever came to appreciate such surprises, but I once again recognized that it was important to adjust quickly to the situation. I also understood that in this case I was being given an opportunity that would be consequential for me in the administration.

Since the budget process was rarely discussed publicly, the announcement of my role received little attention in the press. I had participated in the budget meetings for the previous budget cycles and knew how the process worked under the governor's direction. The governor, Terry, and I met to discuss how they viewed my role this time. I would chair the agency budget review meetings and make decisions on those matters where I was confident I understood the governor's priorities. If I felt there was a potential policy shift being proposed, I would flag that item for the governor's review and decision. How I ran the process with the agency heads was up to me, and on those details I would work with Brian Roherty, the budget director, and Tom Triplett, the commissioner of finance.

This was a fantastic opportunity for me to strengthen the Children's Agenda and the tourism marketing strategy, where I had specific responsibilities. Brian Roherty and I decided to make adjustments in the agency budget review process in those areas. Nan Skelton, assistant commissioner of education and my active collaborator on the Children's Agenda, suggested that we meet collectively with agencies with programs related to child care, children's education, and social welfare programs, to review their respective roles in the Children's Agenda. We wanted changes that would ensure more effective and coordinated programs and responses to the needs of children. We planned a similar approach for the tourism marketing agenda.

Agency heads were told that their agency budget review meetings would include everything except the programs that were part of the Children's Agenda or the tourism strategy. They would then participate in a special review of all the programs that fit those two policy areas with the other appropriate agency leaders.

In the two targeted meetings—for the tourism promotion strategy and the Children's Agenda—the interagency groups would discuss and identify how the various programs connected and find ways to strengthen program coordination and ultimately improve services for children or enhance tourism promotion. There was a new enthusiasm among agencies with child-centered programs as they realized that we would strengthen public visibility for the Children's Agenda. And the "Explore Minnesota" marketing campaign was embraced more broadly among all the affected agencies, producing a coordinated message that we had not previously achieved.

The final review of issues flagged for the governor's decision took one meeting and resulted in no surprises. The governor and I agreed that the process had been innovative and constructive, and had produced a budget that advanced the governor's agenda. My understanding of the state programs and budget had expanded considerably. And my leadership through this budget process had improved policy and program coordination in two of the administration's policy priorities. As we concluded that budget process, I recalled those first budget review meetings four years earlier, when I had arrived with note cards to help me track details and ask appropriate questions. I had come a long way and was in a good place.

The 1987 opening of the Minnesota World Trade Center in St. Paul was another occasion when I found myself grateful for my ability to respond to the unexpected. Governor Perpich had envisioned the center as a symbol of Minnesota's commitment to international trade, an office tower filled with international businesses. Despite considerable political and media resistance, he had garnered both legislative support and private investment for the project, and the Minnesota World Trade Center was built in downtown St. Paul. A grand opening was planned, and several ambassadors to the United States were invited. I was scheduled to attend, but the governor was expected to host the opening-day events.

Then, days before the opening, the governor announced that he was fed up with the criticism he had received over the years about the World Trade Center and had now decided that he would not attend. I was privately outraged and discouraged, as this decision felt like a huge detour in how he approached his leadership role. Previously, he had consistently owned his successes, quietly enjoying them despite any opposition. Having faced down all of the political challenges leading up to the establishment of the World Trade Center, the governor had prevailed. His decision not to attend the opening and celebrate something he had worked so hard for was out of character for him.

Rick Nolan, president of the World Trade Center, quickly announced that former vice president Walter Mondale would host the grand opening. I was furious—not because I didn't want Mondale to play a role, but because Rick had not discussed it with me. I was scheduled to participate, and as lieutenant governor, in the governor's absence, I should have been the host. I called Rick and expressed my outrage in language

I'm quite sure he had never heard me use before. After my ten-minute rant and Rick's apology, we ended the call. Ten minutes later Rick was in my office, apologizing again. We then discussed how we would adjust the program to include me in a fitting leadership role.

To his credit, Rick responded appropriately. And I had expressed my personal views about how my position had been disregarded. It certainly wasn't the first time I had experienced such disregard, but it may have been the first time I had been so honest and direct in confronting the person responsible. It helped that Rick and I were longtime friends, and I clearly felt safe in speaking the truth to him.

In the end, Rick chaired the opening-day events, and St. Paul mayor George Latimer, former vice president Mondale, and I shared the hosting responsibilities. At the final dinner, I was seated beside the Egyptian ambassador. He told me that he was impressed that Minnesota had an international business strategy, and then asked, "Why isn't Governor Perpich here?" I could only share his disappointment that the governor wasn't present, noting that engaging Minnesota in international trade had been his vision, and his tenacity had won the day.

11

Serendipity

As I built my business and engaged in women's political action, my support came from a rich network of friends with whom I regularly shared long walks around the Minneapolis lakes or along Summit Avenue, dinner dates, and season tickets; I had little time left to consider whether I might be lonely. Yet by the early 1980s, I felt increasingly open to meeting someone with whom I could share my life. Acknowledging to myself that I would like to be in a committed relationship was an important step, but I had not met anyone with whom such a commitment felt possible.

For the first fifteen years of my professional life, work and play were indistinguishable. I was totally engaged in building a business, organizing women (in the Minnesota Women's Political Caucus and the National Association of Women Business Owners), and serving on boards of nonprofit organizations. Marriage and children were not on my agenda. Life was exciting and rewarding. Except for a few weekends at my family's lake cabin in northern Minnesota, my first vacation was in 1980, when I joined friends on a ten-day trip to London.

I enjoyed children and loved being an aunt. It was a comfortable role, and if having children of my own crossed my mind, I dismissed the idea, believing motherhood was something I would not be good at. I had limited experience with dating and serious relationships. Being on my own was generally comfortable, and I spent little time expecting things to be different. In business, I experienced institutional biases against single women, such as not being able to qualify for a bank loan without a man's signature, and social biases as well, reflected in few or no invitations to business-related social events because I didn't have a spouse. Since this was my reality, I had only a vague understanding of what I was missing.

My public role as lieutenant governor made it feel even less likely that I would find the space for a relationship or even an opportunity to meet someone. Then, late in the fall of my first year in office, while filling in for the governor in a meeting with Swedish banker Johnny Andersson and his colleagues, I met Peter Frankel. We saw each other again a couple of days later when the governor asked me to cohost a dinner for the Swedish visitors at the Governor's Residence, and then I took them to a concert of the Saint Paul Chamber Orchestra.

A month later, days before I left for Sweden to open the Minnesota Trade Office there, Peter called to suggest that we have dinner on the evening I arrived in Stockholm. We agreed to meet at the restaurant in my hotel. After our meal, Peter and I walked the cobblestone streets of Gamla Stan (Old Town), stopped for a brief listen at a church choir service, meandered through the streets "window shopping," and then walked to Stampen Jazz Club (The Pawn Shop). We were comfortable with each other and felt an emerging attraction as the evening went on. Peter had come to Stockholm from his home in Lund in southern Sweden and was returning to Lund the following morning.

Following the opening of the Minnesota Trade Office, I traveled to Växjö, Sweden, for a few days with Governor Britt Mogård of Kronoberg. A former minister of education for Sweden, she was a highly regarded public leader. I delivered the signed sister state agreement between Kronoberg and Minnesota, and she hosted a luncheon with community business leaders, farmers, and artists. We toured the Glass Museum, the Immigrants Museum, and the Immigrants Research Center for genealogical research. Governor Mogård also proposed an annual Minnesota Day in Växjö and suggested that Governor Perpich or I attend. The day's events would include performances by Minnesotans and presentations about the connections between Sweden and Minnesota.

While I was in Växjö, Peter stopped by for a short visit. The chemistry between us was strong, but it was hard to imagine how we could manage to stay in touch. As I headed back to Minnesota we agreed to write letters and talk on the phone in a week or two. We wanted to stay in contact, but we knew it would not be easy.

The idea of a transatlantic relationship was rather far-fetched, even to us, so we wanted to be intentional about our communications. We began with daily letters written in longhand on thin airmail stationery. We shared details of our days, stories about our childhoods, and reflections—from the amusing to the profound. I learned that Peter strongly disliked fish balls and had tea and porridge for breakfast! We shared deeply personal stories of our families and friends, as well as our joys and fears. We wrote every day and talked on the telephone twice a week. The letters took seven to nine days to reach us, so often we received answers to our questions in our phone calls before we'd seen the written responses. That too became an important part of getting to know each other, as it gave us additional time to reflect on many of our conversations, the details of which might have been lost if we had only been talking in person or on the phone.

Eventually we became impatient waiting for each other's letters to arrive, so we both purchased home fax machines, which allowed us to send and receive our letters every day. It is hard to appreciate now, but international telephone calls were expensive. Personal fax machines were uncommon: they cost about four hundred dollars and used rolls of shiny thermal paper. I was the first person among my friends with a fax machine at home, and it became an amusing dinner conversation topic for weeks.

Besides our letters and telephone calls, Peter and I met in person for long weekends in Lund, London, New York, and Minnesota. Soon we knew we wanted a life together even though our individual professional commitments required that we would not be able to live together all the time. Some friends thought ours was an unrealistic goal. Fortunately, many others, including Peter's sister Antje and my sister Marlys, supported us from the beginning. Of course the weeks apart were challenging, but we also appreciated how enriching it was to learn about each other's cultures. I was experiencing a deep love and support that I hadn't felt before.

We chose September 24, 1988, as our wedding date. Hoping to avoid months of press attention, we decided to announce our marriage at the same time the invitations went in the mail. While Peter had attended some public events with me, our relationship was known mostly to our families, close friends, and my staff, so we shared our plans earlier and confidentially with them, with the pastor at Westminster Presbyterian Church who would officiate, and with Carole Faricy, a close friend who helped arrange a venue for the reception.

The day before I returned to Minnesota from our August 1988 summer holiday in Sweden, I phoned Governor Perpich to tell him that I was getting married on September 24. He asked who I was marrying! He had met Peter a number of times, but one of his sources had told him I was dating a journalist who covered parks and fishing. It was a bizarre rumor that I hadn't heard. The person he mentioned was a friend, a supporter of our tourism strategy, and married. He and I had never even had lunch together. I suggested to the governor that he needed better sources, and that if he was curious about my life, he might just ask me! He took my point, laughed, and wished us well.

As I traveled back to Minnesota, my office announced the date of our wedding. Our secret was so well kept that when he read the news account, the senior pastor at Westminster Presbyterian expressed annoyance that I had not scheduled my wedding at his church. He soon learned that our wedding was on the church calendar under another name. The caterer at the Minnesota Museum of Art, Soile Anderson, was also disappointed that she had not been asked to cater our reception, only to learn from Carole Faricy that the catering contract she had signed for September 24 was for our wedding, not Carole's personal event.

The wedding was modest—most of the people we invited were family and friends I had known before I was a public official. Governor Perpich and the First Lady came to the wedding ceremony but declined to attend the reception so as not to distract from our celebration. I was especially happy that my great-aunt Ruth Wilde, my grandmother's younger sister, attended. She was ninety years old and blind from macular degeneration. She and I were very close. She lived alone in a tiny house on a quiet Edina street, and for a few years I had been visiting her several times a week, bringing her treats, sharing stories, and putting things in order as needed. She adored Peter. She was reluctant to come to the wedding until she learned that her nephew and my uncle, Clarence Nelson, would pick her up, escort her in the church, and drive her home after the ceremony. She sat in the front row of the church to be able to focus on us. It would be the last time she ventured out of her home.

Peter's mother, sister, Antje Frankel, and niece and nephew, Lotta and Krister Frankel, came from Sweden. My siblings and their children and my aunts and uncles joined us, as well as a few friends from Macalester, Denmark, and my community and entrepreneur life. A few friends from my earlier political life were also there, as were William Norris and Leeann Chin, two business leaders I had worked with for many years. Former governor Elmer Andersen and his wife, Eleanor, sent their regrets. An elaborate Swedish smorgasbord buffet was laid out, with gravlax, a variety of salads, and a cake layered with Swedish cloudberries. Sandy Keith made the first toast "on behalf of Beauford" (my father and a supporter of Sandy's run for governor in 1966). It was a lovely moment, further celebrated with the appearance of a rainbow as we stood at the window overlooking the Mississippi River. Three musicians from the Moldy Figs jazz ensemble played the dance music.

Following a two-week holiday and honeymoon enjoying the sunshine and beaches near Marbella, on the southern east coast of Spain, and drives to Ronda and other parts of the Spanish countryside, we settled into our transatlantic life.

12

A Transatlantic Life Together

Peter and I approached managing households in our two countries practically. We both had considerable life experience and professional responsibilities in our own societies. In Minnesota, then Washington, D.C., our home was in my name, and I managed our life on this side of the pond. In Lund, Sweden, our home was in Peter's name, and he managed our life there. Each of us managed the day-to-day chores and created our social lives with our family and friends in both locations.

We generally succeeded in being present for the big events in each other's spaces—from family gatherings to professional and political events. Peter joined me for the farewell dinner for Pinchas Zukerman when he ended his term as music director of the Saint Paul Chamber Orchestra and for an exhibition of art created by men incarcerated at Stillwater State Prison. Later, he attended the event with Professor Anita Hill when I was part of a small group of women who raised funds to establish the Anita Hill Endowed Chair at the University of Oklahoma Law School. When I served as CEO of NAFSA: Association of International Educators, Peter joined me at annual conferences and board dinners. I accompanied him on client trips to Montreal, New Orleans, and the Gold Coast of Spain, and to family weddings and graduations in Lund. Peter was in Minnesota for my sister's big birthday party, a friend's fortieth birthday, and a friend's bar mitzvah, and he went with me to another friend's son's wedding in Wisconsin. For the Christmas holidays, we alternated between Sweden and the United States. It was our normal, and we thrived on the richness of our life.

Our annual summer stays in the Swedish countryside were a firm commitment for both of us. Three weeks of quiet time, enjoying the garden, hiking the forest trails, biking the back roads, swimming at the lake just a walk away, driving through the countryside, and visiting nearby sculpture gardens—these weeks were precious. The time was also a metaphor for a cultural difference between Sweden and the United States. Although summer vacations were generally established habits among my friends and acquaintances and a Minnesota cabin at the lake is relatively common, as an adult I had not taken a vacation of three consecutive weeks until I met Peter. Most Americans I knew hadn't either. In Sweden, a three-week summer holiday and one to three additional weeks during the year is the standard amount of vacation time. Swedes view holiday time as essential to quality family life and as necessary for the health and well-being of all workers. I would come to value the tradition deeply, but it took me a few years to maintain the habit without Peter's coaxing.

While Peter had no previous experience with a political life, throughout our marriage he helped me learn to handle the demands of my public roles. On the occasions when I was attending an event but was not expected to speak, I would often feel uncertain and uncomfortable about how to engage with others. The first time Peter accompanied me to such an event, worrying about how he was doing added to my anxiety. I came home feeling stressed and exhausted. Ever the problem solver, Peter observed that I was approaching these events as if they were parties with friends. He urged me to view them instead as work and suggested that before I left home I should decide what I wanted to accomplish. When he was with me, we should talk about what role he could play to help me. We agreed on signals we could give each other from across the room for "I need help," "Time to go home," or "Things are good." Peter's matter-of-fact support and problem solving were reassuring and comforting.

I was amazed by Peter's capacity for asking questions that got to the heart of my anxiety. When he challenged my thinking, I sometimes became defensive, to which he would simply say, "It's not important to me that you follow my suggestion, only that you understand my point of view." It took me a while to absorb it, but that was exactly how he felt. His consistent support was emotionally comforting in a way I could not have imagined previously, and over time it helped to strengthen my self-confidence.

At times, Peter expressed his views about how I presented myself. My most vivid recollection of such a comment is one that he made after we had attended the opening of an exhibition of art created by men who were incarcerated at Stillwater State Prison. I had supported the planning for the exhibition and spoke briefly at the opening reception, wearing a bright-blue designer dress with a Peter Pan collar. Back at home later that evening, Peter said, "You shouldn't wear that dress again. It's a young girl's dress, not that of a lieutenant governor." I had a limited wardrobe, mostly skirt-and-jacket suits for everyday business, and I found it challenging to choose clothes appropriate for other occasions. With my limited clothes budget, I had been shopping the sales at Frank Murphy, a women's boutique in downtown St. Paul. On this occasion Peter's feedback was hard to hear, yet I understood his point, and on reflection I agreed. I recycled that dress immediately so I would not be reminded of the mistake or wear it again in a pinch. Going forward, I shopped with a consultant at Harold Department Store or with Peter. Fortunately, he enjoyed shopping for clothes with me because he saw it as helping me do my job. Otherwise, he was uninterested in shopping of any kind beyond groceries.

Peter loved spending time with my family and engaging in family gatherings of all kinds. He thought he had the best mother-in-law one could hope for, and she adored him as well. During the final years with my great-aunt Ruth, Peter enthusiastically joined me when I visited her. She was born in Minnesota, but her parents and older sister, my grandmother, were born in Sweden, so she grew up speaking Swedish at home. She loved trying to speak Swedish with Peter, even though it had been eighty years since she had spoken it and Peter couldn't understand much of the dialect she spoke. They enjoyed each other's company very much.

We also had wonderful times with Peter's family in Sweden. He and his sister Antje were close. We spent time with her and her husband each time I was in Sweden, as well as with his mother, who lived close by in Lund. Peter's adult children were establishing their careers and families. We went on nature excursions, attended outdoor musical events, and spent time at the beach with the children each summer. For several years we organized an American-style Fourth of July gathering at our country house, with burgers, potato salad, and watermelon, and a tricycle parade around the flagpole for the youngest children. Peter's son Jonas and his family spent a Christmas holiday with us in Washington that included attending a Wizards basketball game. Grandson Anton got hooked on basketball, joined a team in Lund, and returned to D.C. with Peter to see another Wizards game. Anton remains a Wizards fan to this day.

Peter also wanted my extended family to spend time with us in Sweden. When we converted a workshop building to a guesthouse, we invited my siblings and their families to spend a few days helping with specific projects around the property. Peter's invitation stated: "We want you to leave your mark here, so you and we always remember that you were here, and we hope you'll choose to come back." Many of the signs of their help that summer are still noticeable and bring back wonderful memories: the window shades and mullions they installed to give the windows a more authentic Swedish look, the improvements they made to the dock at the stream, and the work they did to enrich the garden soil to assure a healthier rhubarb crop in the future.

As I've mentioned, Peter and my mother were very fond of each other. She made several visits to Sweden to spend a week or two with us in the countryside and came to see us in Washington a couple of times as well. We spent a Christmas holiday with her in Minnesota, and another time we joined her for a few days at her cabin on Stony Lake. She often talked about the traveling she and my dad had shared and lamented that the one trip they had not been able to do before he died was an Alaska inland boat cruise. Periodically I would mention to Peter that I'd like to take her on that trip. In early 2008, he said, "If you really want to do that, let's do it this year or quit talking about it." He got my attention. Days later I called my mother and suggested the trip, and encouraged her to ask a friend to join us. She loved the idea and invited Gladys Brynoldson. Mother and Gladys had been the first women elected to the board of the electric cooperative that my dad founded. They traveled to national electric co-op meetings together and had become good friends. Gladys accepted the invitation, and the four of us met in Seattle in June 2008 to begin the ten-day excursion. Our two adjacent staterooms had balconies from which we took in magnificent views every day. We visited across our balcony railings, absorbed breathtaking scenery, and shared casual meals as well as formal dinners. When the boat was docked, sometimes Mother and Gladys chose a quiet lunch at the waterfront while Peter and I took a bike ride or a hike in the forest. We all enjoyed a trip together on the historic Alaska Railroad, which we learned had been built by Minnesota workers. This ten-day adventure was one of many ways Peter helped me build a stronger relationship with my mother. I saw her through his eyes, watched her engage with him in conversations on topics she and I had never touched on, and came to more fully appreciate her capacity for learning.

During our first years together, I often found myself comforted by having Peter in my corner—a security I hadn't felt before. I recalled a conversation with the governor early in our first campaign in which he wondered how I managed without a husband. As I grew to count on Peter's support, I had a new appreciation for what the governor had meant.

Although Peter and I didn't have the day-to-day in-person time that many couples count on, I always felt his presence and support. At some point I recognized that our reality was not unlike situations where one member of a couple travels for work, spending weeks at a time away from home for years. Military families and families of corporate executives with extensive travel requirements experience similar separations. While many thought our situation was odd, the separations of traveling corporate or military families are generally seen as normal. I learned that all of us try to manage within our own reality.

Peter and I spoke on the phone every day, often several times a day. We wrote letters, then emails (short notes and longer ones)—whatever worked at the moment. Peter usually worked from Minnesota and later Washington one week a month, between our holidays or our long weekends together in Sweden or other locations. Eventually, we included a winter break in the sunshine on our annual calendar. Our winter destinations included the Canary Islands, the Gold Coast of Spain, Costa Rica, and Saint Martin in the Caribbean. On our first weekends away during my public life, I often arrived at our destination with a very bad headache or other stress-related condition. Peter was a terrific caregiver, even though I was a rather uncooperative and embarrassed patient. Learning how to relax and be cared for in this personal way was yet another of my life lessons.

13

,,\\\\\\\|||||||||////.

Peter

Who was this person who showed up in my office that day in October 1983? Peter was the firstborn of a Swedish dad and a German mom. His parents met when his father visited Norderney, a German island in the North Sea where his mother grew up. She was working at the restaurant her parents owned when Knut Frankel came in for an afternoon coffee and cake. They fell in love, and to her parents' chagrin, Peter's mother left Germany in the mid-1930s to marry this Swede. Immigration restrictions required her to stay in Denmark for several months before she was allowed to immigrate to Sweden.

When Peter was five years old, he and his three-year-old sister, Antje, accompanied their mother on a train trip to Norderney to help her parents in their restaurant. The planned month-long visit was extended when Antje contracted scarlet fever and had to be quarantined; she was cared for at a local convent, where visits from her mother and brother were limited to chats through the window. Three months later, when Antje had recovered, they returned to Sweden. They left for Sweden not long before the official start of World War II, and German troops were already visible on the streets of Norderney. This experience remained a strong memory for Peter.

Peter was a creative and active child, exploring, experimenting, and generally following his own instincts, leaving his parents frustrated about their inability to "control" him and feeling that he needed further discipline. As a young teen, he was sent to live and work on a farm in southern Sweden for several months, then to work as a deckhand on a ship traveling from Malmö to Kalmar. Subsequently, his father sent him to England to live with friends in High Wycombe, where he studied English and art and fell in love for the first time. He had wonderful memories of his time in England, but these experiences of being sent away reinforced for Peter that his parents' approval was elusive—that he wasn't "okay."

With the help of an art teacher, Peter was accepted at the art school connected to NK, the major Swedish retail company. Subsequently, he completed his gymnasium education, then a degree in political science at Lund University.

Peter married in his early twenties, and he and his wife had two children. For three years, the family lived in Germany, where Peter led a medium-size company. He enjoyed living in Germany and speaking German at work. The family then returned to Sweden, and Peter began working on a PhD, but he put that aside to join several colleagues in establishing a consulting group with a shared interest in "action learning" methodology. A core element of action learning is working in a group of individuals from different types of organizations, sharing perspectives with the aim of solving particular problems. The firm that Peter's group founded, Albatross 78, was devoted to facilitating strategic change in mature organizations.

As the managing partner of Albatross 78, Peter was involved in designing a path for the renewal of the Gothenburg economy following the decline of the shipping industry. He created a successful model, the outcomes of which were published, and the project strengthened his interest in helping mature businesses reinvent themselves. The Albatross 78 team embraced the concept of continuous learning and was engaged in the sensitivity training movement that emerged in the 1970s.

In the early 1980s, Peter and his wife divorced; their children were young adults by then, living on their own. As Peter and I spent more time together and our relationship deepened, he explored business opportunities in Minnesota. He established collaborative relationships with a number of business advisers interested in international trade opportunities, including the Minnesota Cooperation Office and the Hubert H. Humphrey School of Public Affairs at the University of Minnesota. Later, he provided consulting services to a biotechnology firm, taking payment in stock in lieu of fees. Peter maintained close contacts with the CEO of that firm. Unfortunately, his other efforts in Minnesota failed to produce substantive business prospects. He found little interest there in the action learning methodology that guided his approach to business development.

In Sweden, Peter purchased the southern Sweden franchise for Hjärntrusten (The Brain Trust), an organization that used an action learning approach to working with groups of six to eight executives from noncompeting companies who shared and supported each other in problem solving and exploring business opportunities. Peter led several Hjärntrusten groups each year, some of which worked together for a number of years. He loved this work and maintained close personal relationships with many of the participants, beyond their professional connections.

Shortly after we were married in 1988, our first granddaughter, Sara, was born to Peter's son, Jonas, and his wife, Helena. Sara was the first of their four children. Peter was an enthusiastic *farfar* (grandfather), often picking up the grandchildren from day care and spending time with them before their parents returned from work. These were treasured memories for him and them. For our youngest grandchild, Theodor, these day-care moments are his only memories of his grandfather, as Peter's brain injury occurred shortly after Theo stopped going to day care.

We spent time with the whole family whenever I was in Sweden, and Peter's children and grandchildren spent a Christmas holiday with us in Washington. Sara and grandson Anton both made trips to Washington with Peter on their own. Later, Sara came to the United States as an American Field Service exchange student; she lived with a host family in Arkansas and spent some of her holidays with us in Washington.

Peter's life experience had taught him the value of following one's dreams, trying new things, and never giving up. His academic and professional experiences had reinforced those values. As our relationship developed, his unwavering support, his compassion, and his deep comfort in always finding a way through a challenge helped me find strength in myself that I hadn't previously known. His guidance helped me to approach my leadership roles with greater intentionality and to accept losses as challenges to be understood and embraced. On occasion, I reacted defensively to his feedback, ready for a fight. He simply reminded me that he wasn't concerned about my taking his advice; what was important to him was only that I understood his perspective as I decided what action to take. Learning to hear feedback in this way has been critical to my various leadership roles over the years, and one of the lessons I often share with those I continue to mentor.

Although Peter did not pursue art as a career, he took watercolor and drawing classes periodically throughout his life. I often found him outdoors, sitting on a rock or a beach, painting. He left a collection of watercolors reflecting the many trips we took as well as his favorite spots in the countryside of southern Sweden. When we were visiting friends, he often painted scenes from their homes or from walks that we shared and left the paintings behind for them as keepsakes. Later, when Peter was living in a nursing home, our friend Marie Bass helped me produce a book of his watercolors to present as a gift to our family and friends.

14

New Ways to Engage

In Minnesota the lieutenant governor's one statutory responsibility is to chair the Capitol Area Architectural and Planning Board, which makes design and location decisions related to the grounds of the Capitol precinct as well as the Capitol and other buildings within the precinct. Additional responsibilities of the lieutenant governor are designated by the governor.

During the years Rudy Perpich had served as lieutenant governor, he and Governor Wendell Anderson had no working relationship at all. Governor Perpich sought a different model for his administration, and that included defining specific roles and responsibilities for his lieutenant governor. I was tasked with serving as cochair of the Open Appointments Commission and with guiding the state's tourism promotion strategy.

My role in the administration evolved as I demonstrated my leadership capacity and learned how to use my influence to advance the governor's agenda. Day to day, agency heads needed to feel that my support enhanced their strategies. Learning to influence others from a position with no authority was my challenge and my goal.

The beginning of my tenure as lieutenant governor was an intense time. The volume of new information and ideas I had to absorb left me excited and at times intimidated by the opportunity to help shape policy. The governor's open invitation for me to participate in the constituent and policy meetings in his office was invaluable. I prioritized joining meetings related to education reform, business development, and the

Children's Agenda, so that I could learn more about those areas in which I had particular responsibilities and could take advantage of opportunities to engage the governor more actively on those issues. It was stimulating to watch him engage with, question, and respond to ideas and then create policy directions in real time. The governor's staff often did not participate in these meetings—a frustration for them, but the governor's preference. On occasion, the governor's staff would check with me about proposals or commitments the governor had made, as my journal notes were often the only record of these discussions.

Judicial appointments are among the Minnesota governor's most important responsibilities. The Governor's Advisory Commission for Judicial Appointments screened potential appointees and recommended a slate of candidates for the governor's consideration. I was not on that commission, but privately Governor Perpich assured me that he expected me to have opinions about judicial appointments, and he asked for my personal recommendation of at least one individual in the first round of appointments to the newly created Court of Appeals. Publicly, he affirmed his commitment to appointing women to the Court of Appeals and the Supreme Court. The governor understood that my choice for the Court of Appeals was Judge Harriet Lansing of St. Paul. He had appointed Judge Lansing to the Municipal Court in 1977, during his first two-year term as governor.

The Court of Appeals would eventually have twelve members, but six would be appointed in the first round. The governor appointed Peter Popovich, a friend of his from the Iron Range, as the chief judge. There was extreme pressure from Popovich against appointing Judge Lansing, so I was staying close to respond to questions and pay attention to the dynamics of the discussions. In a private conversation, the governor asked me, "Why is Peter [Popovich] so opposed to Harriet?" "He's afraid of a smart, strong, experienced female judge. And Peter is anti-choice," I replied. The governor nodded and assured me that "I'll definitely appoint her—just not in this initial announcement." He was referring to the first official statement about appointees to the court, in which Popovich was named as chief judge and the appointment of St. Paul attorney Don Wozniak was also announced. Recognizing the strength of the forces against Harriet's appointment, I stayed in daily contact with the governor to counter any attacks and quietly remind him of his commitment. Harriet was appointed in the first round of six judges to the new Court of Appeals. She ultimately served longer than any of the other initial appointees and was widely recognized as one of the best appellate judges on the court. Judge Susanne Sedgwick of Minneapolis was also among the first six appointees to the Court of Appeals.

Appointments to the Court of Appeals were not the only judicial appointments that faced aggressive pushback from the political establishment. Because the governor had publicly affirmed his commitment to appoint women and people of color to judicial posts, members of the establishment adjusted the tone and language of their opposition to avoid being labeled antiwomen, particularly in areas such as Dakota County that had not yet had any female judges.

When a judicial vacancy occurred in Dakota County, I and others encouraged Leslie Metzen to seek the appointment. We rallied support for her, and I spoke to the governor about her a number of times. He was very interested. Then, late on the day when we expected his announcement, the governor called to tell me that he would not be appointing Leslie. He asked me to call her before the announcement was made to let her know and to ask her to apply for the next vacancy. He assured me that he wanted to appoint her, but he couldn't this time. I assumed he was under pressure from legislative leadership, but he did not tell me that specifically at the time. My call to Leslie was difficult, but we had a good conversation and she agreed to apply for the next vacancy.

Leslie did apply when the next vacancy occurred, and again there was much support in the community for her candidacy. Again the governor told me privately that he was inclined to appoint her. Then, late in the day the appointment was expected to be announced, he called to let me know that House Speaker Harry Sieben, whose legislative support he needed, wanted a different candidate. The governor felt he needed to appoint that person. He told me that yet another vacancy was expected to open up in that district in the coming year and assured me that Speaker Sieben understood that Leslie Metzen would be appointed to fill that vacancy.

This was a low moment in our first term. I was extremely disappointed, even angry. I reminded the governor that being a candidate for a judicial appointment takes a professional and emotional toll that should not be underestimated. I told him I felt that Leslie's appointment had become a pawn in his relationship with Speaker Sieben. The governor acknowledged my dismay, but again asked me to call Leslie before the announcement and relay his commitment to appoint her to the vacancy expected in the following year.

I called Leslie immediately. I shared her deep disappointment and sensed that she did not want to subject herself to this process again. I understood how she felt and appreciated how discouraged she was. She was the only woman with a chance to become a district court judge in Dakota County during our term, so I begged her to keep an open mind about applying again. I told her I felt that the governor had made it clear to Speaker Sieben that he was expected to support Leslie for the next vacancy. She agreed to consider another round.

Governor Perpich personally called Leslie to tell her she was his choice to fill the third vacancy on the Dakota Country District Court. She ultimately became chief judge of that court. I am honored to have played a small role in keeping her candidacy alive during those months of uncertainty. Several years later, Judge Metzen and I encountered each other in the Judicial Building. We exchanged warm memories of our earlier conversations, and I was reminded of that period and that the women judges Governor Perpich appointed rarely forgot the events surrounding their appointments. By 2017 half of the district court judges in Minnesota were women, and I feel pride in having been part of an administration that was so publicly intentional about its commitment to a judiciary that reflected the diversity of the state's legal community.

On occasion, I would receive an invitation from a community leader, with few details about the purpose of the meeting. One such invitation came from Martin Friedman, director of the Walker Art Center. He invited me to lunch at the center's café, mentioning that he had an idea to share. I loved the Walker and enjoyed talking with Martin, so I was happy to accept. Over lunch, he laid out his vision for a sculpture garden in the space across the street from the Walker—land controlled by the Hennepin County Parks Department. He told me that the director of Hennepin County Parks supported his concept, but still unresolved was how a physical connection could be created between the sculpture garden and Loring Park, adjacent to the Walker. The connection that had existed years earlier was destroyed when the interstate highway was constructed through Minneapolis. Martin's vision was a sculptor-designed pedestrian bridge across the interstate. Paying for the bridge was a challenge that currently didn't have a solution, and Martin wanted me to help find one.

I felt that we needed Governor Perpich personally engaged in this project, and within days he and I met with Martin and the Hennepin County Parks director to discuss the proposal. The governor loved the concept and proposed that the project should be paid for out of the federal highway funds designated for highway amenities. Historically, Minnesota had spent the maximum allowed on amenities on federal highway construction, usually for high-quality rest areas. The governor believed that the bridge met the criteria for highway amenities, and he liked the idea that it would be a civic landmark. Siah Armajani, a renowned Iranian American artist who lived in St. Paul, designed the accessible pedestrian bridge to span the interstate that had divided the city. It remains a Minneapolis landmark—a testament to Martin Friedman's vision, the flexibility and enthusiasm of the Hennepin County Parks Department, and Governor Perpich's willingness to see things in a new way. Periodically, when back in Minnesota, I take a walk through Loring Park, across the Armajani bridge, and through the sculpture garden, recalling that initial meeting with Martin and reminding myself that terrific things can happen when we're willing to find new paths and new partners.

Meeting so many different people from all parts of Minnesota society as well as the world was one of the joys of serving as lieutenant governor. Often, I was simply invited to attend events or small gatherings hosted by community leaders. Other times, I created opportunities to bring together diverse groups, from two to one hundred people, to meet around a common purpose or simply for lively conversation.

Informal dinner parties at my apartment were one of my favorite ways to bring women leaders together to share aspects of my work and engage them in broader state policy discussions. In planning these gatherings, I sought to ensure that everyone would meet someone new, and I hoped that all my guests would be exposed to views different from their own. On one occasion, the guest of honor was Governor Britt Mogård of Kronoberg, Sweden, and the rest of the guests were women entrepreneurs, both Republicans and Democrats. I briefed them all about Governor Mogård, telling them that she was currently the political head of a county in Sweden from which many immigrants to

Minnesota had come, and that previously she had been the minister of education of Sweden's Moderate Party. Many assumed that meant she was "conservative." The conversation was lively and informative, as my guests began to understand that Sweden's social welfare system of universal public education and health care, paid family leave, and a social safety net existed within a strong free-enterprise economy. Everyone left that dinner party with a new understanding of political conservatism and social democracy.

In 1985, Anne Morrow Lindbergh, widow of the aviator Charles Lindbergh, was in Minnesota for several days to attend a conference of the Lindbergh Foundation and to take part in other activities. These included the presentation of an award from the Lindbergh Foundation to astronaut Sally Ride and the dedication of a statue of Charles Lindbergh by Minnesota artist Paul Granlund on the Capitol mall. In addition, Anne Morrow Lindbergh spoke at a dinner, and Governor and Mrs. Perpich hosted a luncheon at the Governor's Residence for her, along with her daughter Reeve Lindbergh Brown, Sally Ride, former governor Elmer Andersen, and others. I was Minnesota's official representative at all of these events.

Knowing that Anne and Reeve were both writers, I reached out to the agent who managed their schedule to propose that I host a gathering of Minnesota women writers with Anne and Reeve. He immediately dismissed the idea with "They don't have time." I asked him to extend my invitation anyway, assuring him that of course I would understand if they didn't have the time for another event in the week. Not surprising to me, they accepted, and a breakfast gathering was planned for a private room in their hotel.

I invited Meridel Le Sueur, Patricia Hampl, Carol Bly, Christina Baldwin, Gretchen Beito, and Amy Chao. All were published authors, and as a group they reflected the diversity of Minnesota women writers. Meridel Le Sueur had recently reemerged after being blacklisted during the Joe McCarthy era and was widely embraced as the grandmother of the women's movement; Patricia Hampl had written several memoirs and was subsequently awarded a MacArthur Fellowship (the "Genuis Grant"); Gretchen Beito was the biographer of Coya Knutson, Minnesota's first U.S. congresswoman; Carol Bly was a prolific fiction writer and essayist; Christina Baldwin was a Macalester colleague who had recently written her first book, on journal writing; and Amy Chao, violist in the Saint Paul Chamber Orchestra, had recently published her first novel. After introducing each writer to the group, I encouraged Meridel and Anne to share their thoughts. They connected with each other immediately and guided a conversation among the other writers that was deeply personal and inspiring for all of us. Our gathering was scheduled to last for one hour, but we concluded after two and a half hours, when Anne and Reeve had to prepare for their luncheon appointment.

Weeks later, I received a multipage handwritten letter from Anne Lindbergh, expressing gratitude for the gathering of women writers and sharing that it had been the first time she had felt that level of camaraderie and support from women. Christina Baldwin and Patricia Hampl also sent notes of appreciation and reflection. The gathering was an extraordinary event for me, too. As I recalled my initial instinct to extend the invitation, and then the profound experience of witnessing the exchange among these gifted writers, I became determined to identify any opportunities for such rich engagement in the future. Anne Lindbergh's letter further cemented my resolve.

In early 1990, President Mikhail Gorbachev of the Soviet Union announced that he would be coming to the United States and would travel to cities beyond Washington, D.C. Upon hearing this news, Governor Perpich announced that he would invite President Gorbachev to visit Minnesota. The headlines in the Minnesota press dismissed the governor's idea as "crazy and far-fetched."

A few days later, at a dinner party at the home of Marilyn Carlson Nelson and Glen Nelson, Cargill CEO Whitney MacMillan asked to speak to me away from the table. He told me that he thought Governor Perpich's plan to invite President Gorbachev to Minnesota was an excellent idea. He asked me to share his enthusiasm with the governor and tell him that he (Whitney) would be meeting with President Gorbachev in Moscow the following week and would encourage Gorbachev to accept Governor Perpich's invitation.

I shared MacMillan's comments with the governor and Terry Montgomery the next morning. They understood that with MacMillan's support, Gorbachev would likely accept the governor's invitation. Planning began.

Former U.S. vice president Walter Mondale, Secretary of State Joan Growe, and I would greet President Gorbachev and his wife, Raisa, at the airport. We had no further information about the details of his visit. The published schedule included a luncheon at the Governor's Residence, but the guest list was not made public. There was considerable speculation about the luncheon guests. Senators David Durenberger and Rudy Boschwitz and other public officials had not received invitations. As no additional information about the schedule was released, interest in and rumors about what was happening and who would be included or excluded continued to grow. My office fielded a stream of phone calls expressing disappointment and anger. The governor's political supporters felt that the secrecy about the invitation list was a liability in an already difficult political environment.

I decided to find a way to create a space for political leaders and friends to gather on the occasion of Gorbachev's visit, even if they did not get a chance to meet the president. My friend Carole Faricy, a political fundraiser and event coordinator extraordinaire, and I set about planning an event to celebrate the visit. It would be a luncheon held at the mansion next door to the Governor's Residence on Summit Avenue, the headquarters of the St. Paul branch of the American Association of University Women. We invited Senators Durenberger and Boschwitz, members of Congress, local public officials, administration leaders, and other political friends. Once everyone had arrived, lunch was served, and guests were engaged in conversation, I sent a note through the security officers to President Gorbachev at the Governor's Residence luncheon, informing him that Minnesota's U.S. senators and members of Congress and other Minnesota leaders were next door and inviting him to stop by for a brief visit. Soon I received word that Gorbachev and his wife would greet our guests in a receiving line on the front lawn of the Governor's Residence. It was a generous gesture and warmly received by everyone. In the following days I received dozens of written and verbal expressions of appreciation from those who attended the "event next door" for recognizing the slight that many felt, and for organizing a gathering that had such a positive outcome. Governor Perpich never commented to me about the "luncheon next door," but he certainly played a role in creating the space for the reception line.

For me, the "event next door" became a personal metaphor for creating unofficial ways to recognize and celebrate people and occasions, even when doing so is not one's official role. By creating this event, we acknowledged political and community leaders who had felt slighted, and in the end they felt respected in that brief greeting with President Gorbachev. A potentially embarrassing situation for the administration and the governor was neutralized. In putting on the luncheon next door, we had no support from the administration, but that lack of support also allowed the governor to respond in the moment without losing face. I assumed a leadership role necessary to defuse negative political energy on a day that was a historic moment for Minnesota, and in the process I helped to create a positive memory for many. I am proud of the modest role I played that day.

15

.\\\\\\\\\|||||||///,.

Ending My Time in State Government

The final two years of the Perpich–Johnson second term were tumultu-
ous. The governor's son, a recent law school graduate, had been diagnosed with chronic fatigue syndrome, and the governor was distracted
by his concerns about his son's health; some cabinet members found
themselves pressed to use their positions to find medical treatments
or expert advice. The policy focus, enthusiasm, and energy of the first
term and early second term were gone, leaving the team doing their
best to move the administration's agenda forward without the governor's engagement. The members of the governor's staff were under extreme pressure to support the governor in finding treatment options for
his son. I maintained a schedule of speeches, media events, and visits to
constituent programs related to the Children's Agenda and the tourism
marketing program. Camaraderie between me and the governor's office
was limited.

By 1990, I felt a growing tension with Governor Perpich. He was
feeding rumors about running for a third term, despite many signs that
he could not win. Many of us began to believe that he was losing his
way. The energetic, enthusiastic visionary who ran in 1982 was now re-
active and focused on his son's health.

Early in the year, Peter and I had taken a trip to the North Shore of
Lake Superior for a weekend of cross-country skiing and rest. I needed
time to think about whether I should simply conclude this chapter—
announce that I would not run again—since I felt that we could not win
a third term. By the end of the weekend, I had decided that if I left the

ticket, I would be blamed for the governor's defeat. Whatever support I might be able to generate on the Iron Range for a future run for governor would be gone if I left the ticket now. I decided to stay the course. I never second-guessed my decision, but I understood later that I would always be damaged politically because I had contributed to the defeat of Warren Spannaus. Any support I might have been able to generate on the Iron Range would never have been enough to counter that basic challenge.

During 1990 I had only one private conversation with Governor Perpich about the campaign, which I initiated. I told the governor that I had heard that someone else wanted to be his running mate in the upcoming election. He simply said, "That won't happen," but he didn't pursue the conversation. I concluded that I would again be his running mate, yet I also felt that our collaborative and cordial relationship of the past was significantly diminished.

I was not included in campaign strategy conversations beyond the initial meeting with Peter Hart about plans for the 1990 poll. When Peter presented the poll findings to the governor, unlike during the 1986 campaign, I was not invited to the meeting. Peter Hart was told not to share the results with me. He and I had a cordial relationship, and he had always included questions in the poll about my recognition and role in the administration. Now all he could do was call to let me know that he had been instructed not to share the report with me. I understood, and I asked him a couple of questions that he could answer with one word. I concluded that the governor did not agree with the poll's findings, and they would not inform his campaign strategy.

During the campaign year, I maintained a full schedule of events, greeting workers at manufacturing facilities, participating in daily activities at the State Fair, and attending fundraising events. The scheduling was all done by the lieutenant governor's office, as we had no campaign scheduling staff. All indications were that the governor would be defeated. In a last-ditch effort in the final weeks of the campaign, the governor made a series of personal attacks on the Republican candidate, Jon Grunseth. Several legislative women and I were called to the Governor's Residence, where the governor asked us to publicly accuse Grunseth of not meeting the requirements of his divorce settlement. I felt the strategy would be counterproductive, and I was not willing to carry that message. The governor and I did not speak about this again, but I feel sure he considered my response disloyal.

Ultimately, Grunseth withdrew from the race. State Auditor Arne Carlson, who had come in second in the Republican primary, was selected as the GOP candidate for governor. Carlson was well known and well liked, and he won the 1990 general election. It was not an unexpected outcome, and it was deeply disappointing that Governor Perpich's time in office, which began with visionary leadership, ended with a defeat that he brought on himself.

Following the election loss of 1990, Governor Perpich was bitter and totally disengaged from the representational activities of the transition period, including the traditional holiday observances. I hosted the holiday tree-lighting ceremony and the state employee reception in the Capitol, among other year-end functions, events in which the governor had historically been involved. During our two terms, state employees had felt appreciated and were actively engaged in advancing policy changes in education, child care, tourism promotion, and more. They were genuinely disappointed that they were not able to thank the governor and say goodbye. I shared their disappointment.

Besides fulfilling the obligations of attending these final events, my team focused on preparing our office files for the Minnesota Historical Society's archives and on providing transition planning for the incoming lieutenant governor, Joanell Dyrstad. Of course, my staff and I were facing a big transition as well, so I did outreach to help ensure that all staff members landed in new jobs that were suited to their skills and goals.

The protocol for the lieutenant governor's office archives had been established at the beginning of our first term. Nevertheless, the final execution was an enormous task. Shirley Bonine, my chief of staff, worked tirelessly on this during the transition, and then as a volunteer for several weeks after we left office. It is unlikely that any office delivered a more well-organized documentation of work at the end of a term.

Facilitating a smooth transition with the incoming lieutenant governor was important to me. While the transition with my predecessor in 1983 had been cordial, my role in our administration was to be more robust, so the transition issues were modest. Eight years later, we had established a staff structure, defined policy roles, and created protocols for working with the governor's office that I wanted to share with my successor. She would establish her own protocols, but at least she would have a framework from which to consider and assess options.

I reached out to Joanell Dyrstad soon after the election to discuss general matters related to the role of lieutenant governor. She and I had worked together a number of times: as the mayor of Red Wing, Minnesota, she had supported our tourism promotion strategies; she had joined me in the establishment of the Women Candidate Development Coalition; and she had also been a supporter of the Minnesota Women's Campaign Fund. We had a warm, cordial relationship, and I was pleased that she was succeeding me.

I shared with her the ongoing pressure from the legislature to integrate the lieutenant governor's staff with the governor's staff and my decision to keep my office separate. I wanted her to understand Governor Perpich's and my rationale for a separate office as she contemplated the best option for her leadership role and for the Carlson–Dyrstad administration. Ultimately, she and Governor Carlson chose a joint staffing arrangement; this approach, supported by the legislative leadership, has been the standard in subsequent administrations.

While communication between the governor's office and my office had declined during the past two years, during the postelection transition period we had no contact at all until the scheduler extended an invitation for me to have breakfast with the governor at the Governor's Residence in mid-December. Breakfast was served at a small table in the solarium. Our conversation was casual and cool, in contrast to the warmth and enthusiasm that had existed between us from our first campaign through the early years of our second term. As we finished eating, the governor moved his chair away from the table a bit and said, "Why were you disloyal to me? I heard that you worked against me in this last campaign." I was taken aback, and took a minute to gather my thoughts. I assured him that his information was wrong. In fact, "I can't imagine any conversation I've had during the last years that could possibly have been interpreted to suggest I was disloyal." If anything, I told him, some people believed I had been loyal to a fault: "During our two terms and three campaigns, I have never leaked a detail about you, our policy, or campaign strategy discussions. The press believes I haven't been privy to any policy discussions. As a result, I have not been recognized for my contributions to our administration."

The governor didn't respond. I went on to tell him that I was grateful for the opportunity he had given me to serve as lieutenant governor and to contribute to the administration's accomplishments in education reform, tourism development, the Children's Agenda, pay equity, and more. His record of appointments of women and people of color to the judiciary and boards and commissions was extraordinary, and I was proud to have played a role in helping achieve those outcomes. I paused, hoping for a response. Then I continued: "I am deeply sorry you have believed something about me that is so not true." We shook hands as I left, but he said nothing. As I drove away, I was deeply sad that a partnership that began in 1982 with so much energy, enthusiasm, and warmth could end this way. I realized that this would likely be the last time I would speak to Governor Perpich. And so it was.

In the late fall of 1990, not long before the election, my brother-in-law Bob Nesheim proposed a bold idea for an outlet that could take my mind off the stress of the campaign: I should train to enter the recreational leg of the John Beargrease Sled Dog Marathon in late January 1991. Bob's perspective: he and my sister Marlys owned six sled dogs, and he was interested in having them run the race. Competing in the Beargrease is a huge logistical challenge, and he couldn't do both the planning and the training as the musher. He thought that training for the race would be a great distraction for me. If the Perpich–Johnson team won the election, my participation in the race would bring added visibility to the annual event; if we lost the election, I would at least have a short-term diversion. It was a preposterous idea, but I was ready for the distraction. So, in late October, just before the election, I traveled to Duluth for the weekend for my first training with six huskies pulling a sled. As this was prior to the first snowfall, the sled had wheels. My first hurdle: my generally uneasy relationship with dogs! By the end of that first weekend, I had learned how to lift the dogs up and install them in the kennel on the back of the pickup truck and how to take them out again; I also learned how to harness them to the lead and then to the sled. The work was physical, emotional, and exhilarating. I was beginning to understand why Bob had suggested this as a diversion from the turmoil in my life.

After the election, I spent weekends in Duluth training with the dogs on trails within the city limits. On my last day in office, I said my final goodbyes and thank-yous to my staff, and then stopped at the apartment to change clothes and meet Peter. We headed immediately to Grand Marais, where I would train on a trail that would be part of the Beargrease race the following week. The drive to Grand Marais from St. Paul is more than five hours, so we arrived around 9:00 p.m. My sister's family had readied our cabin, and while their two small boys were asleep, we four adults settled in for a bowl of chili and a conversation about what was ahead for me that weekend. Bob suggested that I do a short training run by moonlight that night. I was bone tired, but I knew the sky would be bright despite the temperature of minus 40 degrees Fahrenheit. So, not wanting to show a lack of enthusiasm, I agreed.

The dogs, always happy to run, were excited as we drove the truck to the trailhead. Bob helped me harness the dogs and hook them to the sled, and I was on my way. Peter and Bob would wait at the trailhead. The plan was that I'd run a loop with the dogs and be back in an hour or so. Then, fifteen or twenty minutes out, the lead dog slowed down, giving a hint to another one that something was amiss. She nipped at another dog—a potential fight! I had successfully intervened in a fight between dogs on the previous weekend's training run, so I wasn't worried. I reached for the stick that is usually stored on the sled handle. It wasn't there. At that point I realized I had neglected to do a gear check before departing. I tried kicking the dogs to stop the fight, but a kick with a two-inch wool-lined boot is of no consequence, and within a minute all six dogs were fighting, and I was on the ground looking up at teeth. I was able to get out of that spot, but there was no way to stop the fight. I put the snow hook in to keep the dogs and sled in that location and started walking/running back to the trailhead. I tried calling for help, but in the wilderness forest, my voice disappeared. Eventually I saw a light heading toward me, but I couldn't determine if it was another dogsled or a snowmobile. Ten minutes later, I met Peter and Bob walking casually along the trail, wearing headlamps. I shared my sad story as we walked by moonlight back to the dogs. The fight was over by the time we got back. There was blood everywhere, the harnesses were a tangled mess, and the dogs were just waiting. Bob untangled one dog and harness at a time, handing over each "rescued" dog to Peter or me to hang on to until we could harness them up again for the run back to the trailhead. One of the dogs was too injured to run, so we tucked him in the sled bag with a blanket. It was amazing to watch the dogs run after an ordeal that had taken my breath away. In twenty minutes we were back, unharnessing them and placing them in their respective kennels for the night. We would take them to the veterinarian the next day, so it was pretty clear that my plans for this adventure were changing.

The next morning at the clinic, the vet informed us that three of the dogs needed antibiotics and wouldn't be able to run in the race the following week. My adventure was over before it began. I was disappointed, and also aware of how tired I was. The concept of a diversion was rational. It was also optimistic to think that I could undertake this kind of a challenge on the heels of such a stressful final chapter to an eight-year public role. I came to see that I hadn't given enough thought to what would be required of me. I loved the idea of participating in something totally new and sharing this adventure with my brother-in-law. But I had failed to recognize my own hesitations and give those doubts a true hearing.

My consolation prize: riding shotgun on a dogsled with a volunteer race manager who kept each rest stop equipped during the race. It was a terrific way to experience the energy, planning, and culture of the race, and to feel the intensity of dogsledding through the night. Bob was right, this was a welcome diversion; he and I enjoyed sharing the adventure, I let go of my uneasiness with dogs, and the physical demands were healing. The experience provided me with invaluable lessons about planning, training, and paying attention to one's personal hesitations. I appreciated the distraction from the stress of those final weeks of the campaign, but I did not fully understand how deeply exhausted I was going into the training or and how demanding it would be. Overall, it was a rich experience.

By early 1991, I found the mental and emotional space to start thinking about my future. Despite the negativity of the recent election, I held on to the possibility of running for governor in the future, even though at that moment it seemed like a long shot. But I assumed I would find a position in Minnesota. I created a list of the many community and business leaders I had worked with, who had observed or experienced my leadership capabilities, to seek their advice and perspective on opportunities that might build on my leadership record of the past eight years and my years in business. Without exception, the conversations I had with them were cordial, but none of them showed any enthusiasm for my leadership potential in the community or in their businesses. Perhaps I was naive about what I could expect from these meetings. Although all of these business and community leaders had worked with me on one or more initiatives during our administration and had seen me in action as we engaged in outreach related to the tourism strategy or the Children's Agenda, their personal experience with me did not translate in their minds into other leadership roles where I might contribute.

When I debriefed Peter following these meetings, he was confused and then outraged by the lack of interest in finding a role for me. He could not comprehend why no one tried to open doors or create an opportunity. Even as his support and reaction to these meetings gave me strength, I struggled with insecurities about what to do next. For the first time, I faced the real possibility that there wasn't a spot for me in Minnesota. Many community leaders had accepted my leadership when I represented the administration, but that did not translate to other arenas.

16

·····\\\\\\\\\|||||||/////·····

New Challenges

Little did I know in January 1991 that in the coming year I would face the first of several transitions I would experience over the next seven years. What I did know was that at the age of forty-five, I had never applied for a job. I had created a position at the Ramsey County Citizens Committee for Economic Opportunity, then been recruited to a new position at the YMCA, then started my own business, essentially creating another job for myself. Then Governor Perpich invited me to be his running mate. I was entering uncharted territory.

For now, while processing the emotional disappointments of the final years of public service, I had to figure out how to support myself. My savings account was modest. I needed income, and I needed to figure out what I wanted to do next. As if she had read my mind, Linda Tarr-Whelan, president of the Center for Policy Alternatives, a state government policy organization that had followed my work on the Minnesota Children's Agenda, called me and offered me a fellowship to help the CPA create a guide for state government policymakers on expanding services for children. This was a short-term concrete opportunity to use what I had learned and provided modest financial support. I would be able to share the story of our work on the Children's Agenda and stay connected to state government policy work. I accepted Linda's offer and agreed to start in March, which gave me a little time to decompress. Peter and I had already planned to spend a few weeks in Sweden and take a short skiing break in Austria. After this break, I would head to

Washington to figure out what a part-time schedule and lifestyle would look like.

This was my first time in Sweden during the winter for more than a long weekend. Also for the first time, I wouldn't be leaving Sweden to return to a full-time position with specific responsibilities. At that moment, I really didn't know what I wanted to do moving forward, and I was financially vulnerable.

Peter was back at work, so initially I spent my days relaxing, going to the gym, reading, and checking in with friends in Sweden and Denmark. One afternoon in early February, I had lunch in downtown Copenhagen with a friend who headed the Danish Refugee Council, and she suggested that I help introduce her management group to the U.S. approach to fundraising. Within a couple of weeks I had a contract to create a development plan for the organization. Learning about the council's work as well as the differences between U.S. culture and Danish culture regarding fundraising was stimulating, and through this cross-cultural exchange, I gained a greater understanding of the U.S. fundraising culture.

During my work with the Danish Refugee Council, I learned to present my suggestions within a Danish cultural framework. My recommendations were well received and many were implemented. It was constructive work, I felt valued, and the earned income reduced my stress. Upon reflection, I realized that my friend had recognized my vulnerability and that her organization's needs could be matched with my skills. For the second time in as many months, a woman friend in a leadership role had created an opportunity for me that provided income and the space to figure out what came next. It was a lesson that I have tried to integrate into my own habits of mentoring and supporting women throughout my life.

During this same period, a Swedish friend, Stefan Holmström, executive director of Individuell Människohjälp, asked me to help develop a fundraising strategy for that organization. Founded by our friend's mother, Britta Holmström, at the end of World War II, IM is an international development organization created to help rebuild education and entrepreneurial programs in countries devastated by war. At twenty-five years of age, Holmström had funded IM through small donations collected in local churches throughout Sweden. By the early

I was honored to serve as a public member of the board of Landmark Center, a historic federal courts building restored as a St. Paul arts center. Other members of the board included Betty Musser (chair, center); John Myers, retired chairman of Waldorf Paper Company; Ruby Hunt, member of the St. Paul City Council; and Tom Swain, chief of staff to former governor Elmer Andersen and executive at St. Paul Companies. I am standing, third from left, in this photograph, with Tom Swain at my left.

The Split Infinitive team gathers in our new offices in the Minnesota Building in downtown St. Paul. From left: my mother, Helen Johnson; graphic designer Esther Malabel; Lena Graziano; me; and my aunt, Ruthie Nelson.

Anne Morrow Lindbergh and I shake hands after my introduction to her keynote speech at the Lindbergh Foundation annual dinner in 1985 during Lindbergh Heritage Week.

Karen Desnick and Jean Heilman join me in counting votes for my unsuccessful campaign for vice chair of the National Women's Political Caucus. The main reason for my loss: supporting a dues increase!

Secretary of State Joan Growe, former vice president Walter Mondale, and I welcome President Mikhail Gorbachev to Minnesota in June 1990.

With the Minnesota Office of Tourism and the Department of Natural Resources, I led the annual Lieutenant Governor's Bike Ride to showcase Minnesota's extensive system of rail-to-trail paths coordinated with miles of back-road bike routes.

On my visit to Sweden to open Minnesota's Trade Office in Stockholm, I met with Governor Britt Mogård of Kronoberg in Växjö for discussions about creating a sister state relationship between Minnesota and Kronoberg.

Astronaut Sally Ride, former governor Elmer Andersen, sculptor Paul Granlund, and I visit at the Governor's Residence luncheon during Lindbergh Heritage Week in 1985.

I was honored to host Coya Knutson, Minnesota's first woman representative in the U.S. Congress, at the celebration for the publication of her biography, written by Gretchen Beito.

At my invitation, writers Anne Morrow Lindbergh and Reeve Lindbergh joined a group of Minnesota women writers for breakfast and conversation during Lindbergh Heritage Week in 1985. From left: Evelina Chao, Patricia Hampl, Meridel Le Sueur, Judith Guest, me, Anne Lindbergh, (unknown), Christina Baldwin, Reeve Lindbergh, Carol Bly, and Gretchen Beito.

I thoroughly enjoyed my role as aunt to nephews Brent Anderson and Andrew Nesheim.

Peter and me at our wedding, with my great-aunt, Ruth Wilde, and my mother, Helen Johnson. Photograph by Charlie Greer.

Peter and me, with his sister, Antje, and her husband, Fredrik, on our second backpacking trip near Abisko, in northern Sweden.

A. M. "Sandy" Keith, a longtime friend and future chief justice of the Minnesota Supreme Court, gives a toast at our wedding dinner "on behalf of Beauford, Marlene's father," beginning with "I've waited twenty years for this moment!" Photograph by Charlie Greer.

I was honored to meet with President Barack Obama and corporate leaders to support the president's 100,000 Strong in the Americas initiative. NAFSA worked with the Department of State and Partners of the Americas to increase college and university engagement in the initiative.

1990s, it had grown into a significant organization that also received grants from Sweden's development agency.

As the original generation of IM donors aged, the organization's leaders recognized that they needed to do more to raise awareness of IM and to generate support for its work among the general public. My key recommendation was to create the Britta Holmström Award, which would recognize young leaders in Sweden who were addressing current needs of the society. The IM staff and board did not initially understand how presenting such an award would benefit the organization, but after several conversations (and with Peter's help), they eventually recognized the potential power of honoring young leaders who were the next generation with a vision for change, as Britta Holmström had been for her generation. The Britta Holmström Award was established and has been presented annually to a young leader who has initiated significant social change in Sweden. Several times I have been invited to meet with members of the IM board and staff to share the story of the award's creation, and on one occasion I was able to attend the presentation ceremony for the award.

In March 1991 I was in Washington, D.C., to begin work on the family policy project for the CPA. I established an advisory group that included former Ohio governor Richard Celeste, with whom I had worked on several activities of the Great Lakes Governors Council during our terms in office. The family policy project produced guidance for the children and family policy agenda that was integrated into the broader policy framework packages that the CPA produced and shared extensively with progressive legislative leaders around the country. I thoroughly enjoyed this recognition of the Minnesota Children's Agenda as well as the opportunity to extend my own engagement in state policy for a short time.

During the time of the CPA fellowship, I rented a small, garden-level apartment at the home of my friend Joanne Howes. It gave me a place to settle in during the one week each month I spent in Washington, and staying there helped me to understand what it meant to live in Washington, D.C.

17

Losing an Election, Leaving Politics, and Landing in Washington

In the late spring of 1993, I was juggling part-time work in Washington with life in Minnesota, trying to determine what opportunities I might find in either place. One morning, as I was drinking a cup of coffee at my D.C. apartment, my friend Carole Faricy phoned from St. Paul to urge me to run for mayor of St. Paul. The current mayor, Jim Scheibel, was not running for reelection, and Carole felt the time was right for a woman mayor. She believed that my twelve years in business in St. Paul and eight years as lieutenant governor put me in a strong position from which to wage a campaign.

Initially, the idea of running for mayor seemed unrealistic. I hadn't been involved in local government or local politics, nor had I spoken out on local issues during my years in business. Several candidates were already announced, all white men—one local businessman and the rest attorneys. Andy Dawkins, a state legislator, was expected to get the DFL endorsement. The perceived frontrunner, Norm Coleman, was anti-abortion and well financed. Although a Democrat, he was not seeking the DFL endorsement and was expected to switch to the Republican Party after the election. Many viewed Dawkins as too liberal to defeat Coleman in the general election. As I would be the only woman in the race, a former St. Paul businessperson and former elected official who was pro-choice and with strong name identification, there was a case to be made for my being a strong candidate against Coleman.

I decided to run, recognizing that we were weeks behind the other candidates in establishing a campaign organization and raising funds. To control expenses, we ran the campaign out of my dining room. Shirley Bonine, who had been my chief of staff and had managed Congressman Rick Nolan's district campaign, became my campaign manager, and Carole Faricy was our fundraiser.

My initial calls to former clients were disappointing. Many businesspeople I phoned had already committed to support businessman John Mannillo, even as they acknowledged he had no public policy leadership experience or visibility. In several cases, these former clients told me they didn't believe Mannillo could win. The primary election was nonpartisan, and the top two vote getters in the primary, whatever their parties, would advance to the general election in November.

Our campaign didn't have the financial resources for major media buys. My friend Ray Strother, a Washington political campaign consultant who had worked for the Perpich–Johnson campaign in 1986, wanted to handle our media strategy, but we didn't have the funds for that expense. Later, Ray told me that my decision not to use his services suggested to him that I wasn't serious about winning. Perhaps he was right. Nevertheless, I participated in all the candidate debates and maintained a steady schedule of candidate forums, community meetings, and the neighborhood door knocking basic to local campaigns in Minnesota. I had always enjoyed door-to-door work, having learned the discipline and value of it when I accompanied Linda Berglin in her first campaign for the state legislature in 1972. As is customary, I was accompanied in my door knocking during the mayoral campaign by a volunteer who worked the opposite side of the street—a strategy that allowed us to cover twice as much territory quickly. In such a door-to-door effort, the volunteer always mentions to residents that the candidate is across the street, so if they want to meet him or her that's possible. As we finished each block, we met up to compare notes and give each other encouragement.

On the Friday afternoon prior to the primary election, I was door knocking in the Frogtown neighborhood of St. Paul when I learned about what would be the final blow to my campaign. I walked up the front steps of a home, and the woman who answered the door greeted me warmly by name. She welcomed my visit and said, "Marlene, I had planned to vote for you until I saw this brochure, which says that Andy

Dawkins is the only pro-choice candidate. I always vote pro-choice." I assured her that I am and always have been pro-choice, to which she said, "I thought you were, but I got confused when this brochure arrived at my door today." She handed me the flyer, a piece produced and distributed by the DFL Party and signed by the St. Paul DFL women legislators; it asserted that the DFL-endorsed candidate, Dawkins, was the only pro-choice person running for mayor. My heart sank as I absorbed the consequences. As I concluded my visit, the woman assured me that she would vote for me because of our conversation. But I knew that for hundreds of others who wouldn't have personal contact with me in the final few days of the campaign, this brochure would be a significant factor influencing their votes, with a fatal result for my candidacy.

A few minutes later, the volunteer I was working with, my friend George Perpich, joined me at the corner of the block. George had been knocking on doors on the other side of the street, and the look in his eyes told me that he had also seen the flyer. We acknowledged to each other that its distribution had eliminated any chance that I could be one of the finalists in the primary election.

Election night made it official—the top two vote getters were Coleman and Dawkins—but I had had the weekend to begin the process of accepting that it was time for me to let go of a possible future in Minnesota politics. Peter was in disbelief. As our supporters gathered at Carole and Dick Faricy's home on election night, he just shook his head as I called Norm Coleman to express my congratulations. Peter and I had been together during the 1986 campaign, but he hadn't been around much or close to the day-to-day campaign activities. This was his first exposure to personal political defeat. Our election victory in 1986 had been expected. The defeat in 1990 was also expected, so while it required adjustments and the closing down of our offices and signified the end of an era, I hadn't felt it personally, since the previous year had been one disaster after another, and I was secondary to the governor. This time, it was my campaign, and the outcome was clarifying.

The morning after the primary, Andy Dawkins asked me to meet him at the coffee shop around the corner from my apartment. Dispensing with casual conversation, he asked me to endorse his candidacy. I took a long minute to compose my response, which was a question: "What made you think it was acceptable to publish a brochure claiming that you were the only pro-choice candidate for mayor? Was that the only way you could win the primary?" He acknowledged that it was a questionable strategy, but he did not apologize. I told him I didn't plan to endorse a candidate for the general election, and all indications were that Coleman would be elected. I reminded him that the combined votes received by the other business candidate and me would have defeated him in the primary.

I understood that the most ardent DFL activists committed to the endorsement process would not support me. But I had not anticipated that they would tell an outright lie. That DFL women legislators participated in the lie was particularly disheartening. Yet I wasn't bitter about the outcome. I felt relief that I had clarity. I now knew that what I had suspected was true: the DFL Party, including DFL women officeholders, would never forgive me for having run and served with Perpich. Our 1982 defeat of Warren Spannaus, their endorsed candidate, would never be forgiven. Despite the monumental role that women and people of color had played in our administration and our extraordinary pro-woman agenda of pay equity, children's health and education, and so much more, their commitment to the party endorsement was paramount. It was time for me to move on, to look for opportunities beyond Minnesota.

As much as I had enjoyed the CPA fellowship and other consulting assignments, and appreciated that the work had been important to my emotional and financial well-being, I did not want to establish a consulting practice. I had built a business once and did not want to do that again. I felt ready for a leadership position, even as I felt at a loss about how to go about getting one.

Once again, my Washington friend Joanne Howes weighed in. She called to check in and to say she hoped I would be interested in a job in Bill Clinton's presidential administration. She knew of a pending vacancy at the General Services Administration, but I would need to have in-person conversations with the appropriate people. I called for an appointment, and Peter and I decided to meet for a long weekend in Washington while I was there for my interview. It would give us a chance to absorb Washington, debrief after my conversations at GSA, and think together about what it would mean to live in Washington. What a weekend that turned out to be! We arrived on a Thursday evening and met at our hotel just blocks from the GSA offices. I had a tentative appointment for Friday, but I was to phone first thing that morning to confirm a time. Shortly after we fell asleep that night, the snow started falling. We woke to a city completely shut down by a major snowfall. There was no city bus service, and businesses were closed, as were all local and federal government offices. Fortunately, our hotel room had a small kitchenette, and we had bought coffee, tea, bread, fruit, and cheese upon arrival. The two people I was hoping to meet at GSA had managed to get to the office, and a meeting was easy to arrange as they had no other demands on their time. I just needed to walk five blocks through the ankle-deep snow to their building—not a serious challenge for a Minnesotan!

I met first with the incumbent, Cynthia Metzler, about the responsibilities of the position, and then with Roger Johnson, GSA administrator. The General Services Administration provides the infrastructure for the government, from property management to technology. The open position had management responsibility for the internal operation. It was one of six positions reporting to the administrator, and the management team also worked with the regional administrators. My conversation with the administrator was interesting and lively. He was the only Republican in the Clinton administration, had been the CEO of a high-tech company in Southern California, believed in government, and had substantive ideas for management changes that would improve efficiencies and government services. By the end of our visit, he offered me the position, pending White House approval.

Trudging through the snow back to the hotel, I felt my body relaxing with each step. I knew I had been stressed about my financial vulnerability and the uncertainty about what came next, but until that moment I had not recognized how much the stress was affecting me physically. I would have much to learn, and I would be working with a team of talented, like-minded people focused on improving the quality of government service and being part of President Clinton's administration. I was excited about and grateful for the opportunity.

By the end of the weekend, the airports had reopened; Peter returned to Sweden and I flew back to Minnesota. I put the apartment on the market and began the process of moving. By April, I was in Washington full-time as assistant administrator for management at the General Services Administration, living in a small rented house on Capitol Hill.

The GSA work was exhilarating and rewarding. My team included the agency controller and the directors of human resources and information technology. We established policies for the regional offices managing federal buildings throughout the country, developing and training for quality improvement strategies. The work provided me with an intense course in continuous improvement and in creating accountability and training systems to improve service quality. I learned a great deal about engaging employees throughout the organization, identifying ways to honor individual contributions, and sharing success. It was an intellectually stimulating and collegial environment, and I made many friendships that continue today.

The one certainty about a federal government politically appointed position is that it is temporary. I learned much at GSA and became a better manager, but I was ready for a new challenge when the job was ending. I had been offered other positions in the Clinton administration, but none were suited to my interests. At the same time, through a referral from one of our training consultants, I was recruited for the position of vice president for people and strategy at Rowe Furniture. It was not an obvious position for me, but there were elements about it that were similar to the work I was enjoying at GSA. Wanting a change and not feeling ready for a gap in my employment at that moment, I accepted the offer, even as I felt it might not be for the long term.

At Rowe Furniture, lessons from my lieutenant governor experience came to mind as I built support among senior managers who did not report to me. The company's chairman wanted me to lead a change process, creating administrative and management systems to support the continuous improvement initiatives under way in manufacturing. The new vice president for manufacturing was from General Electric, trained by Jack Welch. I liked her immediately, but found the "Jack Welch" intensity wearing on a daily basis. Her approach to team building was radically different from mine. Nevertheless, I thoroughly enjoyed my visits to the manufacturing plant and meeting line workers. I was learning about an industry I had known nothing about. This medium-size manufacturing company was a key part of the economic and social fabric of the local community. The former politician in me recognized the tensions between the traditional operation and the new visions for the employees' day-to-day work lives and potentially for the future of their small city.

Rowe Furniture was an outlier in a field where standard production took six to eight weeks after purchase. For several years, the company's model had been two to four weeks, which contributed to the pride workers felt about their products. Second-generation workers were common at the plant, and the pride they took in the company's economic role in the community was obvious. Joining the team at the High Point Furniture Show in North Carolina was also part of my orientation.

Following weeks of on-site observation and research and several planning meetings with the management team, I crafted my proposal with the input of the whole senior management team. The chairman felt the proposed approach was too aggressive, however, and asked me to slow things down. I understood that he was ultimately responsible for the pace of change at the company, but my effectiveness relied on my ability to persuade and motivate. I believed that retreating abruptly from the new direction I had recommended would leave me with no credibility. Sitting across the desk from the chairman, I recalled the conversation I'd had with Peter earlier that morning, in our daily telephone call before I headed to work. I mentioned to him that during the night I'd had a sense that the chairman would not accept my proposal, and I speculated that I would be fired. Peter couldn't imagine that outcome. He reminded me that I had been hired to lead a change process.

Now, as the chairman asked me to slow the pace of change, I paused to collect my thoughts, curious myself about how I would respond. Finally, I answered: "Of course you should have the pace of change you want. But were I to change the pace so abruptly, I'd have no credibility among the team. I think I should leave today." He was visibly surprised by my comment and assured me that it wasn't his intent that I leave the company. As we discussed things further, he concurred with my decision and agreed to an appropriate transition package.

As I returned to my office I felt relief. I had been advancing a strategy without the leadership support that would have been needed. And I didn't feel passionately about this work. I called Peter with the news, aware that I wasn't sad or angry. He was surprised, but recalled my earlier comments. He urged me to call a friend of ours to meet me at the office at the end of the day to help me move my things out after everyone else had gone home. Meanwhile, members of the management team stopped by to see how the meeting with the chairman had gone. All of them were blindsided by the outcome. As surreal as it felt, in that moment I understood it was time for me to embark on a new adventure.

I was in transition again. At least this time, with some savings and the transition support from the company, I felt that I could manage financially for a year or so. I resolved to be more intentional about my next adventure.

18

A Time for Reflection

It was now early 1997. To this point in my life, I had never applied for a job—rather, I had responded to opportunities that had come to me. I had no regrets, and I'd learned much on each leg of my personal journey. But now I wanted to spend some time gaining an understanding of my skills, preferences, and motivations before choosing the path for the next chapter of my professional life.

During the previous few months, Peter had been working with a new client in Germany, an American executive who was making a cultural adjustment to running a German company. Peter was enjoying the work, and he wanted to meet the outplacement consultant who had connected him to this opportunity, Barbara Crenshaw. He first visited Barbara in her New York office, and over time they became good friends. In one of their conversations, Peter mentioned that I wanted to find a coach to work with as I looked for my next opportunity. Barbara referred me to a Washington friend, Nancy Ordway, a career coach.

During 1997, my "job" was to understand what was most important to me and then focus on finding a position that would allow me to pursue my personal goals. While I'd had many terrific and varied opportunities in the past, each of my previous positions had resulted from my spontaneous response to an offer that was presented to me. I wanted to plan my next journey more deliberately.

At my first meeting with Nancy Ordway, I felt comfortable immediately and knew that she would be the perfect guide for this process. We worked together weekly for several months. Assessment tools helped me clarify my interests and skill sets. Nancy gave me assignments to research entire categories of occupations and learn how each might fit my own goals for work and lifestyle. When I was ready to apply for positions, she helped me prepare résumés and cover letters, and she coached me when I was invited for interviews.

Early in the process, I recognized that I wanted a leadership position in a nonprofit organization that was engaged internationally. I learned how to write a résumé that others would want to read and how to supplement it with a letter that spoke directly to the requirements of each position I applied for. The discipline and the time this took for each application reinforced why this process was my sole focus during these months.

I came to recognize that, for my purposes, "research" was defined broadly: obvious steps included reading journals at the Council of Philanthropy's library and poring over newsletter job listings for nonprofit executive positions. Just as important were staying in contact with colleagues who were also exploring new opportunities, joining professional organizations related to my interests, and attending events where I could meet new people and learn more about the huge network of nonprofit organizations in Washington. Another valuable lesson concerned how best to ask for help from my network of friends and colleagues, many of whom would want to help but did not necessarily know how they could.

I made a list of friends and colleagues to solicit for help. But how to begin contacting them? Some advice from Barbara Crenshaw was critical: "Beyond the close friends you can call every day for an update or support, most people on your list should be contacted when you are ready to ask for specific help." She reminded me that "everyone in your network wants to help, but without a specific 'ask,' they'll be unlikely to even notice an opportunity that's appropriate or think of a colleague you may want to meet if you haven't steered them in that direction." That advice kept me on course several times. Over the years, I have shared Barbara's advice dozens of times as I've advised others.

I concluded that I wanted to stay in Washington unless I found an opportunity in Europe. I wanted my next position to accommodate the geographic reality of my marriage to Peter and to include working with people who viewed the transatlantic nature of our marriage as a strength rather than a problem.

Midway through the year, I started identifying positions of interest. As I assessed my personal skill sets in the context of various organizations' needs, I sometimes concluded that a given job would not be right for me. It felt really good to be able to decide not to pursue particular positions. I applied only for those jobs in which I was truly interested.

In the summer of 1997 I was one of two finalists for a position, and the second and final interview took place just before I was to leave for our summer holiday in Sweden. The first interview had gone well, and I was interested in the job. I believed in the mission of the organization, which was due for a renewal and had never had a woman leader, although the majority of its members were women. The chemistry between the search committee and me was excellent. As I left the final interview, the search firm partner and the search committee chair walked me to the elevator and told me to expect an offer in the next day or two. It was a good start to our summer holiday.

Yet as I settled into my airplane seat and reflected further on the opportunity, I felt uncertain. By the time I landed at Copenhagen's Kastrup Airport the following morning, I had misgivings, and when I arrived at our summerhouse in the Swedish countryside, I told Peter I would turn down the offer if it came. Something was off. I felt uncertain about the board's commitment to a renewal effort. The next day, the search firm partner called me and, with tears in her voice, told me that in the end they decided not to offer me the position. The search committee had concluded that the organization's leaders were not ready for the substantial change that my leadership would require of the organization. She was very disappointed. She had felt optimistic about my candidacy from the beginning and knew that several on the search committee concurred. The other finalist was not a strong second choice, so they would restart the search.

I was glad that I could tell her that while I had been genuinely interested in the position, following the final interview I had decided that it wasn't right for me, and I would have turned it down if offered. The outcome was reassuring to both of us. This had been a very instructive process for me, from the initial application to preparing for two interviews and working with the search firm. I was reminded of the importance of taking the time to reflect honestly and not lose sight of my core goals. I looked forward to the next possibility.

Peter had been reflecting on my decision to turn down the offer, and as he listened to my end of the telephone conversation, he understood that the offer hadn't come. He recognized that this meant a restart for me as well. Since we were beginning our summer break, this was the perfect time for me to take a step back from my job search to rest and renew myself for the next round.

It is hard to imagine a better place for a summer holiday than the countryside of southern Sweden. Forests, lakes, and rivers provide a wealth of natural settings for biking, hiking, and swimming. The many local and national art galleries, sculpture gardens, musical performance venues, and museums of all sizes, in addition to the Swedish tradition of *loppis* (flea markets), provide endless options for exploration, relaxation, physical activity, and intellectual stimulation. By the end of the month I was refreshed and ready to return to my "job" of finding the next opportunity.

During this break, Peter proposed yet another activity for me to undertake during the coming months: studying German with a longtime friend, now retired from teaching German to adults. Peter understood that I found language learning intimidating, and learning Swedish wouldn't really be practical for me, since all of my social relationships in Sweden were conducted in English. But learning German would be useful, and he knew that the teaching style of his family friend Krystal would be well suited to my learning style. His idea: We would invite Krystal to stay with me in Washington and give me instruction in German for a couple of hours each day. Then, while I worked on my job search, Krystal could explore Washington as a tourist. Peter believed that this arrangement would give me an alternative model for language learning while also helping me to maintain balance by shifting my focus beyond my job search for a few hours a day. It made sense to me, and I didn't see a downside other than living with another person in the house full-time, which I felt I could manage for a couple of months.

Krystal loved the idea. For her it was an adventure. She had traveled the world on her own, staying in private homes while she explored new places. She had never been to the United States, so the prospect of visiting Washington was exciting. She loved to teach adults, she loved Peter, and she thought that teaching me would be wonderful.

We would meet for two hours every day after breakfast. Krystal would bring worksheets to each session that she had created after our previous meeting. Following the "class," we would have a coffee, speaking only German for fifteen minutes. Then off she would go to explore the city, and I would get to work on my job search.

We maintained this routine for two months, after which Krystal returned to Sweden. Such a short amount of time cannot produce competence in a language, but I liked learning German in this way, which contrasted with my earlier experiences studying Spanish and French. Krystal personalized each lesson and was patient and positive, and I was soon enjoying simple telephone exchanges with Peter in German. The whole process was a terrific break from the demands of my job search.

Soon after Krystal's departure, I received a call from a headhunter for the position of executive director of NAFSA: Association of International Educators. The headhunter, Leslie Madden, had initially approached a friend of mine to inquire about her interest in the position, and after reviewing the job description, my friend recommended that Leslie contact me, as she believed that the position was more suited to my interests and skills than to hers. NAFSA was a fifty-year-old organization with a staff of forty and several thousand members who were college and university staff working in international student services and study abroad programs. The association offered an array of training programs, held an annual conference, and employed a government relations staff.

Leslie and I talked for two hours about the position and the experience and skill sets I could bring to the work. I did not meet all of the published requirements for the position: I didn't have a PhD, and I hadn't worked in higher education or previously led a nonprofit organization, but I had served on several nonprofit boards of directors and had a long-term interest in international education. I also had public policy and leadership experience in government and business. Leslie concluded that my experience would suit the organization well. A couple of days later, we continued our conversation in person. She had further discussions with the board and search committee to explore their flexibility regarding the required qualifications. Later I learned that Leslie asked for a meeting with the full board to discuss their commitment to new organizational models and their openness to a less traditional candidate.

My initial interview with the search committee left me energized and very interested. The board wanted a leader who could stabilize the association's finances following a revenue decline that resulted in an operating deficit. The association also wanted someone who could boost its impact on public policy related to international student recruitment and study abroad, and who could raise NAFSA's credibility within the higher education community.

The more I learned about the organization and reflected on how I could contribute, the more I believed I was a strong candidate. The second interview was followed by dinner with half the members of the search committee. The other half of the committee had dinner with the other finalist, and the full committee met the following day to make a final recommendation. The full board supported the recommendation, and later that Saturday afternoon in early December 1997, in a telephone call from the board chair, Gary Althen, director of the Office of International Student Services at the University of Iowa, I was offered the position. I accepted the offer, to begin in February 1998.

The year I spent finding my way to this opportunity left me rich with wonderful memories. I was supported by many friends and colleagues, Peter most of all. Financially, I lived on the severance from my previous job plus savings. It would have been reasonable for Peter to be concerned about the length of time I was unemployed, but he never expressed concern about my lack of income. He was consistently curious about my process, what I was learning, who I was consulting, and how I was feeling.

It helped that I had the scars and joys of my widely varied life experience to this point. The time I took to think and reflect allowed me to understand what was really important to me in the final chapter of my career. Peter's curiosity about my process, his initiative in finding me a coach and introducing me to Barbara Crenshaw, his idea to recruit his friend to teach me German to help me stay balanced during my search, and so much more reinforced my confidence and helped me stay grounded through the year.

Months earlier, we had scheduled a ten-day break in Spain for late January 1998. Now this would be the perfect opportunity to celebrate and relax before I faced the demands of my new position.

19

\\\\\\\\\\||||||||//////,

Leading NAFSA

Walking in the door of NAFSA in February 1998, I was surprised by the gaps in the organization's management capacity, but on reflection I realized this confirmed the board's recognition of the need for stronger leadership. The management structure was limited to the chief financial officer. There was a lack of clarity about the roles of the staff and the board, and member committees were making decisions with financial implications. The reason for the board's prioritization of a strong public policy function also became apparent when I learned that NAFSA didn't even have a relationship with the Immigration and Naturalization Service. I definitely felt I was in the right place and was excited to get going.

The association's annual conference was just three and a half months away. This key event attracted more than five thousand attendees from higher education institutions in the United States and around the world. Its success was critical to NAFSA's financial stability, as it generated one-third of the organization's annual income. The conference included an exposition hall with booths staffed by representatives of international learning organizations, insurance companies, study abroad programs, and more. The conference's workshops and educational sessions were organized and led by NAFSA members, and the conference planning staff managed the logistics. Traditionally, the opening plenary session featured a well-known speaker.

By the time I joined the organization, the details of that year's conference program were in place and the plenary speaker chosen. This was to be the fiftieth anniversary conference, so some celebratory events were planned as well. As I reviewed the program and thought about the diverse audience who would be attending the four-day conference, it occurred to me that in addition to the dozens of small-venue workshops and educational sessions being presented, more offerings were needed that could be shared by a broader audience. More plenary sessions would bring together attendees from across the many disciplines represented—from study abroad advisers to immigration attorneys to international student advisers and more—and offer them common intellectual and social experiences. At this point, it was too late and would be too expensive to book additional plenary speakers through booking agencies, so I decided to use my network and powers of persuasion to find one or more friends who would "fill the bill" as a favor to me.

I went straight to my Rolodex, and my first three "asks" said yes: former congresswoman Patricia Schroeder, then president of the Association of American Publishers, whom I had known since she did the Great American Family Tour to advocate for stronger child-care programs; former Illinois lieutenant governor and former U.S. senator Paul Simon, who had been a Senate leader on international affairs; and J. Brian Atwood, then administrator of the U.S. Agency for International Development. My intention had been to find individuals I knew were inspiring speakers, and all of them were. I had not anticipated that because I had worked with them previously, all of them would share personal stories of working with me in their speeches, including relating how I had twisted their arms to get them scheduled to speak. The generosity of these three speakers reinforced my credibility and encouraged NAFSA members' confidence in me as the association's new executive director and CEO. Their support would pay dividends in the months ahead, when many of my early decisions disrupted how things had always been done. I have always remembered their willingness to step in on short notice and contribute in this way, and I have tried to pay that forward whenever I've had the chance to step up for others.

C. Peter Magrath, president of the National Association of State Universities and Land-Grant Colleges (now the Association of Public and Land-Grant Universities), also accepted my invitation to come to the conference and introduce Senator Simon. This was the first time that the president of NASULGC had attended a NAFSA conference. Peter Magrath had been president of the University of Minnesota when I was lieutenant governor, and he later married my good friend Deborah Howell, so he had a front-row seat to my job search and my joining NAFSA. He had introduced me as CEO of NAFSA at my first meeting of the Higher Education Secretariat, a network of higher education associations with a Washington office; my attendance was intended to send the message that NAFSA planned to engage actively with the leadership of higher education.

The first management decision I made at NAFSA was to create the position of human resources director and hire Deb Mix for the position. Deb had been a NAFSA member, representing a study abroad organization. She decided to make a career change and earned a certification in human resources management. Her experience in the field and her expertise in HR were exactly what we needed as we created a management structure, and for her this was the perfect opportunity to use her previous experience as well as her newly acquired skills. We began with a clean slate, as the organization had operating traditions but few policies in place.

Strengthening NAFSA's public policy role was the next priority. Historically, the association's government relations role had been limited to staying abreast of policy changes and providing government relations information to members. I spent a few weeks consulting with key board members and other leaders to explore ideas about what an alternative role for NAFSA could be. Subsequently, I created the position of senior director for public policy and shared my decision with board members prior to the conference. Candidates were suggested, and after interviewing a number of individuals, I ultimately hired Victor Johnson. He had been staff director for the House Committee on the Western Hemisphere and currently held an international education role at a Florida university. He was eager to move back to Washington and to be back in the policy arena, and we needed his experience.

The four-day conference was exciting and full of energy, as higher education colleagues from around the world established professional relationships, shared expertise, and renewed friendships. The conference was also a business opportunity for providers of study abroad opportunities and services offered for international students. On any scale, this first conference of my tenure was a success. As we debriefed afterward, however, I recognized several vulnerabilities that needed to be addressed: NAFSA would require new and enhanced management capacity and program expertise to chart a course toward growth and financial stability.

Previously, membership dues and training workshop content and pricing had been set by member committees, with no management oversight of fiscal health or content quality. Building a fiscally sound organization, providing high-quality professional development programs, becoming an effective public policy advocacy organization, and producing an outstanding annual conference required a talented management team that understood and respected NAFSA's culture and had the business skills to execute each part of the organization.

The Asia financial crisis that began in 1997 caused a huge disruption for the tens of thousands of Asian students on U.S. campuses. Our colleges and universities were at risk of losing students and tuition revenue, and this situation raised urgent public policy questions for the United States. NAFSA had not yet hired a new senior director of public policy, so as CEO, I led a network of international education organizations to recommend policies to the administration and worked with universities to create financial safety nets for the thousands of families whose resources for their children's education had collapsed. This was the first time NAFSA had taken a leadership role among higher education and international education organizations in the public policy arena, and it established the organization's new approach to such leadership.

The board had hired William Newman as chief financial officer six months before I joined NAFSA. He had assessed the association's financial health and had begun to understand the organizational history and culture as well as the complexity of the situation. NAFSA is a nonprofit, 501(c)(3) organization, but its income is earned, rather than gifted by philanthropic entities. We needed a management team that understood the inherent demands of a business operation while also respecting the culture of the organization. Upon reflection and with the advice of the CFO and HR director, I concluded that we needed to create two deputy executive director positions, both of which should be filled by individuals with NGO management experience. In addition, at least one of the two needed to have experience in generating income, and at least one should have deep roots in NAFSA's membership. I was eager to hire individuals I trusted and who knew me.

From my first day at NAFSA, Peter served as my personal consultant. He loved our conversations about my work. For more than twenty years, his professional consulting practice had focused on helping reinvent mature businesses. He loved the creativity and learning required of each leader among his clients, and he used "action learning" methodology to help clients build internal teams whose members could learn from each other as they tried new approaches, reviewing and revising as necessary at each step. As I worked my way through the myriad challenges at NAFSA, Peter's questions helped me clarify the issues and ensure participation from my own team. His enthusiasm for my work sustained my energy.

My concept was that we would manage the organization as a team: two deputies, the CFO, the senior director for public policy, and myself. All members would report to me, and we would make strategic decisions and oversight assessments as a team. I was excited about the plan, and Peter was enthusiastic and supportive. His view was that this approach would work well if I trusted each person implicitly, as that would also reinforce trust among the team members.

My choices for the two deputy executive director positions were Betty Soppelsa, then director of the very successful Applied English Center at the University of Kansas, and Bob Stableski, deputy executive director of AFS-USA. Betty was a longtime NAFSA member and currently served on the NAFSA board of directors. I knew Bob from my years on the AFS-USA board. Betty was on the board that hired me, so I had observed her capacity to influence her colleagues, and I knew that she had built an innovative and financially successful language center with active engagement of the faculty at the University of Kansas. Bob had major responsibilities for an organization with one of the more complex management structures in the nonprofit world. Both had been involved in international education throughout their personal and professional lives.

I left the office on a Friday afternoon with my talking points ready for the telephone conversations I would have privately with each of these candidates over the weekend. From my kitchen table in Washington, D.C.'s Foggy Bottom, I placed both calls the next morning. I had talked to Peter earlier, to review the approaches I planned to take and to confirm that he would be available to talk after I had completed the calls. There was a lot at stake. I did not have a backup plan if either or both of them turned me down.

Fortunately, both were interested, flattered to be asked, and comfortable with the plan. But for both of them, accepting would mean geographic relocation and leaving comfortable positions in organizations that they had helped build. I shared my enthusiasm for the challenge and my conviction that each was the perfect person for this moment. I also shared with each of them that I was making an offer to the other one at the same time, so I very much hoped they would both accept. Being the cautious individuals they are, they both asked for a day or two to think about it, but they also indicated how interested they were. The decision was a bit less complicated for Bob, as he was an empty nester. For Betty, accepting the job meant disrupting her life as well as the lives of her husband, her son, and her mother, who had recently relocated to Kansas—many pieces to juggle. In the end, both accepted the offer and within two months were in place at NAFSA.

Among the logistical and financial issues of that first year was office space. We had three years remaining on the lease for our offices, but another tenant in the building was expected to exercise an option to take our space at the end of our lease. Even if that did not happen, there was no room for us to grow in our current space. Then, as if on cue, Peter Magrath called to ask if NAFSA would be interested in being a tenant in a new building co-owned by four higher education associations that had previously occupied space in the higher education building at 1 Dupont Circle. Because the purchase of the new building had been financed with tax-free bonds, the owners had to rent to nonprofit organizations, and our rent would be nontaxable, unlike our current rent. The move would be financially beneficial for NAFSA, with the added advantage that we would be next door to other higher education associations with whom we might find opportunities to collaborate. Our current landlord was happy to let us out of our lease, so within a year we were settled at 1307 New York Avenue Northwest, Washington, D.C. The new office was excellent for NAFSA: logistically, we were now between two Metro stops, a huge benefit for our commuting staff, and strategically, the location raised NAFSA's profile on international education and policy advocacy among university presidents.

We then built staff capacity to produce an annual conference that would ultimately serve ten thousand attendees and generate 40 percent of the association's annual income, offer high-quality and expanded conference learning programs, increase year-round professional development offerings, and build an advocacy staff to place NAFSA among the key national advocates for international education. Later, our expansion of public policy staff allowed NAFSA to include international education issues in the immigration reform policy debates.

My vision for a team-managed organization improved NAFSA's productivity and creativity. With talented senior managers in each area of the organization, our weekly management team meetings focused on strategic issues, collaboration among the departments, and problem solving as needed. Because the annual conference was essential to the success of every aspect of the organization, each manager understood the benefits of internal coordination and collaboration to strengthen the conference program and increase revenue.

Early in my tenure we concluded that future conferences should be held in convention centers rather than hotels, to meet the expectations of annual growth in the numbers of attendees and the increasing demand for participation in the exposition hall. The expansion of the conference was an adjustment for an association that had been defined by its intimate culture of member-organized presentations. In the larger configuration we now needed to ensure that attendees could find their professional peers and have intimate interactions. At the same time, the increasing demands of their own work required that they learn more about global issues and find common ground with others whose responsibilities differed from their own.

Plenary sessions were on important way to create common experiences among our diverse attendees. I decided that every NAFSA conference would have a plenary session each day. My personal role would be to choose the plenary speakers. As a group, the speakers needed to bring a range of views to our audience.

Over the course of my nearly twenty years at NAFSA, conference plenary speakers included Nobel Peace Prize laureates Wangari Maathai, Kofi Annan, Shirin Ebadi, Leymah Gbowee, Tawakkol Karman, and Óscar Arias; former president of Ireland Mary Robinson; journalist/ authors Robert Kagan, Judy Woodruff, David Brooks, Gayle Tzemach Lemmon, and Salman Rushdie; Kenyan educator and entrepreneur

Kakenya Ntaiya, founder of Kakenya's Dream school for girls; author and human rights activist Ishmael Beah; former U.S. secretaries of state Madeleine Albright and Colin Powell; anthropology professor Jack Weatherford; basketball legend and author Kareem Abdul-Jabbar; Swedish diplomat Jan Eliasson; and Bryan Stevenson, founder of the Equal Justice Initiative. The opportunity to engage with these extraordinary leaders and share our vision for international education was a highlight of my tenure and generated great excitement and critical learning among attendees.

Among the changes my team undertook at NAFSA, governance issues were critical, as the organization had lacked clarity regarding the specific roles of board and staff. From the association's founding, member expertise had been shared through regional meetings and the annual national conferences. The small staff, board members, and committee members created programs, built networks, and shared day-to-day operational work. Under our leadership, members continued to develop training materials and other resources, and the staff was responsible for the delivery and marketing of those services. We needed the board to focus on strategy and future directions, to understand the financial requirements and opportunities of the organization, and to recruit future board members capable of handling the strategic and fiscal responsibilities of a growing NGO.

With the revision of our bylaws, we had the exciting opportunity to add three board members from outside the NAFSA membership. For these positions we sought experienced, strategic thinkers who had a passion for international education and could bring new perspectives and management oversight capabilities. During my tenure, among the board members were Debra Stewart, president of the Council of Graduate Schools; Lars Heikensten, president of the Nobel Foundation; Peter Robinson, president of the United States Council for International Business; Simon Adams, executive director of the Global Centre for the Responsibility to Protect; Joy Olson, executive director of the Washington Office on Latin America (a NAFSA collaborator on immigration policy issues); Doris Meissner, Senior Fellow at the Migration Policy Institute and former administrator of the Immigration and Naturalization Service; Jody Olsen, former deputy director of the Peace Corps and faculty member at the University of Maryland, Baltimore; Jolene Koester, president of California State University, Northridge; Earl Potter, president of Saint Cloud State University; William Holmes, vice provost of the Sheridan College Institute of Technology and Advanced Learning; Keith Stock, CEO of First Financial Investors; and Robert Pastor, former national security adviser to President Carter and faculty member at American University. Each brought fresh ideas and rich understanding of organizational leadership, consistently asking questions that deepened the board's discussions and informed our efforts to play a more significant role in debates on immigration reform. The participation of outside board members also strengthened NAFSA's credibility in the larger higher education community and enhanced members' pride in the association's relationships beyond the field of international education.

The board's priority directive to strengthen NAFSA's advocacy leadership role remained in the forefront of my goals throughout my tenure. We determined that NAFSA should take a strategic approach to advocacy, and our statement defining the value of international education to society became the frame for every aspect of our advocacy program.

It was an exciting time for this work, as the Clinton administration's Departments of State and Education were led by individuals who believed in international education and worked with us to strengthen international education programs and national support. In our first year, Secretary of Education Richard Riley and Secretary of State Madeleine Albright embraced our recommendation for a National Policy on International Education, adopting NAFSA's language as the policy of the Clinton administration, which was articulated in an executive order.

The international education policy remained on the books during the Bush administration and provided the critical framework for NAFSA's work following the terrorist attacks of September 11, 2001, when U.S. society was profoundly challenged and NAFSA contributed to the public discourse about the role of cross-cultural learning. Amid government demands that Middle Eastern students be sent home, NAFSA actively articulated the importance of international students and scholars to our society and urged university leaders to maintain their commitment to welcoming these students to our campuses. Our relationships with university presidents and associations such as NASULGC, the American Association of State Colleges and

Universities, and the American Association of Community Colleges would be tested during those months as NAFSA led higher education efforts to influence Congress and the Bush administration, reminding them of the value of international students to our society. Robert Gates, at that time president of Texas A&M University, worked with us to write an op-ed for the *New York Times* in support of our policy recommendations after 9/11.

NAFSA actively supported the 100,000 Strong in the Americas initiative, the Obama administration's strategy to increase student engagement in Latin America. We worked closely with Roberta Jacobson, head of the Western Hemisphere Bureau at the Department of State on the public–private model for implementing the initiative. Partners of the Americas shared the role of advocacy and managed the program implementation. Along with the administration, we encouraged corporate investment in the program, joining President Barack Obama at the White House for meetings with corporate leaders. Later, in 2015, I attended President Obama's meeting with corporate leaders at the Summit of the Americas in Costa Rica to encourage them to commit to this forward-thinking education initiative. At the request of the White House, NAFSA hosted a reception for the executives later that day to help promote further conversations about the initiative. The program grew and continued during the Trump and Biden administrations.

The rhythm and pace of my life during my years at NAFSA were all that I had hoped for when I was defining my hopes and aspirations in 1997. I was leading an organization focused on international issues, with an advocacy role that put higher education in the broader conversations of immigration policy and international affairs; international travel was an important part of my responsibilities; and I was working with a talented management team that managed the day-to-day demands of the organization. Identifying opportunities to strengthen the organization and taking action to implement the changes was some of the most rewarding work I'd ever done. From improving individual and group skills to increasing the gender and ethnic diversity of the staff to expanding NAFSA's public visibility and credibility among policymakers and other international organizations throughout the world, I felt energized by the work and grateful to have the board's support.

Peter and I were in a very good place. He had arranged his consulting schedule to allow a week each month for writing, which he did from

Washington. Since NAFSA's board meetings and conferences were set a year or more in advance, he was able to be in Washington for most of those gatherings. He enjoyed cohosting the board members for dinners at our home and attending the annual conferences. Learning about the organization, its management structure, and the role of members in developing many of our products was exciting for him. He enjoyed getting to know NAFSA staffers when he dropped by the offices, board members at our dinners with them, and association members during the annual conferences. And the more he learned, the more questions he had for me, and the more ideas he had that strengthened my own capacities. His support during these years continually reinforced my management skills and confidence.

On several occasions Peter was able to join me on work-related international travel. He accompanied me on trips to China and South Africa, visiting university campuses with me and doing his own sightseeing while I attended private meetings or made presentations; we would often add a few personal days to a trip to visit sites together. A number of times during these years, we were able to meet at European locations where I and others on our team were attending the annual conference of the European Association for International Education (Vienna, Turin, Tampere, Porto, Madrid, and Kraków). Peter would join us for special programs, cohost small gatherings with me, or go sightseeing with the spouse of one of our staff or board members. These were very special opportunities. Peter appreciated establishing closer bonds with the staff and board members who traveled with us, and the experiences enriched his understanding of NAFSA and my work. Even when I was not around, Peter went out of his way to engage with any of my friends and colleagues who happened to be in Sweden, including introducing Betty and Bob Soppelsa to a Santa Lucia candlelight service followed up by a traditional *julbord* (Christmas table) at a classic countryside restaurant.

My years at NAFSA: Association of International Educators were more fulfilling than I could have imagined possible. Every day was stimulating and challenging, and I felt supported by the board and staff throughout my service. In the community of international educators, my transatlantic marriage was of interest but not a sensation. Until I lived with this reality, I did not fully appreciate how stressful it had been to cope with the lack of acceptance I had felt in Minnesota.

20

\\\\\\\\|||||||||////,

Learning from the Unexpected

Sometimes unanticipated events occur that are clearly related to one's role, while at other times they are more peripheral. Regardless, embracing unforeseen opportunities can bring a richness to one's life and a deeper understanding of oneself and often the larger world. Four such moments in particular stay with me.

One of these took place during my first term as Minnesota's lieutenant governor, when Jehan Sadat, widow of Egyptian president Anwar Sadat, invited me to bring a group of Minnesota women leaders to Egypt. I met Madam Sadat on her visit to Minnesota in 1983. We were seated together at a private dinner, and during our conversation she extended the invitation: if I would bring a group of Minnesota women to Cairo for a visit, she would host us and help arrange for us to meet government officials and business leaders and visit historic sites. It was a spontaneous and generous gesture, and of course I accepted. During the next several months we chose a date for the visit in the following year and identified the women leaders I would invite to participate. Among those who joined us were First Lady Lola Perpich and her chief of staff, Maureen Flahaven; Karen Desnick, owner of Metropolitan Picture Framing; Roxanne Givens, Minneapolis entrepreneur and philanthropist; Kathryn Koutsky, developer of International Market Square; Sarah Solotaroff, artistic administrator of the Saint Paul Chamber Orchestra; Judge Harriet Lansing; Vivian Jenkins Nelsen, diversity, equity, and inclusion consultant; and art consultant Char Hovy.

The day of our arrival in Egypt in October 1984 was the anniversary of President Sadat's assassination—a day of national mourning. Lola Perpich and I were honored by an invitation to a private visitation at the Sadat residence, where we greeted Madam Sadat and joined the other women mourners seated around the edges of the grand receiving hall. It was my first exposure to this gender-specific Muslim tradition, and it led me to recall the separation of genders (women hanging out in the kitchen and men in the living room) that I often saw in my childhood during social times in people's homes, on holidays or on occasions such as funerals.

During our week in Cairo, we visited women-owned businesses, government leaders responsible for social welfare programs, and historic sites such as the pyramids; at one point, I tried riding a camel. This was my first visit to Africa, and I had to make some cultural adjustments, as did other members of our group. The first came when we were required to give up our passports when we checked in to our hotel. We would not get them back until we left the country, so the hotel clerk had to see our return plane tickets to mark the date in the hotel's calendar for the return of our passports.

At that time, Cairo's infrastructure was in development. This affected us primarily in two ways: moving around the city was difficult, and it was almost impossible to schedule meetings by telephone. Walking anywhere was physically dangerous, as there were few sidewalks— pedestrians took their chances in the street among the cars. And the telephone network was unreliable. We tried to make arrangements by phone, but if we called someone and the telephone wasn't answered, we could not assume that no one was available at the other end. It was more likely that the phone wasn't ringing there. In practice, this meant that our meetings had to be scheduled in person, so for each appointment we had to visit the location twice—once to schedule the meeting, and then to attend the meeting. In addition, it was expected that meetings would rarely begin sooner than half an hour to an hour after the scheduled time. Fortunately, I am generally a patient person, and I quickly recognized the reality and understood that one meeting a day was all we would be able to do. For a few of our highly organized colleagues who were accustomed to being in charge, the "inefficiency" of this was difficult to accept. Clearly, we had not provided an adequate predeparture orientation for the members of our group regarding cultural values and differences. Years later at NAFSA, I would reflect on my experience in Egypt and appreciate even more the cultural orientation sessions that our members provided for American students studying abroad and for international students studying in the United States.

In 1986, I received a call from the executive director of the American Refugee Council, who asked me to join him on a trip to Sudan to visit refugee camps. ARC was providing medical services in refugee camps in Thailand and Cambodia at the time, and was now being asked to do so for the expanding refugee population in Sudan. The director wanted a public official to join him on this visit, to help raise awareness of the need, believing that the increased visibility would help with future fundraising efforts. I was the last person on his list—the first three or four elected officials he had invited had turned him down. I would need to cover my own costs for the trip and be away for seven to ten days. I accepted immediately, with the caveat that I would need a couple of days to figure out how I would pay my way, as I didn't have the personal resources, nor could I use state funds.

Two friends who had supported my political committee immediately agreed to share the costs of my trip, and within weeks we were on our way to Sudan. We spent a few days in Khartoum, adjusting to travel fatigue, meeting with USAID officials, and making arrangements to take the regional bus for the several-hour drive out to Showak, where we would stay in the regional rest center for medical staff working at the refugee camps.

Each day of this trip was beyond any experience I had ever had. I was definitely out of my comfort zone. This was the first time I understood that I could not rely on my instincts in a culture so different from my own. We were the only two non-Sudanese on the bus, which was also shared with chickens and other animals. Packages were stacked high on top of the bus, and the windows were kept open, providing air circulation but also allowing desert sand to blow over us. Other travelers were kind, if a bit amused to see us there. As the bus bounced along on the narrow, two-lane highway without shoulders, the often-heard saying that "the journey is more important than the destination" took on new meaning for me. Over the next few days, we traveled in a caravan of two open jeeps across the desert to various refugee camps, each vehicle following the tracks of previous ones unless the winds had blown sand across the path. Then the drivers were on their own, hoping that a larger wind would not cause sand to clog the jeeps' engines. At each camp, I met the aid staff, medical workers, and many residents. I was struck by the dignity and tenacity of the refugees, who, despite their profound suffering and displacement, carried out the myriad tasks of everyday life—caring for their children, establishing an economy, creating hair salons under the trees, organizing sports games, doing laundry, preparing meals, and more. I had never known or seen such remarkable courage and determination.

I have often been reminded of the impact of this experience on my way of thinking. My understanding of the wider world was critically influenced by this exposure to another culture and the tragedy of war, as well as to government and civil society systems working to address the human suffering resulting from that unrest. The Sudan experience continues to reinforce for me the value of pursuing new opportunities, recognizing the growth that comes from stepping outside one's comfort zone, and expanding one's influence when possible.

Accepting the invitation to make this trip also required that I answer questions from those who felt it was a distraction from my responsibilities as lieutenant governor. I told them that I was grateful for the exposure and the experience, and glad to be in a position to generate public support for ARC's work. After we made our trip, Senator Ted Kennedy traveled to one of the same refugee camps with his children for a holiday visit, and two months later Minnesota's WCCO-TV sent a reporter/photographer team to that camp. The media coverage stimulated further interest in the refugees' situation and ultimately led to the Minnesota State Legislature's appropriation of $100,000 for the ARC medical program in Sudan.

Another unexpected moment came in 1984, during my first term as lieutenant governor. At the time, there was considerable speculation about who Walter Mondale would choose as his running mate in his bid for the U.S. presidency. Governor Ann Richards of Texas had shared with me and a few others in a private meeting that in her view Mondale's only chance of winning the election was to have Lloyd Bentsen as his running mate. Active Democratic feminist leaders had another idea, and worked tirelessly to promote the choice of Geraldine Ferraro.

During the weeks leading up to his decision, Mondale phoned

Governor Perpich to ask him why he had thought that having a woman running mate would be a strategic advantage. Perpich told Mondale that my presence on the ticket had been a key factor in our primary victory. I've always felt that the governor shared this anecdote with me because he was surprised—and pleased—that Mondale had called him. Governor Perpich had told me more than once that he and Mondale were not close. The Humphrey–Mondale wing of the DFL Party had never trusted the Perpich brothers' Iron Range organization. Our defeat of Mondale's close friend Warren Spannaus in the 1982 primary had reinforced the distrust. While Mondale had known me since I was a student, I wasn't a Mondale insider. Governor Perpich and I were invited to join Mondale at the Minnesota State Capitol when he announced Ferraro as his running mate. Later we were among the luncheon guests at the Mondales' home in North Oaks. It was an exciting day filled with optimism.

The out-of-the-blue moment during my years at NAFSA came at the end of the Clinton administration. The NAFSA management team had scheduled a meeting with Secretary of Education Richard Riley to express our appreciation for his extraordinary leadership in helping to establish a U.S. international education policy and working with us over his two terms to promote a variety of initiatives to advance international education. The day before the meeting, I was on an airplane with the leaders of several other higher education associations, returning from a funeral in Minnesota. One of my colleagues commented on how much we would miss Secretary Riley and voiced the hope that he would find a way to stay in Washington and continue working on some of our issues.

As our NAFSA team visited with Secretary Riley the following day, I shared with him the conversation we'd had on the plane and told him how much we all hoped to continue working with him. He looked at me and asked, "Do you have something specific in mind?" I replied, "Give me a day or two, and I will!" Riley's policy director, Terry Peterson, followed me to the elevator and probed further. I told him that we weren't in a position to offer a salary, but we would definitely think about opportunities for collaboration. We agreed to talk the next day.

Back at the office, I gathered the management team and told them about our meeting with Secretary Riley. After a focused, one-hour conversation, we all agreed that if he would provide periodic consultation regarding our policy agenda, we could make room for him to have an office for himself and an assistant, and we would give him the title of special policy adviser. I insisted that it was important for Secretary Riley to come to our offices before he agreed to this arrangement. We all loved our space—it was energetic, light, and well designed, but modest. It was unlike the typical law firm or even the offices of other higher education associations. Our staff was made up of talented and creative people, and I felt sure Secretary Riley would enjoy the team. But I wanted to be certain that he would be comfortable in our space.

He came by the following day, which was also the day NAFSA's regional leaders were in town for a meeting. He loved our space and welcomed the idea of having policy discussions with us; he was excited about an affiliation as our senior policy adviser. His home was in South Carolina, but he would be in Washington periodically; his assistant would work from our offices most of the time.

Secretary Riley didn't stay for our leadership reception, but he was happy for me to announce our arrangement to the regional leaders that day. His involvement would be a huge asset for NAFSA, and we had secured it only because I had followed an instinct in real time. Days later, when we made the public announcement of his new association with NAFSA, I received several calls from colleagues at other higher education associations who wanted to know, "How did you accomplish that?" My reply: "I asked." Secretary Riley was an adviser to NAFSA for several years, and he has remained a good friend.

21

Life Changes in a Flash

In his work with Hjärntrusten, Peter had guided several groups of executives, some of whom had been together for three or four years. He loved the work and kept records of the action learning process of each participant as the group members engaged in addressing each other's challenges and outcomes. He was documenting theories of change and would research them further in his PhD thesis. It was inspiring to watch him move from practice to theory and back, and I shared his enthusiasm and was continually amazed by his insights. By the summer of 2010, his PhD adviser was chosen and his project accepted. He spent the summer completing his research proposal, which he would present during the first week of the fall session at Lund University.

During our summer holiday that year we talked about what our retirement might look like, exploring different time frames and transitions that might include part-time work. I wasn't ready to leave my position at NAFSA, but I thought I might be ready within two or three years. At that point I would have been in my job for fifteen years, and Peter would have finished his PhD and perhaps written a book. I had recently been invited to join the board of directors of Kakenya's Dream, a school for girls in rural Kenya. It was a new organization, and the opportunity to be involved establishing its foundation and helping raise financial support for its important work would keep me in an international and educational network. We made no decisions, but we felt optimistic about the possibilities.

Friday, August 12, 2010, would be the last day of our summer holiday. The next day I would fly back to Washington and return to work at NAFSA on Monday. Peter would present his research proposal to his faculty adviser on Tuesday, August 16. We had thoroughly enjoyed our three weeks in the countryside. Peter had spent mornings writing, and I had worked in our garden and taken long bike rides. In the afternoons we took walks in the forest, drives in the countryside, and day trips to Louisiana Museum of Modern Art in Denmark and Wanås Konst sculpture park in southern Sweden; we visited friends or relaxed with a book and a coffee, and we swam at the small beach on the lake just a short walk from our house.

Our holiday guests had included Graham and Kathy Collins. Graham was my AFS exchange brother in 1967. They had visited us often over the years, both in Sweden and in the United States. Peter and I had met them in London during the years they lived in Margate, England. During their visit this year, Peter had experienced dizziness, prompting Kathy (a nurse) to insist that he go to the hospital for an MRI. Peter had the test, and everything was okay.

Thursday, August 11, was a warm, sunny day. Peter always began his days with a short walk to the lake for a morning swim. Usually he did this on his own—I was often already on a bike ride. But this morning I joined him. I'd never absorbed the morning swim ritual as my own, but I appreciated the joy it gave him. I am grateful that my many treasured memories include sharing this morning swim on our final day before his fall.

Refreshed from the cool water and morning air, we walked back to the house along the forest path. Peter made porridge, and we sat down at the balcony table to enjoy the garden view and the sounds of birds and cows in the pasture across the stream. I had stopped eating the porridge Peter prepared every morning when I was diagnosed with celiac disease in 2008. He wanted to cook gluten-free porridge so I could have some, but I resisted; gluten-free oats have a smoother grain, and I was reluctant to have him give up the texture of his favorite meal and ritual of the day for my sake. In retrospect, I regret my attitude. It wouldn't have bothered him at all. Rather, he consistently viewed such situations as opportunities to learn something new, and I'm quite sure he would have found a way to enhance the oats' texture.

Following breakfast on the deck, Peter spent a couple of hours on his research proposal. It was written, but he was still thinking through his presentation to the faculty committee on the coming Tuesday. In the early afternoon we drove around the countryside for a couple of hours, exploring a few more of the endless back roads through the forests, finding remote cottages and gardens—further signs of the rich texture of Sweden's summerhouse culture. Later in the afternoon, seeming a bit tentative, Peter wrapped himself in a blanket and settled into his favorite chair, the Danish classic Hans Wegner "bear chair," with a book. He didn't want an evening meal. He said he didn't feel sick, but he was unusually quiet—not his usual energetic self.

At 8:00 p.m., Peter joined me on the deck for the final evening of our summer holiday. The sun had set, but the sky was still bright, and the evening chill was a hint of autumn. We lit a candle and sat at the table wrapped in blankets. We reflected on the past three weeks, recalling visits with friends and quiet moments together, then made a list of the practical chores we would do the next morning—cleaning the house, putting the garden tools in order, emptying the refrigerator, packing the car—before heading for Lund and dinner with his sister Antje and her husband, Fredrik. Our summer holiday was over, and on Saturday morning I'd take the train to Copenhagen's Kastrup Airport for the flight back to Washington, D.C.

Peter's tone changed as he reached for my hand, looked directly into my eyes, and reminded me how much he loved me and admired my leadership. "Don't forget what a terrific leader you are. You're doing a great job at NAFSA. You have special leadership capacities, a team that respects you and thoroughly enjoys working with you, and you've earned their trust." Peter had made similar comments to me previously, but this time I was taken aback by the intensity and clarity of his words, his quiet smile, and the urgency of his tone.

We went to bed around 10:00 p.m. I was ready to sleep, Peter brought his book. I lamented that the heavy fog settling over the landscape was denying us a favorite aspect of the Swedish summertime—the view of the moon and stars from our bed.

Hours later, I was awakened by a loud thud. Sitting up in bed, I saw that Peter wasn't beside me. I heard his snoring, so I assumed he'd fallen out of bed. But he wasn't there. The heavy fog made the bedroom unusually dark, so I had to turn on the lights as I jumped out of bed and moved to the top of the stairs. Peter was on the floor at the bottom of the stairs!

I made my way down the stairs and tried to wake him, but he didn't respond. In my anxiety I couldn't recall the emergency telephone number. I phoned a neighbor but got no answer. Then I called Peter's sister's number, told her husband what had happened, and asked for the emergency number. Within twenty minutes the ambulance arrived. The medics called the hospital, described the situation to the attending doctor, and were directed to take Peter to the regional emergency room at Kristianstad Hospital.

As they lifted Peter onto the gurney, the attendant quietly told me, "Our emergency vehicles are smaller than U.S. ambulances, so there's not room for a passenger. You'll have to drive to the hospital on your own." In the stress of the moment I couldn't find the car key, causing me further panic. The medic calmly encouraged me to sit for a moment, assured me I would find the key, and reminded me, "There's nothing you can do for Peter right now, so take your time, come to the hospital ER, and you'll learn more then."

For ten minutes I ran around in a panic, trying to figure out where the car key could be. We each had a car key and a personal habit for where we kept our own. Neither key was in its designated place. I searched the pockets of all the jackets either of us had worn recently, checked the shelves near Peter's desk and my desk, and then tried to recall when we had last used the car. The day before, we had been out for a drive and did food shopping. When we arrived at home, I was late for a conference call with my office. Peter urged me to do my call and he would empty the car. The keys were in the ignition where I had left them the day before, when I raced to my phone call. (After a couple of years I found Peter's car keys—in a pocket of his computer case.)

A few minutes later I had dressed, locked up the house, and was on my way, only to discover I couldn't remember the route to Kristianstad! I called my sister-in-law, who reminded me where I would find the sign toward Kristianstad and assured me there would be further signs along the road directing me to the *sjukhuset* (hospital).

That was the longest half-hour drive I have ever taken. I felt numb, scared, and aware that I was entering very new emotional territory. I sensed that our life had changed, but I could not imagine beyond that.

What I thought I knew was that Peter had fallen down the stairs as he returned to the bedroom after using the toilet. As bizarre as that thought was, I knew this wasn't a dream.

Walking from the car to the emergency room, I was struggling to comprehend or define the destination. I had not been inside a Swedish hospital since 1991, when I needed treatment for a knee injury I'd sustained on a ski trip to Austria. Until this moment, Peter had been my guide for each new experience I'd had in Sweden during the twenty-seven years we'd been together. I was very much alone and felt disoriented and terrified about what lay ahead. I introduced myself at the intake desk, and a nurse came immediately to talk to me; I was told that Peter was in a coma, and they had no way of knowing how long he would be unconscious.

If this was a dream, I wanted to wake up. But I had taken enough steps to know that this was some kind of reality. As much as I wanted someone else to take charge, at that moment I made a list of the people I needed to call immediately: Peter's son and daughter, Jonas and Katarina; my mother; my deputy at NAFSA; and my two closest friends in Scandinavia. Jonas and his family had moved to Nairobi, Kenya, just two weeks earlier; he was beginning a three-year term as head of the Swedish School there. Understandably, he felt conflicted about coming back. I encouraged him to wait until we knew more—Peter would want him to focus on his new responsibilities in Nairobi. Jonas volunteered to phone his sister.

I dreaded calling my mother. She and Peter had a lovely relationship and had shared many private conversations about life and values. We had visited her in Minnesota many times, and she had stayed with us in Washington and Sweden. Her last visit to Sweden was two years earlier, when she was eighty-five and experiencing vision loss due to macular degeneration. When she left Sweden then, she acknowledged that she probably wouldn't be physically able to make the trip again. Now she felt so sad when I called to tell her about Peter; she offered to call my siblings, and we agreed to talk again later in the day. Next I called Betty Soppelsa, my deputy at NAFSA, to let her know what had happened and to delegate the leadership role to her for the moment; later, during the weekend, she would work with me to develop a plan for informing the board. Then I called my Danish friend Lis Frederiksen and my Swedish cousin Elisabeth Dahlgren. Lis called back later in the day with a pro-posal for the following day, and Elisabeth reminded me that her daugh-ter Louise was a doctor at this hospital, and she would have her check in with me later in the day.

At 9:00 a.m., the ER doctor confirmed that Peter had suffered a se-rious brain injury. It wasn't possible to tell from the CT scan whether a stroke had caused the fall or the fall had caused the brain injury. The re-sults were being reviewed with the neurological team at Lund University, and meanwhile Peter was medicated to sustain the coma. The doctor told me that Peter was in the intensive care unit; I would be able to sit with him and take breaks in the patient family sitting room. The hospital case manager showed me the family sleeping rooms and told me I would have one for the night. These two conversations were my introduction to the "care of the family" that is part of the Swedish health care system.

I was anxious to be at Peter's bedside in the ICU, to hold his hand and talk to him. I also needed to make sure the nursing team under-stood that Peter has no hearing in his left ear, so they must direct all communication directly to his right ear. Peter's breathing was heavy, his eyes were closed, and he showed no signs of awareness. Watching him "sleep," I instinctively spoke to him, despairing that his hearing impair-ment further reduced the likelihood that he could "hear" me. I stroked his hand, told him where he was and what had happened, reminded him that I loved him, and implored him to please wake up. How impor-tant it was to be there, to help Peter and stay calm—I held his hand, rubbed lotion on his hand and arms, cut his fingernails, talked to him, and played music (Leif "Smoke Rings" Anderson), hoping to get a reac-tion. Despite my anxiety, the rhythm of his breathing and the sounds of the hospital machines were steady and quiet and reassuring.

The day is a blur in my memory. Even though there was no news, I took breaks from sitting with Peter to make follow-up calls—to Peter's sister Antje, my sister Marlys, my mother, Lis, Elisabeth, and Betty at NAFSA. We all needed to hear each other's voices and words of love and encouragement.

Throughout my adult life, daily journal writing has been the vehicle through which I've processed and understood what I'm feeling. On this day, that's just what I wanted to do, but I didn't have a notebook or even a piece of paper with me. At the hospital gift shop I found a small journal adequate for my first notes of this journey: initial diagnosis and treatment in the ICU, plans for the first day, lists of people I wanted to contact, questions to ask when I next talked to the doctor or nurse, things that came to mind as I understood I would be staying in Sweden for the foreseeable future rather than flying back to Washington the following day. For more than forty years my journal writing had helped me clarify, find courage, acknowledge fears and joys, and in many cases determine what I was feeling. Once again a journal provided a space of comfort.

I met with the doctor in the midafternoon. Peter's daughter, Katarina, and her mother had arrived by then, so they joined me for the meeting in a quiet, private room with a sofa and chairs—another reflection of the pace and culture of Sweden's medical care. As we gathered, the doctor indicated that this would be the only time he or anyone else in the health care system would communicate with family members other than me. Their obligation is to speak to Peter's wife, and in the future, family and friends would get their information from me. Despite my stress and anxiety, his direct comment reaffirmed my responsibility for managing Peter's care and the health care system's responsibility to me. I might feel like a foreigner, but the system was honoring my role and responsibility. I would find the strength to step into that role, learning each day—about the Swedish health care system as well as about what Peter needed at each turn. I would come to appreciate that I was on a long journey in a system that consistently engaged with me in understanding Peter's situation and his recommended care.

Later in the afternoon, our niece Lotta and her husband, Krister, stopped by the hospital to give me a hug and bring me pajamas, a toothbrush, and a change of clothes. They lived near our summerhouse and kept a key, so they had taken the initiative to tend to these practical matters. I will always remember their helpfulness.

Lis was in touch throughout the day, confirming that she would be at the hospital Saturday morning when Peter was to be transported to Lund University Hospital by ambulance. She suggested that Antje meet Peter at the hospital in Lund and she and I drive back to the summerhouse to pack up and check in with our neighbor/caretaker before going down to Lund. She would stay with me in Lund for a few days. Her clarity on the practical matters was a huge gift as I struggled to figure out what my next steps should be.

Things were in slow motion during the late afternoon, as I sat at Peter's bedside, talking to him, getting no response. The family sleeping accommodations at the hospital provided incredible comfort—by early evening I was in a deep sleep. When I woke during the night, I walked down the hall to check on Peter. As expected, there was no change. Early in the morning I awoke to find a note from Louise Moberg, my cousin's daughter, a hospital doctor on the night shift. She had stopped by to check on me while I was sleeping, so I returned her call and we had a brief conversation before she went off shift. Lis arrived from Denmark, and we stayed with Peter until he was taken to the ambulance to be transported to Lund; we then left for the summerhouse.

By midafternoon, Lis and I had cleaned and packed up at the summerhouse—chores that Peter and I had planned to do on Friday morning before we left. I checked in with our caretaker neighbor to tell him what had happened and to confirm that he would oversee our summerhouse as needed. When we arrived at Lund University Hospital, Antje was with Peter in a double ICU room. He was allowed one or two family visitors at specific hours each day. Initially I felt considerable anxiety about the limited time I was allowed to be with him, but I came to appreciate that I needed breathing room as well. At that moment, Peter's recovery was out of my control. I needed to create the space for myself to cry and reflect.

The thirteen days Peter was in a coma felt like months. By the second week, his blood pressure and fever spiked, then he squeezed my hand when I spoke to him. Days later, he wiggled his toes when prompted! The doctor observed Peter trying to respond verbally. By the tenth day, he was responding to requests to squeeze my hand and periodically opening his eyes for a second. A slightly opened eye, a small squeeze of my hand, a relaxed muscle—signs of recovery. By the end of the second week, he was briefly opening his eyes more frequently, and when he fully opened both eyes for the first time, the physical therapist and I were on either side of his bed. He looked at her and broke into a big smile! She exclaimed, "In my thirty-five years in this field, I have never before felt a patient's spirit so strongly when he woke from a coma!" Her words strengthened my resolve and hope for weeks.

The uncertainty left me exhausted and terrified. I struggled to sleep, tried to make a few decisions about my life in Lund in the short term, and determined how to manage my work responsibilities in Washington. I had lived alone much of my life, but I had never spent a night alone in Lund, nor had I managed our daily life in Sweden. Throughout our marriage, our shared responsibilities were generally based on our current location, so I had few responsibilities in Sweden over the years. Now there were so many decisions to make. Years before, Peter had insisted on putting my name on his bank accounts. At the time, I wondered what the rush was, as we had given each other legal, financial, and medical power of attorney. At this moment I was grateful, as it meant I had no legal issues to settle before I could tackle the daily business of our lives.

Sitting at Peter's desk in our Lund apartment, I made a list of tasks related to his work and my work that needed immediate attention. The call to Peter's thesis adviser to let him know that Peter would not be presenting his research proposal on Tuesday was surreal. Just days before, they had spoken on the phone to confirm the time for the presentation. Peter was excited to be back at the university and glad to have found an adviser interested in his work. He had presented his theories at an international conference the previous summer and was eager to complete this work and write a book. When I told his adviser the news, he was in a state of disbelief as he felt this compelling project implode. My second call was to Peter's business colleagues, as they would have to distribute his current workload and start planning for a very different future for the firm.

Meanwhile, one of Peter's close friends and colleagues came by to check on both of us. An experienced international entrepreneur, he helped me understand Sweden's requirements for managing Peter's business affairs. He gave me a short list of "must do" actions. Over the next months, he revisited that list with me to make certain that I had the help I needed—from communicating with the bank to paying bills on time to understanding the tax filing requirements. His generous guidance and regular follow-up over the next several months were immeasurably important. He didn't offer to take on tasks for me; rather, he ensured that I understood what needed to be done and had the tools to do it. I deeply appreciated this kind of support, and I have tried to follow his example by providing others with the tools they need in similar situations.

22

A New Chapter in Lund

Each day after Peter awoke from the coma felt like an adventure: more questions than answers, a search for signs of improvement, uncertainty at every corner. Although he remained in the ICU while waiting for a bed in Ward 26, the neurological ward, the physical therapist worked with him daily. There was always something for me to do—answer Peter's questions, assist with physical therapy, hold his hand and feel him squeeze my hand, read to him the notes from friends and family. That first day, his eyes were open for twenty minutes. Mostly he slept as I sat with him and played his favorite music—Wynton Marsalis, Monica Zetterlund, Benny Goodman. When he was awake, his eyes followed me as I moved around the room, and he squeezed my hand periodically or tried to pull tubes out of his nose. Each day he made more eye contact, but he was still sleeping a lot. His involuntary body motion increased—a troubling sign. The physical therapist helped him sit with his legs over the side of the bed, and then he was able to get his legs back onto the bed on his own—a good sign. My emotions went from fear and discouragement to excitement.

On day 16, I awoke from dozing in a chair beside Peter's bed to see him opening his eyes; he looked at me and moved his lips, making sounds, trying to speak. The next time he opened his eyes, he started speaking to the nurse as she removed the oxygen tube—a heart-skip moment! As I leaned over him to talk closer to his ear, he raised both his arms and wrapped them around my back, gave me a hug, and said, "I love you"—the first physical and verbal expression during those first weeks. We sat for a few minutes holding hands while he dozed a bit. I told him I would leave now so he could sleep and that I was having dinner with our friends Boris and Lena Levin at their restaurant, Ringsjö Wärdshus. Boris was Peter's childhood friend from when their families lived in Helsingborg. I knew it would give him comfort to know I was with them.

Despite the uncertainty of those early weeks, the medical staff and I felt optimistic. Peter continued to sleep much of the time, opening his eyes once in a while and sometimes giving my hand a squeeze. His body was rolling back and forth constantly, and his legs and arms moved up and down. By the third week, he was sitting in a chair a couple of times each day, and sleeping there as well. The neurologist assured me of his progress. His routine: meals, physical therapy, sleep. He was eating two thousand calories of real food each day, and he responded to questions from the nurses and me in short sentences. His involuntary body motion continued, whether he was sitting in a chair or lying in bed. It was exhausting for him and hard to watch. There were many heartwarming moments as well: Peter greeted our Danish friend Ulla with a broad smile, he accepted grandson Anton's help with eating, and he gave granddaughter Sara a huge smile the first time she visited. Reminded that his friend Lars Risberg would be visiting, he nodded and smiled. These moments felt almost "normal."

On day 26, Peter was moved from the ICU to a private room in the neurological ward. When I initially told him that he would be moving to another ward in the hospital there was no response. A few minutes later I told him again and asked if he understood. "Yes, I think so."

The medical team provided a consistently high quality of coordinated care for Peter and the family. They treated me as a member of Peter's care team and considered me a guide to Peter as well. I was learning from them and helping them know Peter—who he'd been, what his passions and interests were, from action learning to jazz to his relationships with his children, Jonas and Katarina, and grandchildren, Sara, Anton, Fabian, and Theo. I shared our love story to help them understand how this "foreigner" wife was in the picture. I was Peter's voice, his chief advocate. Mine was an evolving and essential role, and appreciating the full impact of this was an ongoing process.

Each day I absorbed a bit more of the uncertainty that was the new normal. Peter seemed to be aware of his surroundings and to recognize his family and friends, yet it was hard to know if he understood how his life had been before. I was learning how to be present without adding to his stress, what it meant to monitor and manage his care, and how to take breaks in order to fulfill my responsibilities at NAFSA. Finding a daily rhythm that worked for me was essential. I needed to be with Peter—for my own comfort and to assure him. I needed to communicate regularly with the medical team to understand what they were learning and recommending for changes in Peter's care. And I also needed to provide consistent leadership at NAFSA.

The hospital routines defined the parameters of my schedule. Communicating with the medical team required that I be at the hospital first thing in the morning during the doctors' rounds. Noon to 2:00 p.m. was the "quiet period" in Ward 26: no visitors were allowed. The six-hour time difference between Sweden and D.C. dictated that I conduct my work with the NAFSA staff in the late afternoon, Sweden time. For the first month, I spent mornings at the hospital. After consulting with the medical team, I stayed with Peter until noon. He slept a lot and had physical therapy, and I talked to him whenever he was awake. During the break from noon to 2:00, I managed our personal matters and prepared for my NAFSA workday. By 3:00 p.m. in Lund, I met with the NAFSA team—our regular 9:00 a.m. management team meetings in Washington. While I was in NAFSA meetings, Antje was with Peter. It was a schedule with parameters and flexibility as needed. Antje's consistent support ensured that we were always available for Peter and for the hospital team.

The established patterns of our time together helped me maintain a sense of equilibrium as I tried to help Peter connect with memories of our time together and with family and friends. I shared news and read him the dozens of emails and cards we received. At times, he didn't seem to connect at all. Then one day I read him an email from my sister's son Matthew in Minnesota. Peter had known Matthew since birth, and over the years they had spent time together in Minnesota, Sweden, and Washington. Peter had introduced Matthew to golf, and they had played at Washington's Hains Point golf course near our home. At the time of Peter's hospitalization, Matthew was with his parents in Duluth, getting ready to leave for a Peace Corps assignment in Paraguay. The email read:

For Peter:

I am in Duluth preparing for my two year Peace Corps assignment in Paraguay, feeling pretty stressed about everything.
Yesterday I played golf with my godfather. I reached into my golf
bag for a ball, and the ball that I brought out had the Frankel
name on it—one of the balls you'd given me. I saw it as a sign
that my worries are inconsequential compared to the challenges that you are facing right now, and I just want you to know
that I'm sending you strength and love for all that you must
go through.

—Matthew

As I finished reading the note, Peter nodded. Tears were streaming down his face—and mine.

As I left Peter at the end of each day, I always shared my plans for the evening, whether I would be on my own or having dinner with family or friends. One evening I told him I was having dinner with Elisabeth Dahlgren and Krister Moberg, my cousin and her husband. Peter and I had shared many good times with them over the years, and earlier that summer had visited them at their summerhouse in Båstad. Their Lund apartment was a short distance from the hospital, so I told him that I would be walking there when I left him. He nodded in understanding.

Peter's involuntary body movements had been severe that day. It was hard to know how much pain he was in, but it was certainly exhausting and uncomfortable as his whole body turned back and forth continu-ally. About two hours after I'd left the hospital, the nurse called to tell me Peter was asking for me. He seemed in pain, his body motion was increasingly severe, and he hadn't yet slept. She felt it would help him if I could return and spend time with him. I quickly finished my meal and headed back to the hospital. Elisabeth walked with me to ensure that I took the shortest route and avoided getting lost on the dark backstreets. We arrived at the ward at 9:00 p.m., and I settled in with Peter, lying on the bed with him, my arms around his upper body and a leg across his legs to try calm his movements. By 11:30, his body relaxed and he fell asleep. I stayed with him for another half hour, until I felt sure he was asleep for the night, and then took a taxi to Peter's apartment. As we drove through the city, I felt grateful that I'd been able to be with Peter that night, and anxious about how such nights must be for him when I could not be there. The logistical dilemmas of our transatlantic marriage felt infinitely more daunting at that moment.

Peter responded positively to the daily physical therapy sessions, so of course I wanted him to have more. Ingrid Lindahl, the physical therapist and a most trusted member of the team, reminded me that Peter was exhausted after each session, and his meals, showers, and moves down the hall were all physical therapy as well. He needed more sleep, not more PT. The staff also reminded me that personal contact with family and friends was important for Peter's relearning, his recognition of people and events, and his ability to speak. While he might sometimes recognize people he knew, he might need reminders at other times. It was challenging to absorb the extent of the memory loss Peter had suffered and to understand how much he would have to relearn. It was hard to accept that the pace of Peter's journey was not up to me. I needed heavy doses of patience. Learning to let go of those things I can't control is one of the most important lessons of my life. In this latest challenge I was getting mountains of practice.

The weeks in the neurological ward at Lund University Hospital were intense. The nurses, physical therapists, doctors, and occupational therapists were enthusiastic, supportive, and caring, and without exception treated me as a partner. They were consistently responsive to my questions and open to my ideas. One day, as I sat watching Peter sleep and observing the staff as they went about their work, I noticed that nurses were emptying the trash and serving Peter's meals in addition to carrying out their regular nursing roles. It reminded me of an observation Peter made when I was a surgery patient at George Washington University Hospital years earlier. He commented on the number of individuals with no caregiving role who came into my hospital room for various reasons, creating endless noise and disruption in my space without acknowledging my presence. Here at Lund University Hospital, each time a nurse or nursing aide entered Peter's room, her or his priority was caring for Peter. While keeping his room clean and orderly was part of the nursing staff's responsibilities, they were also checking on Peter, without unnecessary disruption. I came to recognize that these contrasting approaches to care are the result of basic cultural differences between the two societies, differences that may not even be generally acknowledged.

Peter's awareness and engagement varied: he might nod in acknowledgment when I talked to him about someone who had been in touch, or he might speak briefly, sometimes saying, "I'm tired." Periodically, in response to my question "Do you want to go to bed?" he'd answer, "Yes." Another time when I leaned over the side of his bed to say good night, he threw his arms around me, hugged me long and hard, and said, "I love you." It was impossible not to feel hopeful at that moment.

By the fourth week in Ward 26, Peter was responding with enthusiasm and energy to the physical therapy challenges. He stood at the standing podium for a longer period each time and smiled at his successes. He "walked" his wheelchair the length of the hallway and back. Then he "bicycled to Stockholm"—his answer to the physical therapist who asked him if he was bicycling to Barsebäck. With the occupational therapist, he wrote his name and my name by hand and on the computer. He could lift a glass of water and drink it on his own, and eat a spoonful of cereal from a bowl. One day, when he woke from an afternoon nap, he spoke clearly to the nurse: "Am I doing good?"

By the end of that first month I felt an urgency about getting back to my office in Washington for a couple of weeks. I had scheduled conference calls daily, made decisions as necessary, guided the team in daily management, and communicated with my board about the adjustments we were making. It had been working well, but I wanted in-person time to discuss with the team how we would manage going forward in the face of a longer recovery and rehabilitation period for Peter. While I was away, Antje saw Peter each day and communicated with me by email and telephone; we arranged for Peter to hear my voice on the telephone periodically.

Peter's medical team felt that he was an excellent candidate for rehabilitation. He was likely to achieve significant improvement and ultimately be able to live at home with assistance, so they sent a request for an assessment to the rehab center. I was back in Lund from Washington in time for the rehab medical director's assessment meeting with Peter's medical team, and his interview with Peter and me. He agreed to consider admitting Peter to rehabilitation and would be kept informed by the medical team about further developments in Peter's recovery. A couple of weeks later, the rehab center confirmed that Peter was accepted, and his move to that facility was scheduled for mid-October. Then, a few days before the move, as I was helping Peter eat his breakfast, he took a spoonful of porridge and stopped breathing. I screamed for help, and within seconds the nursing staff took Peter to his room, where the doctors met them and had Peter breathing again in less than a minute. The episode demanded that further tests be conducted, so Peter's admission to rehab would be rescheduled.

Later, as I sat with Peter, he asked, "What happened?" I told him that he had stopped breathing for a few seconds, so they would do a few more tests, and that the start of his rehabilitation would be postponed a few days. He sighed and squeezed my hand. A week later, Peter was transferred to rehab. His entire team gathered for his departure, with hugs, good wishes, and smiles. Peter's demeanor was calm, although he must have been pretty anxious. I was terrified but dared to be hopeful.

23

We Are Optimistic

Peter was transported from the hospital to the rehab center on a gurney rather than in a wheelchair, by means of a special taxi. Later I would understand that this decision meant that he was not able to watch the familiar landscape roll by on the half-hour journey, and as a result, his sense of control was diminished. Antje rode in the taxi with him, and I drove ahead to guide the taxi driver to the admission entrance to avoid confusion for the driver and potential added stress for Peter. I parked my car and met Peter as the taxi driver opened the door and lowered the gate. Immediately I saw that Peter's involuntary body motion was about to cause him to fall off the gurney. I intervened with my own body weight to hold him in place until the safety straps could be adjusted. He didn't seem to know it was a near miss, so I was the only one who had to recover.

Within a few minutes we were meeting the staff and getting Peter settled in his room. Days later, as we struggled to feel confident in this team and environment, that anxious arrival would register as a sign of the challenges we would face during the entire rehab experience. At that moment, though, I wanted to feel hopeful, so I sought to find optimism at each step of the settling-in process.

During the first hour we learned that Peter's ICU roommate, Samuel, was now his neighbor in the next room. Samuel had suffered a brain injury and multiple broken bones in a serious fall, and he and Peter and our families had built a lovely rapport. Now Samuel was undergoing long-term rehabilitation, and he was excited to reconnect with Peter.

While Peter was at the rehab center, he and Samuel shared mealtimes in addition to other periodic contact.

As we got Peter settled in his large, sunny room with a TV and stereo, seating area, and private bathroom, I felt uneasy about the staff's initial response to Peter. They understood that his body motions posed a threat to his safety were he to roll out of bed. But rather than lowering his bed and putting a mattress on the floor alongside his bed, as the hospital staff had done, they installed a second bed parallel to the bed he slept in, leaving him a bed-width away from whoever came to help him. He clearly felt isolated and vulnerable. I came to realize that this initial decision by the staff was the first of several that caused Peter to feel unsafe in this facility. During his six weeks at the rehab center, he never slept while in bed, only while sitting in his wheelchair.

On his first day there, I stayed with Peter until it was time for him to go to bed. I wanted to observe the routines and shift changes, meet as many staff members as possible, and support Peter's adjustment. As I wasn't allowed to accompany him to meals in the dining room, I took walks and spent time in his room, reflecting and reading, when he went to lunch and supper. Later in his room, as he sat in his wheelchair dozing, I adjusted the chair to a reclining position, so his body could relax as he slept. When it was time for me to leave that first evening he became upset and tried to articulate that he didn't want me to leave. It was dark outside, so I initially assumed he was concerned about my driving in the dark. But it was something more. By asking more questions that he could answer with a yes or no, I understood that he was worried because he thought I had a long drive home—the thirty-minute taxi ride from the hospital must have felt like a much longer trip to him. I sat with him for several more minutes and talked about how close we were to Lund, telling him that we were just ten minutes from our friend Boris's restaurant. I told him that I would stop there for a meal with Boris and Lena before driving the final twenty minutes back to our apartment. I promised him I'd drive carefully and not be late getting home. Was that okay? He relaxed and nodded in agreement. He accepted a goodbye hug, and I assured him I'd be back the following day.

Peter approached his physical therapy sessions in rehab with enthusiasm. He walked the length of the parallel bars in the gym, used the stationary bicycle, and participated in a range of other therapies. His friend Boris Levin visited often, and when the weather was mild they would walk in the garden. During indoor visits, Peter and Boris bounced a ball back and forth between them, with Peter catching and throwing the ball consistently.

Peter's lack of sleep was a constant concern. Brain-injured individuals in recovery require considerably more sleep than the eight hours most of us need. Peter was not sleeping at all when he was in bed during the night. The medical director's response was to instruct the staff and me to keep Peter from sleeping in his chair during the day. I rejected that directive, and my objections created turmoil among the staff. Since Peter had never slept in his bed at the rehab center but slept comfortably in the reclined wheelchair, I finally prevailed on the doctor to allow him to stay in the chair—reclined—during the night, to ensure that he would sleep. An attendant would stay in his room to ensure his safety. The first night of this arrangement, I sat alongside his chair until he fell asleep, then watched him sleep for several hours to feel comfortable that this might be a short-term solution. Shortly after midnight, the night nurse came by and assured me that she would stay with Peter and not allow him to be put in the bed, supporting the goal that he would sleep through the night. I hadn't met her previously, but I sensed that she understood the tension between me and the medical director and was supportive of my view. The stress of the day left me in tears as I walked to the car, where I sat and wept for a few minutes before driving home.

Days later, I arrived in the morning to find Peter very upset and unable to express himself. He was angry, but I couldn't figure out why. As we sat together holding hands and looking at each other, I realized that his bushy eyebrows were gone! "Did someone shave off your eyebrows?" I asked him. "Yes!" he responded angrily. In all the years we had been together, Peter's bushy eyebrows were his signature, reflecting his creative and spontaneous personality. I could only imagine what a scene it had been when the nurse shaved them off. I told him I would talk to the head nurse and immediately went to find her. The head nurse told me that Peter had actively resisted when the nurse helping him with his morning hygiene had attempted to trim his eyebrows, and the nurse had responded by shaving them off entirely. I was furious, and eventually the head nurse acknowledged that what the nurse had done was inappropriate. I took my concerns to the staff psychologist, who shared my outrage, acknowledged that this should never have happened, and agreed that he and the head nurse would individually talk to Peter, apologize, and acknowledge the huge mistake. They also agreed that the nurse who had behaved so badly should not care for Peter again.

By the end of Peter's fourth week in rehab, the medical director told me that the team had concluded that Peter was not making adequate progress to warrant continued time there. I suggested that it was unrealistic to expect progress when Peter wasn't sleeping—I pointed out that if the director or anyone else on the staff had as little sleep as Peter was getting, they wouldn't be able to do their jobs. The rehab center team recommended that Peter be moved to a short-term nursing facility to try to address the sleep issue, and a decision would be made later about a possible return to rehab.

I met with the team and learned that the decision was unanimous. The physical therapist who had seemed optimistic about Peter's progress now agreed that Peter needed more sleep in order to improve further. The team members did not feel obligated to address the sleep issue at the rehab center. I told them that I would tell Peter that it was my decision that he leave rehab because I felt this team was not giving him the level of support he needed. Peter had been working hard, and I didn't want him to take the move to the nursing facility as his personal failure. I knew that he didn't trust many of the rehab staff. Having to leave there was deeply disappointing and meant making another adjustment, but on some level it was also a relief for both of us.

My journey as an advocate was testing me, and my insights about leadership were giving me much to reflect on. During Peter's hospital stay, I was consistently a member of his team in my advocate role. I never encountered anything other than a team approach to his care. But during rehab, I rarely felt part of a team approach; rather, I generally felt that I was a challenge or disruption for the staff. I never observed staff members engaging with Peter to try to understand his desires and needs. Despite the heartbreak of this outcome, I was relearning to recognize those things over which I had no control and the importance of staying the course in my primary role as Peter's advocate above all else.

24

Another Turn

Soluret is a community nursing home for individuals requiring transitional care or whose at-home caregivers need a break. It is a small facility near the center of Lund. Peter's post-rehab transfer to Soluret was seamless, requiring no logistical effort on my part. The health care system arranged for this short-term nursing home placement within days of the rehab center's decision. Peter's southern-exposure room was centrally located in the building, and within minutes of his arrival there, Peter and I were both feeling calmer.

Each transition in Peter's care required me to reflect on my role, learn another aspect of Sweden's system of care, and adjust my expectations. I wanted to get acquainted with the new team and help Peter do the same. I also needed to let go of my anxiety enough to be comfortable leaving him for a couple of weeks while I returned to Washington for a meeting with the NAFSA board of directors.

The nursing staff stopped by to meet Peter, and I went to introduce myself to Fanny, the head nurse. I shared the "Background Memo about Peter" that I'd written months earlier—my way of providing some orientation for those on Peter's care team. She was very happy to receive it. She had read the report from the rehab center and understood that I'd had concerns about Peter's care at that facility. She was aware that Peter hadn't slept in a bed for several weeks and acknowledged that was not sustainable. Her first goal was to help Peter sleep. She had already concluded that Peter had not felt safe at the rehab center. Her plan was to meet with Peter in his room shortly to talk with him about his lack of sleep and explain her commitment to helping him overcome his sleep deprivation.

At that first meeting, Fanny proposed to Peter that after lunch she would personally come to his room and help him get into bed. She would leave him in bed to relax for twenty minutes, then return, at which point he could decide if he wanted to try to stay in bed and sleep for a while in the afternoon. If he didn't want to stay in bed, she would help him get up. If he chose to stay in bed to rest and sleep, she would personally return to help him get up when he was ready. Whatever he decided, it would be just the two of them working on this together. He nodded in agreement.

That first day, Fanny came to Peter's room after lunch and helped him get into bed. At this point, Peter was able to push himself out of his wheelchair and turn to sit on the bed, raise his legs onto the bed, and lie down on his own. When Fanny returned after twenty minutes, as they had agreed, Peter told her that he wanted to stay in bed. As she left the room, Peter's eyes were closing, and he was soon sleeping—the first time he had slept in a bed in more than six weeks. He slept through the night in bed, and for the rest of the time he lived at Soluret, he slept an hour or more during the day and more than eight hours each night in bed.

What a difference one person can make. The quiet yet strong demeanor of this head nurse was truly remarkable. I assumed that Fanny must be the most experienced person we would work with, but I soon learned that this was her first job out of nursing school! She was a kind, thoughtful, and aware person without biases about how things must be done. She used her core knowledge, assessed Peter's situation and history, reflected on the options, and relied on her personal judgment and engagement with Peter as she developed an approach that would meet his needs. The immediate relief that Peter and I both felt on his first day at Soluret gave me confidence about his care that I hadn't felt during his weeks in rehab. This experience would strengthen my focus on human resources development at NAFSA and provide a powerful story about the impact that one person with thoughtfulness and judgment can make.

Despite the lack of a physical therapist at Soluret, the staff regularly guided Peter on walks in the hallway, as he was motivated. Some days he was willing and able to do a short walk with the parallel bars or using the standing walker, and other days just getting in and out of bed was as much as he could do. His involuntary body movements continued. Most of the time, he responded to my questions with a yes or no, most days he told me he loved me, and sometimes he asked a question. Yet I had a nagging sense that my husband was slipping further away.

As always before leaving Lund to fly to Washington, I talked to Peter about my upcoming trip and reminded him that Antje would be with him every day while I was away, that we would talk on the phone, and that I would return before Christmas. I shared news about NAFSA and mentioned the staff members he knew. I also reminded him that the NAFSA board would be meeting while I was in Washington. Peter had consistently been in D.C. for my board meetings and thoroughly enjoyed hosting the board for dinner at our home. He was a terrific host, and often teased out details about people that I hadn't heard before. His curiosity was infectious, so everyone made a point of spending time with him. It was lovely to watch and a great help to me in nurturing those relationships.

Recalling those good times with the board, it was hard to envision hosting the annual dinner without Peter there. I knew the guests would also miss him very much. As I said goodbye that afternoon, I couldn't know how much he understood, but I sensed that he felt a familiarity in the conversation.

During my three and a half weeks in Washington, I began each day with a call with Antje (and sometimes Peter as well). If there was an issue she needed my help with, she would still have time in her day to take action. Otherwise, the call was a check-in that gave me a sense of comfort as I began my Washington workday.

As the NAFSA management team and I made final preparations for the board meeting, I considered how to frame my thoughts about Peter's care and how I was managing my work. The board would have legitimate questions. At the meeting, I reviewed the status of the organization's financial health, program performance, and strategic plans for the coming year. Then I described how I was managing between caring for Peter and doing my job. I shared details about the logistics, noting that I was working every day from Sweden or Washington, and that our weekly management team meetings were providing the framework that enabled me to assess how the business was doing and what matters needed my personal attention. The management team members had always attended board meetings and presented their respective parts of the management report, so the board was familiar with each manager's portfolio and leadership capabilities. During the executive session with me at the end of the meeting, the board chair expressed the board's confidence in my leadership and support for the day-to-day adjustments I was making. While I had felt comfortable with how I'd been managing, at that moment I was more than grateful for the generosity of their assessment.

I was back with Peter for the Christmas holidays of 2010. This had always been a favorite time for me, with the glow of holiday lights along the streets and in the windows of businesses and homes throughout the city. When I arrived in Lund, I dropped my bags at the apartment and had a short visit with Antje before heading to Soluret to let Peter know I was back. The staff and Antje had told him I would be returning. By now I'd learned that instinctively he would be anxious until he saw me. On these initial visits after being away, Peter greeted me with a smile, a nod, or a slight wave of his hand—any of which touched my heart. He seemed content, and his good sleeping patterns had remained consistent while I was gone.

Later, on my way back to the apartment, I stopped to buy a small Christmas tree. Peter and I had shared the ritual of putting up a tree each Christmas, whether we were in the United States or Sweden. Now, installing and decorating the tree gave me a sense of normalcy in the midst of so much uncertainty. I missed Peter terribly as I carried on our tradition. Peter loved trimming the tree—stringing the electric candles, putting angel hair on the candle bulbs, and hanging the icicles once all the ornaments were on the tree. Over the years we had collected ornaments on our travels, and unpacking them and finding the best spot on the tree for each one was a lovely shared time. This year, the angel hair and icicles wouldn't adorn the tree—placing them had been Peter's job, and right now it was more than I could handle. But the lighted tree with some of our favorite ornaments was a comfort. A few days later, on Christmas Eve, after I visited with Peter at Soluret, Antje and her husband came by to share a modest Swedish Christmas meal and enjoy the small tree.

On Christmas Day, Peter seemed to be feeling low. A couple of times during the day he had a slight fever, but it didn't last. He was definitely quiet. I spent several hours with him, mostly just being nearby as he dozed. The next day his symptoms were similar. A couple of hours after I left him on December 26, the Soluret head nurse called to report that Peter's fever had spiked, so she had sent him by ambulance to the hospital emergency room. She suggested I meet him there.

The ER was busy and arriving patients were being triaged, so Peter had not yet been prioritized for further diagnosis or admission to the hospital. But he was in a private room, where he slept most of the time. I was stressed and anxious for him to be admitted to the hospital. By 9:00 p.m. they had decided to admit Peter but had not found an available bed. I urged the attending ER doctor to tell the head nurse on the neurological ward that the patient needing admission was Peter Frankel, and that his wife was here with him. Within half an hour, Peter was admitted to Ward 26. He recognized the head nurse immediately, and she welcomed him; she then wheeled him to an empty room and explained that it would be another half hour before they could make up the bed for him. She asked him if he would be okay on the gurney in the meantime and promised him she would personally be back to get him settled. "Is that okay, Peter?" He nodded. It was now 10:00 p.m. Peter had had nothing to drink for a few hours, and neither of us had eaten since noon. The nurse gave Peter juice and suggested that I go home, assuring me that they would take care of Peter shortly. I asked Peter if it was okay if I went home. He took my hand and nodded. I was relieved and comforted, and I struggled to hold my emotions in check as I found my way to the car. Despite the emergency that brought us here, Ward 26 was a safe place. We knew the team and trusted them. As I drove home, I felt our reality shifting.

Back at Ward 26 the following morning, I was greeted as a member of the family—everyone was happy to see me, yet they all had looks of deep disappointment and sadness on their faces. They had last seen Peter two months ago when he left to go to rehab. They had expected to next see him walking after having made significant progress toward an independent life. This was a different reality. Through their eyes I began to see a different future. At that moment I understood at yet another level that I was losing my husband.

Over the next few days I accompanied Peter to a series of follow-up tests. His involuntary body motions remained a huge factor, making some of the tests challenging for the technical team. For one test I physically laid on top of Peter to help his body be still. At other times I simply talked to him about what was happening and how long it would take, assuring him that I was with him. It was impossible to know what he understood, but he visibly relaxed as I stayed close and spoke quietly to him. After each test, he was exhausted and slept for a while.

Once the tests were complete, Dr. Widner, chief of neurology at Lund University Hospital, met with me. I asked Antje to join me. The head nurse, a physical therapist, and a social worker were in the meeting as well. With tears in his eyes, Dr. Widner told me that Peter's outcome was not as they had expected earlier last fall. He explained that it was now clear that Peter would not be able to make further progress cognitively or physically, that he would not be able to live independently or live at home with assistance. Peter's requirements for care could be met only in a nursing home. As I heard his words and looked at his face, tears filled my eyes as well. I struggled to stay in the conversation and avoid collapsing. Dr. Widner told me that he understood the brutal emotional toll of having no other option, as he had recently faced a similar decision regarding his elderly mother—although Peter's situation was much more unexpected, given his relatively young age.

I asked Dr. Widner if I should get another opinion, and even as I said those words they felt hollow. During the past few weeks, several American friends had urged me to seek opinions from U.S. experts, each one convinced that Peter could recover. My friends were well-intentioned, but I also felt an undercurrent of "America knows best, and we can always find a solution here!" Dr. Widner's response was kind. "I understand what you're asking. I worked at a hospital in the United States for a few years, and I recognize it's the American way for many patients and their families to insist on more opinions. Of course, if you want to, you should. But I also want you to know that in Sweden we consult widely among all the experts in our medical system, so I already have the benefit of several perspectives when I bring this recommendation to you." As he described Sweden's diagnostic methodology, I felt my body relax. I accepted his recommendation. For a few short minutes we both cried quiet tears. My husband was slipping further away.

The social worker broke the spell to tell me that I would be contacted by a community caseworker later that day and would have her guidance for all the decisions I would need to make, including a nursing home placement. In the meantime, Peter would return to Soluret (his room had been held for him during his hospital stay), where he would live until a nursing home was found that suited Peter and our family.

As promised, the caseworker stopped by Peter's room at Soluret to meet us and begin the process of finding a suitable nursing home close to the center of Lund, where several members of the family lived. She had read Peter's file and seemed sensitive to his particular needs. Antje and I consulted a colleague of Peter who managed nursing homes and reviewed a list of facilities that met our needs. We visited several and identified three or four that we felt would be good options. I shared the list with our caseworker. Days later, she stopped by to tell me that there were no vacancies at the facilities on our list, but there was one at a nursing home close to the city center that she felt would suit Peter well. She had placed a forty-eight-hour hold on the room for Peter, giving us time to decide if this would work.

Within an hour, Antje and I were visiting Ribbingska Nursing Home, a ten-minute walk from the train station. We met the staff on the morning shift and returned in the afternoon to meet those on the later shift. The administrator showed us the room and commented that Peter would be able to live there for the rest of his life. Her comment caught me up short. Absorbing the reality that this would be Peter's final home and that it would also be the last place that he and I shared took my breath away.

This was a good space for Peter. The French doors of the corner room opened to a small park where families with children enjoyed quiet play and university students relaxed outdoors. Peter would be able to watch them as he sat in his wheelchair in front of the window. Another decision made.

25

Managing from Two Continents

Monday, August 15, 2010, was to have been my first day back in the office following our summer holiday in Sweden. In a flash, on August 12, Peter's fall and hospitalization changed everything. Over the weekend, I stayed in touch with my deputy, Betty Soppelsa, and we ultimately determined that the planned Monday morning NAFSA management meeting would be held, with me calling in from Sweden. I could not have envisioned at that moment that this would be the first of hundreds of telephone meetings over the next few years, and that we would be creating protocols for a generation of remote work.

I was the leader of an NGO in Washington with a staff of one hundred people. My responsibilities included management and public representation. I had been in the position for more than ten years and had built a talented management team; the board of directors had supported the many bold changes we had made during my tenure, and the organization was financially strong.

In the meeting that Monday morning, my priorities were to inform the management team about the situation with Peter, talk through the issues requiring immediate attention, and establish a framework for maintaining good communication between myself and the team during the coming weeks. Since the team members knew that Peter was in a coma, there were obvious unspoken questions about how long this arrangement would last. For now, though, we needed to make plans for sharing information with the NAFSA board: I would be working from Sweden for the time being, meeting with the management team in weekly group and individual phone calls, with more frequent meetings as needed. We would determine on a case-by-case basis which external meetings would be delegated and which I would conduct by phone.

It helped that the staff and board knew Peter. Over the years, Peter had thoroughly enjoyed his informal conversations with staff whenever he met me at the office to go out for lunch or to walk home at the end of the day. He had developed casual but personal relationships with many staff members through these visits to the office and through his attendance at NAFSA events such as holiday parties and summer baseball games. Our annual conferences were on his calendar most years, and he also cohosted board dinners in our home, so board members had personal memories of conversations with him. These many nuggets of goodwill contributed to the extraordinary support the staff and board showed toward me during the years I was managing NAFSA "remotely," long before Covid-19 made remote work a standard practice for many organizations.

Eventually, I established a schedule that allowed me to do my work in Washington while also overseeing Peter's care: I would be in Washington for three weeks at a time, and then in Lund with Peter for ten days. Finding a rhythm for those ten days each month was key. The six-hour time difference between Washington and Sweden dictated the basic framework of my days. My workspace in Lund was the corner of my bedroom, with a computer that duplicated the one at my D.C. home. We used telephone and Skype for regular meetings—Zoom was not on the horizon at that point.

In the morning, I would first respond to emails that had come in during the night, and then write letters and prepare for staff meetings that I would have later in the day. Then, over breakfast, I would watch the previous day's *PBS NewsHour* online, a daily habit I'd had for years that now provided a moment of welcome normalcy. By 10:30 a.m., I would head out for the thirty- to forty-five-minute walk to Peter, a journey that ensured minimal daily exercise as well as reflection time.

I would usually spend a couple of hours with Peter prior to lunch. We'd share a game, I'd give him news from family or friends, or we'd take a walk in the neighborhood (with me pushing his wheelchair). I would serve him lunch, and then while he took his afternoon rest in bed, I'd walk home for a rest and lunch, and sometimes the first management team meeting of the day. I would then return for another hour or more with Peter, including serving his evening meal. Back at the apartment by 6:00 p.m., I would meet with my administrative assistant to review future scheduling, read and write emails, or read relevant materials.

At the end of the ten days, I would remind Peter I would be flying to Washington the next day to take care of my responsibilities at NAFSA. I often shared a few details of the trip, describing how I would take the train to Kastrup, fly from Copenhagen to Washington, and take a taxi from Dulles Airport to the apartment, and how I would spend my days at the office.

The pain of leaving him never lessened, and during his first few months at Ribbingska, Peter was clearly angry with me each time I returned. It took me a couple of hours to assure him that I was now staying for ten days, to remind him why I'd been away, and for him to relax. Antje and I concluded that Peter needed to hear my voice more often while I was away, so we arranged that she would facilitate scheduled telephone calls with me two or three times each week. The Ribbingska staff would fill in when Antje couldn't be there. From the time we started this new habit, Peter accepted my absences without anxiety or anger. It was a relief for everyone and a reminder to me how important it is to pay attention to the nonverbal cues that people send out. With Peter, reading such cues was essential, and, as I was learning, the ability to understand what people are communicating nonverbally is just as important in managing people and organizations. During the nine years in which I traveled back and forth between Sweden and Washington every month, board members and staff often shared with me their favorite memories of conversations they'd had with Peter that I had not heard previously. He made an impression on so many individuals with his deep curiosity and charisma.

As we all became comfortable with the rhythm of my schedule, I came to appreciate that my ten-day stays in Lund gave me valuable time and space to reflect; the geographic distance from the Washington office helped me to clarify challenging personnel issues and to take action more promptly than I likely would have done if I had been in the office full-time. Having the distance and privacy to assess and consider options, and to consult with the human resources director and our attorney—all without the interruptions of daily life in the office or the anxiety that my being in the office with a closed door for a couple of days could cause for others—allowed me to make decisions and act on them with expediency once I was back in Washington.

26

\\\\\\\\\\|||||||||////,

The Final Move to Ribbingska

It had been eight months since Peter's fall. He had been hospitalized in a coma in the ICU and then treated on the neurological ward, sent to a rehab center, and then to Soluret, hospitalized again, and then back to Soluret. Now Peter would move to Ribbingska Nursing Home, where he would live for the remainder of his life. I tried to focus on the practical issues that morning as I headed for Soluret to say goodbye to the staff and support Peter in this transition.

The plan was for Peter to ride in a taxi for the short trip from Soluret to Ribbingska, but the bright sunny morning prompted Soluret's head nurse to adjust the plan. She decided a walk in the sunshine would provide Peter with a lovely transitional journey. The nursing staff would push Peter in his wheelchair through the nearby churchyard cemetery, with its paved walkways, blooming daffodils, tall shade trees, and peaceful fish pond, and then along city sidewalks for the final four blocks to Ribbingska. Peter's parents were buried in this cemetery, and he and I had walked there many times. The new plan offered some familiarity that could help Peter feel comfortable and secure in his adjustment to his new environment.

We shared the plan with Peter, assuring him that I would meet him at his new home when he arrived. He nodded in agreement. After a round of goodbyes and thank-yous to the head nurse and staff at Soluret, before I drove away, I watched as Peter was being wheeled along the walkway toward his new home. I tried to focus on the task at hand, but I let myself cry as I drove those few blocks, arriving just in time to enter Ribbingska with Peter.

Ribbingska Nursing Home had six wards, each housing eight residents. Every resident had a private room and private bathroom, the Swedish standard. It was the most intimate nursing home environment I had ever seen. Each ward included a dayroom, a dining room, and a three-season veranda and was staffed by a dedicated team of two to three workers on three shifts throughout the day. Meals were served in the dining room, where the staff knew each resident well.

Ribbingska's beautiful architect-designed garden included a small fish pond, a variety of flowering bushes, raised gardens for strawberries and other plants that the residents could tend, and shaded areas with benches, tables, and chairs. A four-meter-long set of parallel bars was available for wheelchair users, and spaced across a large patio area were several tables and chairs where twenty to thirty people could gather for visits over afternoon coffee.

The staff welcomed Peter to Ribbingska and showed us his studio—a large, sunny corner room with north- and east-facing windows, a private bathroom, a small refrigerator and microwave, and plenty of storage space. The day before, we had moved in a table, lamps, guest chairs, and bookcases, as well as Peter's favorite paintings and sculptures. By now I had learned that each physical move and change of staff were stressful for Peter, so helping him get acquainted with staff members, his room, and the common areas felt urgent, even as I knew it would take time. The Ribbingska staff also had to become comfortable with Peter, as his needs were quite different from those of the other residents.

I had learned that my usual fast pace added stress for Peter, so as I began to organize and arrange things in his room, I heard my mother's voice in my head reminding me to "take it easy." I moved Peter slowly around the room in his wheelchair before positioning him in front of the French doors, through which there was a view of a small park. I sat close by for a few minutes to absorb the moment and be conscious of the view from this vantage point. From here Peter could see neighbors enjoying the sunshine, children playing, and dogs romping. Peter had always preferred living on higher levels in apartment buildings, so I had initially been disappointed that there wasn't a vacancy on a higher floor. Now I saw that this first-floor room was the perfect location for him to see the garden from his wheelchair. He would be comfortable here, and the world outside would be in his field of vision.

This would be Peter's home for the rest of his life, and it would be a significant part of my life during those years as well. Peter took a long look through the open door, but soon wanted the door closed. He continued to look out toward the garden, appearing calm, if a bit tired. I unpacked his things and described to him what I was doing. His involuntary body movements were active while he was sitting in his wheelchair, so each time I came close to him, his arms swung back and forth, at times grabbing my arm with a strong grip. I often had a few bruises by the end of a day with him. Peter had always had a firm grip and had learned to take care when he shook hands with others, especially individuals with small hands. Now he had no concept of his strength, so the staff and I had to be alert and make adjustments.

During Peter's first months at Ribbingska in the spring of 2011, being among other residents at the dining table during meals was more stimulation than he could tolerate. His involuntary body movements increased, and he verbalized loudly, distracting other residents. So, for the first several weeks, his meals were served in his room. Family and friends did not join the Ribbingska residents for meals, but an exception was made for Peter from the beginning. His need for help was a significant additional demand on the staff, and having me there to serve him his meals was reassuring for Peter and provided brief relief for the staff as well.

On his first day at Ribbingska, I served Peter lunch at the table in his room. It took trial and error to find the approach that worked for him. At times, he'd grab the plate or glass and throw it or not cooperate when I tried to get him to take a bite or a drink. I learned that he needed the table space in front of him free of plates, cups, and cutlery. That space was for him to "polish the table" throughout the meal. The plate of food and the glass of milk or juice had to be kept out of his direct vision. The person serving him (whether it was me or a staff member) needed to stand on Peter's right side to minimize the visual stimulation and to be able to speak to him in his good right ear. This protocol was necessary throughout his years at Ribbingska, even after he was able to eat with the other residents in the dining room.

I shared with the staff Peter's long-term habit of "polishing" the edge of the table at the end of a meal and as the dinner conversation continued. He had been lovingly teased about this habit over the years. Now, although the situation sometimes resulted in spilled juice, recalling that endearing habit touched my heart and helped the staff connect to Peter's past.

The staff and I worked hard to identify routines that worked for Peter and were within the frame of Ribbingska's protocols for caring for all residents. I also confirmed which supplies I needed to provide, from sheets, towels, and personal hygiene products to clothes, and familiarized myself with the staff's routines for laundry and cleaning. The attention to personal detail that I observed in the staff for this "community" of eight residents increased my confidence in Peter's care.

As I had done in each new facility where Peter had lived, I reviewed my memo about Peter—his life before the accident, his business, his children, our marriage, our lifestyle, and his watercolor painting—with the Ribbingska team. I told them about our summerhouse and the rhythm of our lives and encouraged them to talk to him about any of those details. I explained that I continued to work in Washington, D.C., that I would be traveling back and forth each month, and that it was important that we all acknowledge this to Peter. When I was in Lund, I would be with him daily, often twice a day, so I would meet the staff on both shifts and help serve his meals. When I was away, Antje would assist Peter in talking with me on the phone. The team welcomed my perspective and assured me that my memo would be kept in Peter's file so the staff could review it regularly.

Peter usually greeted me with a slight nod and small smile, sometimes a "Hej" when I arrived. Then, one day, in response to my comment that it was about time for lunch, he said, "Say that again." A few days later, I arrived to find him sitting in the dining area watching the staff bake a tart, looking content and having no involuntary body motion. When I greeted him with "Good morning, how are you today?" he responded, "Fine," and gave me a small smile. I commented that it looked like he might have been flirting with the staff, and he smiled again and nodded. Such moments invoked memories of playful times, glimpses of the person I had married, and these brief, intimate connections buoyed my spirit as I sought to ensure that Peter received the love, respect, and care that he deserved.

In those first months, Peter's capacities were erratic from day to day, and week to week. One moment he would hold a glass of milk and drink it on his own in a most normal way, and the next minute he'd pick up the glass and throw it across the room without apparent awareness of what he'd done. The staff and I got quite good at intercepting these involuntary motions, mostly saving the room and Peter's body from being splashed with whatever food or drink was involved. One minute, following a comment I made about the next meal or a suggestion that we go outside, he'd say, "Say that again," as clearly as could be. Then, when I repeated what I'd said, he'd retreat to a nonverbal response indicating only yes or no. My emotions bounced from excitement to despair as his responses ranged from clear comments to no reaction at all. I was learning that many of Peter's responses were beyond his control and often had nothing to do with me.

In his early months at Ribbingska, when I first returned to Lund from Washington, Peter would lash out at me. Antje and I decided to schedule telephone calls with Peter while I was away, so he could hear my voice and respond to questions as he was able. If his response to one of my questions was simply a nod, Antje would relay that to me. As our calls became regular, Peter seemed to accept my absences without the stress that he had experienced earlier.

During my weeks in D.C., my personal anxiety and sadness increased. The periodic telephone conversations helped both of us. I often called as I walked to work. It was a route that Peter and I had frequently taken as he walked me home at the end of my workday. It felt good to remind him of a bit of our history even as I faced his lack of memory. I would remind him of my work at NAFSA, share greetings from those he knew, and ask him questions that he could answer with a yes or no. After we concluded our visit, I found that the final blocks of my walk provided a space for deep breathing as I parked my sadness and sense of loss and prepared myself to attend to my professional responsibilities.

Several of Peter's friends—men he had known a long time—visited him regularly at Ribbingska. Each was comfortable sitting with Peter in silence, holding his hand or sharing stories. It was beautiful to watch and to hear about. When these visits occurred while I was in Washington, Antje told me about them in her periodic emails; she also shared anecdotes about her walks around the garden with Peter and her conversations with the staff.

Initially, some of the Ribbingska staff were intimidated by Peter. Their training had not prepared them fully to manage someone of his height (six feet, three inches) and physical strength who made sudden involuntary motions, sometimes grabbing at their arms or pushing food off the table. Peter also made verbal "comments" that they didn't understand. Peter's inability to communicate through speech left him at the mercy of the staff's capacity to notice or anticipate his needs. If he wanted a glass of water or to listen to music, if he was uncomfortable in his wheelchair or wanted to take a nap, if he preferred to be out of the sun or to watch TV—it was impossible for him to make a simple request. Aides had to check on him much more often than they checked on other residents—a huge additional demand for the team of two to three caregivers. It was stressful for everyone, including Peter. I felt another approach was needed.

Antje and I met with Doctor Winge, the on-call doctor for Ribbingska, to review Peter's situation and to suggest that Peter needed a personal care attendant, or PCA. Dr. Winge had been Peter's private doctor prior to his injury and knew him well. Having met with Peter at Ribbingska and reviewed his care plan, he understood our concerns and concurred that Peter needed more support. He recommended to the administrator that a PCA be assigned to Peter as soon as possible.

A few days later we met with the administrator, who had already reviewed Dr. Winge's recommendation. She acknowledged Peter's special needs and agreed that his situation warranted the presence of a personal care attendant for several hours each day. Within days she was recruiting candidates for this assignment, and she invited me to participate in the interviews. I tried to imagine such a quick, nonbureaucratic response in the U.S. health care system. It was a reminder to me as an organization leader how important it is to hire and support individuals who take personal initiative, who are willing to adapt standards as needed, focus on the goal (in this case, patient care), exercise judgment, and act promptly. Many Americans consider the Swedish health care system to be the ultimate bureaucracy. Yet this was another example of an on-site manager making independent decisions to ensure the delivery of patient- and family-centered care. I was personally grateful and relieved for Peter, and this administrator's actions would inform my own management decisions many times in future years. I was thankful that Peter was receiving care in the Swedish system. While there were challenges for me in learning a new culture and balancing the travel back and forth between Sweden and Washington, my active engagement was welcomed as I monitored and supported Peter's care in Sweden's patient-oriented system.

Once two shifts of personal care attendants were in place, Peter's care became more consistent as the PCAs gained knowledge and identified techniques that supported him. Regularly on the agenda were physical therapy routines, walks around town with stops for coffee or ice cream, and visits to the churchyard—places that were familiar to Peter. The attendants suggested options and encouraged Peter to choose. They engaged him in conversation, helping him to verbalize. They also developed strong skills of observation, coaching, and discipline, which strengthened Peter's confidence and sense of safety. He clearly relaxed with them.

During most of his life at Ribbingska, Peter expressed a preference when asked a direct question—whether it was which door to use when leaving the building, which route to take for a walk, whether he wanted a soda or ice cream or simply to sit in the garden and watch the birds and fish. But first, someone—the PCA, another staff member, or I— needed to ask him a question.

When I was in Washington, the PCAs would often write emails to me to share anecdotes and to process what they were learning about working with Peter. Their insights helped me reflect on my own interactions with him. As one attendant wrote:

Today I learned that one must not be in a hurry when helping Peter. . . . Of course it is impossible to know exactly how much he understands—we try to figure out a way to communicate. . . . I see this as an important lesson—that one needs to be calm with Peter and also to know one's own limits, according to how much power and strength one has at a particular moment. It is a demanding job. Yet interesting, and stimulating.

On a lovely, sunny day, one of Peter's PCAs, Alex, took Peter on a walk to the city library, to enjoy the beautiful, contemplative garden and fountain behind the building, then for a coffee in the library café. Many of the regular staff at Ribbingska felt uncertain about how Peter would handle having a cup of coffee away from the nursing home, so they were not comfortable taking him on such an excursion. For Alex, it was a regular part of life in Lund, and thus an obvious activity to do with Peter, who felt the normalcy, was completely relaxed, and enjoyed his latte as he always had.

The PCAs developed many effective strategies for working with Peter that often elicited spontaneous comments from him; he showed enthusiasm for using the parallel bars in the garden and for making decisions about which direction to take on a walk. As the regular staff observed the PCAs' approaches to working with Peter and his growing comfort, they gained confidence and new energy for providing Peter's care when the attendants weren't present. I now dared hope that Peter would become a part of a small community that shared space, staff support, and daily life.

With the PCAs, or after they had left for the day, on his own, Peter spent time in the garden every day during the warm months, watching the fish in the pond, observing the other residents and guests, just relaxing, or napping. It was also a lovely place to meet with friends who visited. The architect-designed garden included parallel bars at a height for those in wheelchairs. Initially, Peter enthusiastically pulled himself through the four-meter length of the bars, with one hand grabbing each bar. The aide or I would then do a bit of steering and turn the chair around so he could complete a return lap. He would do five or six "round trips" during an outing. By early fall of 2011, however, we observed a reduced enthusiasm. Then one day he just looked at the bars, seeming to have no clue what to do. The aide placed his hands on the bars, and he pulled himself through, but a few weeks later, he didn't know what to do even after his hands were placed on the bars.

By late summer of 2011, one year after Peter's accident, the first individuals hired as personal attendants were leaving to return to medical school. Each of them commented that the experience of working with Peter had been important to his development as a physician. Each talked directly to Peter about why he was leaving and shared how he felt about the time they had spent working together. It was lovely to watch Peter listen and look at them directly, nodding in response to their questions, once in a while saying "Ja."

I had observed their professionalism as they became aware of how Peter communicated with them, how they explored new ways of relating to him, and how they never stopped trying. The quality of the care they provided, their commitment to trying new approaches, and their willingness to reflect on how things were working contrasted with my experiences and observations in U.S. institutions.

During the first year at the nursing home Peter was quite verbal, loud, and often incomprehensible. To an inexperienced listener, the sounds he was producing seemed to be nothing but noise. But the doctor assured us that Peter was stuttering, trying to get words out. As I absorbed this important detail, I learned to "hear" Peter's comments and ask questions that he could respond to with a yes or no or sometimes find the word he was trying to articulate. If I misunderstood, he'd let me know. I shared the doctor's comments and my tactics with the staff and encouraged them to be intentional in asking Peter's opinion and offering him choices. I believe that my ongoing coaching helped to build a stronger team for Peter and helped the staff members become more effective as caregivers overall. Because of this experience, I became a more intentional "lead by example" coach in my leadership at NAFSA as well.

As friends visited Peter, I observed that sometimes visitors and staff would have conversations in front of him as though he didn't understand or hear their comments. Also, first-time visitors were often unsure about how to engage with Peter. Because of this, Antje and I made a point of trying to be sure that one of us was present whenever someone came to visit for the first time. We would show these friends how to include Peter in their conversations and encourage them to take Peter to the veranda or the garden. By being there, we could also observe whether Peter was paying attention to the conversation and ask him if he wanted a break from talking. In most cases, friends who had visited once or twice with Antje or me returned regularly to see Peter on their own.

Peter spent many hours of each day without a personal attendant. When he watched a champion *fotboll* (soccer) game on television, a visit from me or anyone else was an annoying interruption. It was obvious Peter understood the game and who the teams were. When he watched skiing races or hockey games, he knew which skiers or teams were competing, and he reacted with irritation to anyone who distracted him from his viewing, responding to questions about teams or individual players with only a nod or a "Yes" or "No."

Staff changes were inevitable, and they always created anxiety for Peter, and for me. Gratefully, the late-summer transition to Linda, the new personal care attendant, went very well. Linda was outgoing and opinionated. She engaged with Peter from the first day, not at all intimidated by him, and with no preconceived notions about what was or wasn't possible for him. Within days she was taking him shopping at the supermarket, asking him to hold the basket in his lap while she filled it. A few weeks later, she took him for lunch at the pizza restaurant down the street—a place we had walked by many times. The restaurant had outdoor seating, and one day as they were walking past, Linda asked Peter if he would like to go there for lunch one day. He responded with an enthusiastic "Yes." Her initiative reminded me that people who are new to their jobs often bring new approaches with them. I was in Washington on the day of their lunch expedition, so Linda texted me a photograph of them sitting outside at the restaurant. That photograph provided me with another metaphor to use when I coach others about the importance of applying new perspectives to day-to-day problem-solving, as well as to larger challenges.

27

The Support of Family and Friends

Getting Peter settled in at Ribbingska found me balancing the practical aspects of arranging his space (collecting the appropriate supplies, clothes, books, music and art) with profoundly emotional moments as I faced the reality that this would be his final home. This would be where we would share the time we had left.

Through much of the last months, I'd clung to the possibility that Peter would recover enough for us to live together and share a relationship, even though life would be different. When things aren't great, my general approach is "Things will get better—I can manage." Now such hopes were gone. My role now was to ensure Peter's care and give him as much personal attention and support as possible while also creating a new life for myself. The loneliness I felt was beyond anything I had experienced previously, and I couldn't find words to articulate my feelings to myself, much less to others.

Walking has always been my go-to activity for staying healthy. Now while in Lund, the thirty- to forty-minute walks back and forth from my apartment to Ribbingska were essential to my well-being. On the morning walk, I'd reflect on the previous day and make a mental list of chores or issues to discuss with the care staff. On the walk home, I'd often smile recalling a special moment with Peter that day, and the next minute cry for the future we wouldn't have.

Once Peter was settled at Ribbingska, I established a rhythm for the ten days each month I spent in Sweden. Between being with Peter and doing my NAFSA job remotely, my days became very compressed. I had little time or energy for personal conversations. I was exhausted, but also I couldn't figure out what to say to friends. My American friends generally wanted a "progress" report. There wasn't any "progress" to report, and the nuances in Peter's situation were difficult to articulate and to place in context for friends to understand.

Fortunately, several friends did more than their share to keep me on their radar. Longtime Denmark friends stayed close and visited Peter and me each time I was in Sweden. On occasion, I'd make a quick train trip across the bridge to Copenhagen for lunch or dinner with them. Lund friends and relatives invited me for lunch or dinner or to visit them at their summer homes. Their support helped get me through those early months. Others too far away to be in physical contact sent emails or letters to Peter and to me. We were in their thoughts, and they wanted to share family news or simply acknowledge our challenges. These gestures made a deep mark, and knowing how much they meant to me, I now try to be more consistent in sending notes to family and friends facing challenges of their own.

During our marriage, we hosted many friends at our summerhouse in southern Sweden, enjoying the countryside and taking short day trips in the area. Now, these friends wanted to visit Peter and me in our new situation. I learned from experience how important personal visits to Peter at Ribbingska were to our Scandinavian and American friends. Seeing Peter in his new home helped them better understand our journey. Prior to their first visits, it was often difficult for them even to know what questions to ask. Most commonly they arrived with an expectation that Peter would "get better," which was difficult for me to respond to, as that wasn't the context of Peter's life now. Whenever friends came to visit and share time with Peter and with me, it was a gift of support; these visits also helped them understand our reality and take a step toward facing their own loss.

Several close Swedish friends visited him regularly: Stefan Holm-ström, Dan Nordström, Lars Risberg, and Bo Hellborg. All long-term friends, they were matter-of-fact, patient, and at ease sharing news of their lives and recalling mutual experiences or just sitting with Peter, as the situation required. I was often present for their first visits to show them around and introduce them to the staff. They became very comfortable spending time with Peter on their own, and often after they visited, they would let me know, so I could talk to Peter about their interactions in subsequent conversations.

The first summer Peter was at Ribbingska, our friend Linda and then my mother, my sister Marlys, and her husband, Bob, came to visit, staying with me at the summerhouse and seeing Peter during the day. In subsequent years numerous other friends and family members came, adding a day or two to business trips or visiting during the summer when they could stay at the summerhouse. I was deeply touched by each visit, even as I felt anxiety about how it might go.

Each person dealt differently with our new reality. I was grateful that many simply walked right in and engaged with Peter, holding his hand, tossing a ball to him across the table, sharing a cup of coffee, sitting with him in silence or sharing thoughts—whatever worked at the moment. For others, seeing Peter in his wheelchair and recognizing the limitations in his ability to communicate was more than they could handle. I couldn't anticipate how any one individual would react.

Linda Winslow was very happy to see Peter, and he greeted her with a nod and small smile, responded to her taking his hand, answered her questions with a nod, and kept his eyes on her. She spent a week with us—hanging out in the country, visiting Peter several days, and walking around the city on her own when I stayed a bit longer with Peter. Other days she just enjoyed the countryside and the garden and had dinner ready when I returned from Lund.

My mother had visited Sweden several times over the years, the first time in the 1970s after my father's death. She had established ties with cousins on both sides of our family. After Peter and I were together, she visited us three times at our summerhouse, traveling on her own or with a cousin. Her last visit had been in 2008, on her own at eighty-five years of age and with declining vision due to macular degeneration. The trip had been exhausting. As she left that year, she said she felt this was her final visit to us in Sweden. Yet she made the trip one more time in 2011, with Marlys and Bob accompanying her, because she wanted to see Peter. She was deeply sad about the situation, missed Peter in her life, and wanted to tell him that she loved him and be present for me.

Waiting at Kastrup Airport for the arrival of my mother, sister, and brother-in-law, I realized how stressed I was about their visit. I had strong memories of my mother's last time with us in Sweden and had accepted that it would be her final visit. Now, seeing the three of them walk through the arrivals door, I was reminded of my mother's strength, and of the stability, kindness, and capacity of my sister and her husband for managing in a range of situations. They are kind and generous, and have extensive experience working with individuals with special needs. Their capacity for helping and caring was apparent from the moment they arrived.

For the duration of their stay in Sweden, my sister took charge of our mother's care and suggested the details for her visit to Peter. We drove directly from the airport to our summerhouse, with a short detour through Lund to show them where Peter was living. We arrived at the summerhouse with time for rest, a meal, and a walk around the garden. The following day we spent at home in the countryside. They were tired from the trip, and I needed the rest as well. Antje and Jonas, Peter's son, visited Peter that day.

Bob went with me to Lund the following day, while my sister and mother stayed home. At this point, Peter was limited to one visitor at a time (in addition to me), to minimize the stimulation to a level he could handle. Bob and Peter had always enjoyed each other's company and appreciated each other's senses of humor. Bob was comfortable with Peter, and Peter was calm and responsive. His arms and legs were in motion a bit, but he also took Bob's hand and held it for a while, looking at him hard as if trying to figure out who this was. I reminded him that Bob and Marlys had come to Sweden with Helen (his mother-in-law), and that Marlys and Helen would be visiting him another day. It was hard to know if he recognized Bob, but he was calm—a good sign.

When Marlys came to see him the next day, Peter clearly recognized her. He responded to her greeting and easy laugh with an infectious smile that lit up the room. Marlys's professional background is in early childhood and parent–teacher education. She is a gifted observer of nonverbal communication and engages patiently. She brought those skills to her visit with Peter as we sat in the garden around the patio tables, enjoying the sunshine, passing a ball back and forth across the table or bouncing it on the ground. Watching Peter respond to her questions and comments was heartwarming.

Our mother visited on the third day. She'd had a few days to rest, but I knew this would be an emotional visit, and perhaps physically difficult as well. Peter's involuntary body movements could be physically difficult for a frail person to handle—they were often too much for the Ribbingska staff to manage. Mother took care to sit where Peter would have a clear view of her, and as she spoke to him, she put her hand on his arm. He looked toward her without moving his arm and placed his left hand on hers. She continued to talk to him. At one point I cautioned her, concerned that he might grab her arm with too much strength. She ignored me and continued talking to Peter. During her half-hour visit, his body was still and he was attentive, nodding a couple of times in response to her questions and tilting his head to see her better as he listened intently. It was lovely to observe.

We all spent a couple more days relaxing in the garden and had a visit with Antje, and then I drove Mother, Marlys, and Bob to Kastrup for their flight back to Minnesota. There are not adequate words to describe what their visit meant—it was a generous act of love and support for Peter and me. I recalled times as a young woman when I had underestimated my mother. In this moment, I experienced her raw courage and commitment to doing the right thing for her family. I wanted to absorb that quality as my own.

My family's visit coincided with the early weeks of Peter having personal care attendants. During these weeks, Antje, one of Peter's children, Jonas or Katarina, or I visited Peter each day after the PCAs had left so we could observe how Peter was adjusting to the special support they were providing. We all learned much, and sharing our insights during this period strengthened our family communication about Peter's adjustments.

During the fall of 2011 the European Association for International Education held its annual conference in Copenhagen, Denmark, just a forty-minute train ride from Lund. I regularly attended the association's conferences as part of my NAFSA representation responsibilities. This time I stayed in Lund, took the train to attend each day of the four-day conference, and returned to Lund in the evenings to be with Peter and sleep at my apartment. Debra Stewart, a close friend who attended the conference in her role as president of the Council of Graduate Schools and a NAFSA board member, visited Peter during this week as well. Her visit was brief, quiet, and intimate. Peter held her hands, responded with a simple word or a nod to her questions, and watched intently as Debra and I talked. We took a short walk in the garden and then sat in the patio and passed the ball while we had a brief conversation. Later that evening, Debra said to me, "Peter is working as hard as he can, as he always has, with what he has." The clarity of her comment gave me great comfort, and it has stayed with me throughout my journey.

28

Establishing My Life in Sweden

For the first time in our years together, I was in Sweden without Peter as my guide. I faced huge cultural adjustments during the first eight months of Peter's hospitalization and rehab. Later, I took a further leap into the unknown as I absorbed the reality that Ribbingska Nursing Home would be Peter's home for the rest of his life. I had much to learn about Swedish society and the various aspects of the nation's health care system. I would have to educate myself about how I could best support Peter appropriately in each of these environments.

But first I had to tend to the practical matters of real estate, Peter's business, and determining where I would live after Peter's apartment was sold. Peter's business needed to be closed, and I needed to sell the apartment and purchase another, smaller flat so I would have a place to live while in Lund. Years before, Peter had put my name on his bank accounts, made me a voting member of his business, and introduced me to his accountant. There was much to learn about Swedish legal processes, but Peter had kept me well informed and positioned to work my way through the details. We had discussed his business over the years, and I knew his colleagues and many of his clients. Peter's colleagues needed an update from me. In August I had informed them of Peter's fall. Now I had to let them know that the business would be closed, and give them the information they required to continue the client work they had collaborated on.

My cultural learning continued in modest and grander ways. A friend recommended a real estate agent to sell the apartment, and as I showed the agent the property, I shared with him the historic detail that the building was the last in Lund to install indoor plumbing and noted that the original outhouse was now the building's trash shed. When I showed him the laundry room, a lower-level space accessed from the interior garden of the property, he was pleased to see that it included a mangle iron—a device I had used only once to iron linen place mats and napkins, mainly just to see how it worked. I asked why it was important to him that the building laundry room had one, to which this young man replied, "How else would you iron sheets?" Needless to say, I asked him if he ironed his sheets, to which he said, "Of course—everyone does!" I told him I didn't know any Americans who ironed their sheets, and that I knew of no home or apartment building in the United States with a mangle iron. He shook his head in amazement, and I was reminded again of the practical lifestyle differences between our cultures.

Lund is a university town with a thriving high-tech economy, and the apartment sold in a couple of weeks. My immediate challenges then were downsizing, including distributing Peter's books, and finding another place to live.

Peter had spent the summer of 2010 writing the final draft of his research proposal for the completion of his PhD. His academic adviser requested a copy of that proposal for the university archives, thinking that another student might build on Peter's work. Our grandson Anton stepped up to find that research document on Peter's laptop and forwarded it to the adviser.

The distribution of Peter's books was an emotional undertaking and a practical chore. Sorting through the books jogged so many memories, and sharing them with others was an early step in a years-long process of saying goodbye. Peter was a prolific reader, often reading several books a week. We had talked about his favorite books, and I'd read many of them as well. It was hard to part with them, but it was also terrific to share those books with family and friends. Peter's library reflected his diverse interests: political history, mysteries, political biographies, business development, change theories, leadership, and more. Peter's thesis adviser took the titles he could use at the university, and then friends and family made their selections. One friend took Peter's early edition of Winston Churchill's history of World War II, and others found books of interest. I kept a couple dozen that held particular meaning to both of us. The twenty or so books remaining in the end went to a secondhand store.

Finding a new place to call home in Lund was particularly difficult at the time Peter's apartment was sold, as I was still holding out hope that Peter would live at home with assistance following rehab. That meant I was looking for a unit that was accessible in all aspects and convenient to the center of the city. With the help of Antje and a friend of Peter who had real estate and renovation experience, I searched for weeks but found nothing that felt like the right fit. As an interim solution I looked for a short-term rental, but came up empty again. Lund's real estate market is always challenging, given the presence of the university and the city's dynamic economy, but my situation was further complicated by a deep uncertainty about the future.

Ultimately, Antje proposed that for a few months I stay with her and her husband during the ten days each month that I was in Lund, giving me a supportive space from which to face the next few months as we gained more clarity about Peter's prognosis. Her generosity relieved me of myriad challenges during those early months.

When the decision was made that Peter would live in a nursing home, I wanted to find a permanent apartment as soon as possible, but the market was still very tight. I liked the building where Antje and Fredrik lived—it was a fifteen-minute walk from the center of town and a thirty-minute walk from Peter's nursing home. Antje and Fredrik had a three-bedroom unit, but the building also had twelve studio, or two-room, apartments, none of which were currently on the market, however. But I woke up one morning in Washington with an idea: I called Antje to propose that she put a note under the front door of each of the smaller units in the building, indicating that her sister-in-law was interested in buying the apartment and would be happy to make a direct purchase. If interested, the unit owner should contact Antje.

Within twelve hours, a neighbor responded, and when I was back in Lund a week later I met with her, a woman ten years my senior. She was planning to move to a new assisted living facility in the center of town, but her new unit wouldn't be ready for three months. With a handshake, we agreed on a price and settled the details: I would buy her apartment as soon as we could arrange the closing, and she would live there until her new unit was ready. It was a perfect arrangement for both of us. Her son, who participated in our meeting, was appreciative that his mother was able to make this change with minimal stress. I was thrilled as well. And it was special for both of us that we had accomplished this transaction on our own and in a matter of an hour. For the next few months, I continued to stay with Antje and Fredrik.

Moving into my own small apartment in the spring of 2011 brought a level of comfort that I hadn't anticipated. I now had a designated space for my work and a place to relax surrounded by furniture, art, and books that Peter and I had lived with for more than twenty years. I looked forward to inviting friends and family over for meals and to eventually bringing Peter there as well.

During my ten-day monthly stays in Lund, I established personal routines, in addition to my daily routines with Peter, that were critical for my own well-being. My walks to and from Ribbingska took me through the market square, a favorite spot for buying vegetables, fruit, and flowers. At least once a week I would walk to Godiva Boutique, a shop Peter had introduced me to. The owner became a friend and reliable adviser on wardrobe choices, which was important to me, as this was the only time I had for such shopping during those years.

Each month I had lunch with my friend Inga Persson, a university professor. We met when she presented her research at the University of Minnesota during the New Sweden '88 celebrations. We stayed in touch and became good friends, and during the nine years I was living part-time in Lund she tracked my schedule and consistently arranged for us to meet for lunch. A cousin who now lived in Lund did the same, making sure that we met for dinner each month.

Another monthly stop for me was a gluten-free bakery in Malmö. Peter found this shop after my celiac diagnosis in 2008, and he often brought gluten-free bread from the shop to Washington with him. Now I became a regular customer, enjoying talks with the owner about her family's summer holidays in her native Yugoslavia and her children's transitions to young adulthood.

29

Adjustments and Routines in Peter's Care

As Peter adjusted to living at Ribbingska, he became comfortable beyond the parameters of his room. I would suggest going outside to take a walk or to sit in the garden and ask him which he'd like to do. Initially, he often responded with a word: "Garden" or "Walk." As we headed out, I'd ask him which door we should use, the back door or the front door (which required taking the elevator). He'd usually say "Lift" or "Door." In later years, I needed to ask yes-or-no questions. Once outside, I would ask him where he wanted to go, always offering choices that he could answer with yes or no. On occasion, when I neglected to ask, he let me know—with a wave of his hand or a loud "No"—that his choice was not the one I'd made. It warmed my heart that he could convey his opinion.

Despite the emotional turmoil that was my constant companion that first year, Peter didn't seem stressed by the physical changes or aware of his limited capacities. His expressions of frustration were related to confusion or conflicts with the staff and his inability to make himself understood. His smiles or laughter always lit up the room, often the result of teasing by a staff member or a visiting friend who brought their own smile.

Peter also often smiled or laughed when we watched comedy films or television programs together. Among his favorites were *I Love Lucy* episodes, the German classic *Dinner for One*, and, during his first Christmas at Ribbingska, *Home Alone*. Those who have seen that film will recall the scene when the thieves break into the house, crushing all the Christmas tree ornaments, and then are comically assaulted by the many obstacles the young boy has installed throughout the home. Peter and I both laughed several times while watching the film. I came to understand that the shared experience and my laughter reminded his brain how to laugh as well. *Home Alone* became an annual tradition for us, creating shared smiles and laughter.

After Peter's weeks in rehab, he enjoyed the shared activity of bouncing a soccer ball back and forth on the floor with me or another visitor, or rolling a smaller ball across a table. Building with Duplo blocks initially occupied him for fifteen or twenty minutes at a time, and he would periodically welcome "help" from me or others. During those early months he regularly "read" the newspaper—paging through, pausing at headlines that caught his attention. A year later, he had no interest in the newspaper and tossed it on the floor. About that time he also lost interest in tossing the ball or building with Duplo. I missed sharing these activities with him, but Peter didn't seem distressed. Rather, he now was experiencing less involuntary body motion and was generally more calm.

Peter's doctor helped me understand that the activities (passing the ball, building with Duplo blocks, reading the newspaper) had helped Peter adjust to the new environment. Physically engaging with me or others he trusted was his way of being okay during the very stressful transition. Now that he was comfortable and felt safe, he didn't need the focus that those activities required.

In Peter's first months at Ribbingska, standing therapy was part of his routine. The personal care attendants always asked Peter if he wanted to use the standing platform, and initially he responded enthusiastically with "Ja." At the platform, he quickly raised his arms to begin. Some days he would stand for four to six minutes, sit for a few minutes of rest, and then stand again for a few minutes. Another day a ten-minute stand seemed effortless for him, yet he wouldn't try a second time. On occasion, sitting in front of the standing platform waiting for the staff to get the straps in order, he'd reach out to inspect parts of the apparatus, as though trying to figure out how it worked. I'd known Peter's curiosity well, and even now I could see that curiosity occasionally coming through. But on other days, he showed no interest.

One day that summer, Peter was preparing to do standing therapy when his personal attendant, Erik, took a short break. I told Peter that Erik would be back in a minute, and he responded, "Okay." A minute later, not waiting for Erik to return, he stood, rested his arm on the platform, and put his head in his hand, much as he'd often done in the past while sitting at his desk contemplating an idea. I commented, "It looks like you're thinking 'I'm going to walk again one of these days'"—to which he responded, "Yes." Just days later, he struggled to stand, and once up, stood for only a couple of minutes. A few months later, he couldn't stand at all. The physical therapist concluded that a physical therapy program was no longer appropriate for Peter. I agonized about the end to his PT sessions, understanding that each time he stood I had allowed myself to hope that the earlier diagnosis might have been wrong—maybe he would walk again. Who knows what else he might be able to do?

Music had been an important shared experience for us throughout our relationship. We attended a Saint Paul Chamber Orchestra concert together within days of our first meeting, and weeks later we listened to Dixieland jazz at Stampen Jazz Club in Stockholm. Peter's personal music collection favored piano and jazz clarinet and classical orchestra. He usually had music playing while he was writing or reading. At Ribbingska, the staff and I regularly asked him if he wanted to listen to music.

He often listened to music in the mornings while the aide helped him with hygiene and getting dressed, and after breakfast as he sat in front of the French doors in his room. During winter afternoons, when we sat together in that corner of his room, specific music—by artists such as the Swedish singer Monica Zetterlund, Duke Ellington, or Benny Goodman—provided topics for me to share memories of our times at Stampen Jazz Club and other venues.

When Peter was annoyed, he found ways to express it. He would remind me to ask him a question through his tone or his facial expression, or by grabbing my arm. I would ask, "Do you want different music?" or "Do you want the music turned off?" He would respond with "Ja" or "Nej," and we'd take it from there. "Hearing" his opinion, experiencing Peter making me understand and being able to respond, affirmed an important role I played for him and reminded me of the richness of our journey together.

Lund is full of neighborhood parks and city squares. The city park Stadsparken lives up to its name as a park for the entire city, with a solarium garden, multiple and unique flower gardens, a large duck pond, spaces for playing bocce, coffee and ice cream shops, a larger restaurant for seated meals, a swimming hall, paths for walking and bike riding, a climbing wall, a skateboard park, a small stage, and endless spaces for gathering and relaxing on the grass or on benches or hammocks under the trees. All of the city's parks feature spaces for events such as flea markets and food markets, along with places for visiting, reflection, and enjoyment of the sunshine, the flowers, the art, or the water. Peter and I had spent time in many of these parks over the years. Now during his years at Ribbingska, we frequently visited Stortorget (The Large Square), the library park, the botanic garden, Grand Hotel square, and the Skissernas Museum sculpture park—each within a short walk of the nursing home. Stortorget has rows of benches and reclining chairs facing the sun, where sun-starved Swedes sit whenever the sun shines, regardless of the time of year. For several years Peter lived in a nearby flat. The small arcade park across from the train station also had benches facing the afternoon sun. On occasion, we'd eat an ice cream as we watched people walking across the square or passing by on their way to the train station. At the library park, we enjoyed the fountain and watching young children play in the water. These were all places we had spent time together before, and I hoped the familiarity would give him comfort, as it did me.

Grabbing my arm or shoving me away was Peter's way of getting my attention. My job was to figure out what he wanted. "Is it time to go outside for a walk?" "Do you want the TV turned on/off?" "Do you want to listen to music?" "Do you need to use the toilet?" "Do you want me to quit talking?" If I was paying attention to what was going on, I rarely had to ask more than one or two questions to get to the one on his mind. On our walks to the town center or the churchyard, I'd often comment on the flowers, a nice path, or something else of interest. Once in a while he would repeat what I'd said—"Nice path" or "Yes, flowers." These moments with Peter were precious to me.

During the months that Peter had the support of personal care attendants, he adjusted well to the Ribbingska environment and was able to spend more time in the common areas. Regular staff gained confidence in supporting Peter as they observed how the PCAs engaged with him. His involuntary arm and leg movements continued, but the staff members were less intimidated. They began to see Peter's personality and learned to engage with him in ways that would prompt responses from him. It was a relief to see them become more comfortable with Peter. Supporting them in this work would continue to be my priority throughout his time at Ribbingska.

Linda's resignation as Peter's personal care attendant in early 2013 was met with an immediate staff response. Kerstin Nilsson, the senior nursing aide on Ward 1B, made the case to the administrator that she and the entire staff team now felt they were capable of managing Peter's care as part of their regular duties and were willing to do so. They felt he no longer needed the added support of a personal care attendant. Their recommendation was based on Peter's adjustments, a significant reduction in his involuntary body motions, and his general calm around other residents. Given these developments, they believed that they could care for him successfully.

Initially, I was anxious about this change, but I had tremendous confidence in Kerstin's skills and leadership, so the idea also felt exciting. As much as Peter had needed and benefited from the personal care, I had been concerned that because Peter was not included in Ward 1B's regular routines, he might never be fully integrated into the culture of the ward. Now, the staff were embracing Peter and the challenges he brought to their work, and they wanted to step up to care for him on their own.

Kerstin became Peter's lead staff person, both because of her seniority and because she connected with him in a special way. She usually worked the morning shift, and so was with him when he woke up. At that time of day, he was well rested and most able to respond verbally. Kerstin reported that she and Peter had clear conversations; he helped with brushing his teeth and washing his face, and would speak in short sentences—"What time is it?" or "A nice day." At the breakfast table in the early months of 2014, Peter would pick up a cup of tea or a sandwich and eat on his own. Even as my brain told me that these actions did not indicate major changes, they were moments of special connection that gave joy to the staff and me.

Kerstin observed that Peter was more calm when I was physically in Lund. Each time I flew back from Washington, she would tell Peter on the day before my return that I would be coming to see him the next day, and she noticed that he would visibly relax at the news. I recalled how he worried about my driving back to Lund on the evening of his first day at the rehab center, so it wasn't surprising that his instincts might include concern about my safety on the transatlantic flight, a flight he'd taken himself dozens of times during our marriage. So I established the habit of stopping by to let him know I'd landed first thing after I dropped my bags at the apartment. I'd spend a few minutes holding his hand and talking about the trip, and then go home for a couple of hours of sleep and return after lunch and his afternoon nap. We would spend the rest of the afternoon together and I'd serve him supper. Usually I'd leave him after supper, but if he seemed uneasy, I would sit with him and watch TV or listen to music until he relaxed, asking him every now and then if it was time for me to leave.

There were days I would shed tears as I walked home or to the car at the end of the afternoon visit. Tears for the husband I missed, as I reminded myself yet again that he wasn't coming back and that this new normal would continue to require much of me.

I was regularly grateful for the matter-of-fact way the staff responded to my questions and requests. When Peter needed a haircut I just asked the staff to arrange it, suggested a monthly appointment, and ensured that his cash account had the resources to cover the cost. A hairdresser came to Ribbingska regularly to provide services for the women residents, but there was no similar arrangement with a barber. Responding to my request, one of the staff stopped at the barbershop across the street to ask the barber to come to Ribbingska to cut Peter's hair and to set up a monthly appointment schedule. I made a point of being there for his first visit, to help him get acquainted with Peter and to ensure that the barber understood that Peter didn't want his eyebrows cut. The barber took one look at Peter and exclaimed, "Peter, it's so good to see you. I was wondering why you hadn't been by the shop for so many months!" It turned out that he had been Peter's barber for years, working at a different shop. I had met him during those years, and had walked by that shop a few weeks earlier but didn't see the familiar barber. As that barbershop was several blocks from Ribbingska, I didn't pursue it. Now, here was a person familiar to Peter, available to walk across the street and cut Peter's hair on a regular basis. It was a lovely reunion that added consistency to Peter's care and reminded the staff of Peter's many relationships in the city.

Peter had had regular pedicures for many years, so it was welcome news that pedicures were scheduled every six weeks for all residents. While some activities caused Peter stress and increased his involuntary motions, he was calm and attentive while his feet were being tended to, as though recalling all the good feelings he had experienced during pedicures in the past.

Antje visited Peter regularly while I was in Washington, and her time with him often produced new ideas for engaging with him. She had been a dentist in a care facility for many years and was intimidated by nothing. She consistently worked to make Peter's life better, trying new tactics until she found something that worked, from a small pillow that improved his ability to nap in his wheelchair to a longtime favorite snack that could be left in his refrigerator. Antje and Peter were very close, their trust deep, and he had no trouble expressing disagreement or dissatisfaction with something she might try.

One of the gifts of Antje's partnership with me was that she had informal conversations with the staff in Swedish. While most of the staff understood English and many spoke it fluently, when I spoke to staff members in English and they responded to me in Swedish, there were times when none of us were certain we had understood everything. When Antje and I met with staff together, I felt confident that we weren't missing nuances or details. In her regular emails to me she described her visits with Peter in depth, telling me all about her activities and Peter's responses to them, as well as relating her interactions with the staff and the substance of any reports they shared.

Understandably, it was difficult for other residents to initiate conversations with Peter or even stop by to visit him when he was on his own. Serving Peter's meals was a favorite time for me, and it created opportunities for other residents to engage with Peter in the dining area. Often when they left the table before he did, they would stop at his chair to greet him. My serving Peter his meals also relieved the staff, as there were often two or three other residents who needed help at mealtimes. Between meals I also initiated conversations with individual residents who were sitting near us in the dayroom, in the garden, or on the veranda. This allowed them to feel more comfortable stopping to talk when they saw us. They would ask Peter questions or comment on the day, and Peter would usually listen, often responding with a nod and sometimes a one-word answer.

Sven, Peter's neighbor across the hall, was a special exception. A quiet man, small in stature, recently widowed, Sven consistently reached out to Peter, introducing himself, touching Peter's hand, and speaking of things on his mind. He seemed to understand instinctively that he and Peter had much in common. There's no question that earlier in his life, Peter would have thoroughly enjoyed visiting with Sven. In this situation, Sven was completely comfortable. When I was present, he engaged with me as well. When he learned that I was from Minnesota, it brought a smile to his face and recollections of the year his family had lived in Maple Plain. Sven's comments about Minnesota caught Peter's attention, so I asked him if he'd heard Sven talking about living in Minnesota. Peter nodded and said, "Yes."

Sven often stopped to greet Peter when he was in the dayroom or in the garden with me or a staff member. He also visited with Peter when he found him sitting alone. Sven was a gardener, and he carried trimming shears on his strolls around the garden; he pruned bushes, cleaned out dead leaves, and generally enjoyed the role of resident gardener. As we all became better acquainted and I shared with him details about Peter's work and our life together, Sven began to integrate some of those anecdotes into the comments he made to Peter. It was lovely to watch. Sven was a generous and intelligent person.

Over time, Sven shared that he and his wife had lived in Ethiopia for thirty years. He had been a university professor there, and their children had grown up in Ethiopia. He and his wife had moved back to Sweden after his retirement. He often invited us to look at his Ethiopian art, sharing stories of that period in his life. During the years we knew Sven, he was inducted into the Ethiopian Academy of Arts, the first non-Ethiopian so honored. The Lund newspaper carried a story when he received that honor, prompting a Ribbingska party in celebration.

Sven's death was a loss for both of us. His capacity for kindness and his consistent engagement with a person whose ability to reciprocate was limited were powerful reminders of the impact each of us has on others. Sven found Peter's humanity and, in doing so, showed it to others.

30

.\\\\\\\\\|||||||||////,.

Sustaining Traditions

By the fall of 2011, I felt ready to expand the geography of our walks, and decided to try reminding Peter of some of his favorite spots. I asked him about taking a walk along the Malmö waterfront and having a coffee at the bathhouse café. Over the years, Peter had spent many Sunday mornings when he was alone in Sweden having a swim at the bathhouse, then calling me from the café, where he enjoyed a latte and read the paper.

He responded affirmatively to the idea of the Malmö walk, so I decided we should do it on a weekday when Linda, his personal care attendant, could join us. I hoped this excursion could become a regular one for Peter and me, so having Linda's help the first time would give me a chance to observe the process and outcomes and plan for future trips. We scheduled a taxi with accommodations for a wheelchair, setting our departure and pickup times in advance. In Sweden, this type of service is available to elderly and disabled people at minimal cost.

Linda had never been to this part of Malmö, so she was excited to accompany us and helped with the logistics for a destination Peter and I had shared many times over several years. We pushed Peter's wheelchair along the seaside promenade toward the city. In view was the towering building known as the Turning Torso, an iconic, internationally recognized part of the Malmö skyline. Peter and I had visited the skyscraper when it opened years before, so when I asked Peter if he could see it, he responded with an enthusiastic "Yes."

From the promenade, we walked to the restaurant at the end of the pier, where we ordered lattes and sat on the outdoor veranda. The café staff and other guests seamlessly helped us move tables to find shade and make room for the wheelchair. The kindness of so many people in a variety of public spaces reinforced for me how individual personal acts of kindness have impacts on the recipients far beyond what we appreciate when we extend ourselves for others.

Subsequently, Peter and I managed this excursion on our own each summer during Peter's life at Ribbingska. I couldn't discern how familiar the Malmö coast felt for Peter, but I hoped that being together in a place that he had loved might jog a memory.

Peter's daughter, Katarina, visited her dad regularly. She had relied on him a lot over the years. He had been an active advocate for her as she faced her own disabilities, which sometimes limited her opportunities and often limited what others expected of her. That was not the case with Peter. He had consistently encouraged her to complete her education and try new things. In the 1980s, he brought her to Minnesota for two summers to intern at Camp Courage, where she was expected to support campers who had challenges far beyond her own. That experience increased her personal confidence, motivated her to further her education, and ultimately led her to write a memoir about growing up with a disability, which was published. For Katarina, her father's support had been an important part of her successes. Now she sought to provide a level of support for him and comfort for herself.

One day, Katarina proposed to the Ribbingska nurse that she and her husband take her dad for a day trip to a campground area by the sea. She had attended a program at the campground and felt it would be a perfect place to visit with her dad. The site, which was an hour's drive away, had a network of paved pathways that would make it possible for Katarina to give Peter a lovely day in an outdoor setting near the sea.

It seemed like this would be a very long day for Peter without the possibility of rest or eating or using the toilet. In my anxiety, I focused on the risks. The nurse heard my apprehension, but was confident that this could be a positive experience for Peter. She was familiar with the facility and knew that it was staffed by well-qualified people. She also felt that Katarina was appropriately comfortable with taking her dad on this day trip. Despite my anxiety, I understood that Katarina's idea was a good one, and this was exactly the kind of initiative that would have made Peter very proud of his daughter. Were I to interfere, *I* would be the problem.

The excursion was a huge success—photographs from the day confirm a happy Peter. His reaction reminded me of his capacity for adjusting to new experiences and his comfort in being with Katarina. I was also reminded that Katarina and others often had ideas for Peter's care that were different from mine and could be positive for him. I would continue to relearn the value of listening to the ideas and perspectives of others, in the care of Peter as well as in doing my job as an organization executive.

For Peter's first Christmas after moving to Ribbingska in 2011, I wanted to bring him to the small apartment where I lived. He had never lived there, but he had lived for years with the furniture and art the apartment was furnished with, most of which we had selected together. I hoped that visiting me there would connect him with our life together and help him feel comfortable about where I was living.

For years, Peter's Christmas tradition had included sharing a lutefisk meal prepared by his sister, Antje, and her husband, Fredrik. The years we spent Christmas in the United States, Peter shared the lutefisk meal with them before he left for the States. When we spent Christmas in Sweden, the lutefisk meal would wait for me. We had always trimmed the Christmas tree together in Sweden, Minnesota, and Washington. Our tree was a combination of Peter's tradition of Swedish electric candles, sparkling icicles, and angel hair and my tradition of adding at least one new ornament each year from the ornaments we collected in our travels. Peter had particularly enjoyed stringing the lights and putting on the angel hair and icicles, the two tasks of this tradition requiring considerable patience.

Bringing Peter to my small apartment for a midday lutefisk meal with Antje and Fredrik and to see the Christmas tree would combine these traditions. I had already decorated the tree, as Peter wasn't able to engage in such tasks. Linda, Peter's personal attendant, would join us.

The lutefisk meal was simple: baked cod, boiled potatoes, green peas, melted butter, and a mustard cream sauce—one of Peter's favorites. Dessert would be another Peter favorite, either crème brûlée or *ris à la malta* (rice pudding with extra whipped cream) served with black currant sauce made from berries I picked at our summerhouse garden.

That first Christmas was a success, and we maintained this tradition until 2018. The scheduled taxi service brought Peter and me from Ribbingska to my apartment, where Antje and Fredrik prepared the meal. Peter sat in the kitchen to watch the final food preparation, including the flaming of the top of the crème brûlée. In the dining/living room, I showed him around, commenting on his favorite Josef Frank upholstered sofa and the Peter Dahl prints, which had hung in Peter's apartment for several years.

Peter was generally calm for these visits. He often made direct eye contact with Antje and me and periodically reached out to hold my hand or grab my arm. His appetite was good, but he showed little awareness of eating one of his favorite meals. We hoped that this small ritual from his previous life would reinforce that we were there for him and create a new memory for me as I accepted our new reality a bit more each day.

This simple holiday excursion required planning, created additional tasks for the Ribbingska staff, and risked creating anxiety for Peter and leaving him exhausted. The seemingly simple activities of putting on winter coats and moving his wheelchair in and out of the taxi took considerable energy. The ride was only fifteen minutes long, but I realized that from the taxi, Peter was seeing the city differently than he saw it during the short walks we took near Ribbingska. We were passing by places that he'd known for years, yet it was impossible to know what he was recognizing and what his reactions might be. At times he looked straight ahead intently, then bowed his head and closed his eyes, as if to have a rest from it all. While with him in the taxi for these outings, I tried to "see" the city from his perspective, but was also reminded of my own loss.

Peter and I had always enjoyed hosting parties, so during the years at Ribbingska, I initiated annual social events for all the residents of the ward, to create memories among this new "family." Peter's birthday parties were afternoon gatherings of residents and staff of Ward 1B as well as our family and friends from Lund and Denmark. The staff prepared a long table in the dayroom with porcelain plates, cups, and saucers. I brought bouquets of tulips, candles, and coffee cakes and chocolate cake from the local *konditori*. Peter sat at the head of the table, and we sang the traditional Swedish birthday song. And every year, from the first party, we also shared a special gift from Minnesota: a video recording made by my sister Marlys's husband, Bob Nesheim, of himself playing "Happy Birthday" on his ukulele as he sat in front of their window in Duluth overlooking Lake Superior.

Early in October 2012, during a visit with Peter at Ribbingska, his childhood friend Boris Levin, the owner of Ringsjö Wärdshus, a very special restaurant where we had eaten many times, mentioned the restaurant's preparations for the annual Saint Martin's meal—a Swedish tradition of roast goose, roasted potatoes, brussels sprouts, cooked red cabbage, and a special apple cake unique to southern Sweden. The Saint Martin's meal was the restaurant's exclusive menu during November.

I asked Boris if it might be possible to bring the meal to Ribbingska for all the residents and staff of Ward 1B. He loved the idea, and for several years this special Saint Martin's dinner was served at Ward 1B as our gift. A few family and friends from Lund and Denmark joined us as well. Peter and I were the hosts, Boris and his wife, Lena, delivered and served the meal, and Boris shared stories of growing up together with Peter in Helsingborg. For many of the residents, it was their first Saint Martin's dinner in years. Between these special social events and increased contact with Peter at meals and in the common areas, the other residents became increasingly comfortable with Peter.

It was difficult to gauge how much Peter understood, but in comparison with those early months, when being in the same space with three or four other people would have been impossible, his calm demeanor and observation throughout the first party, and each year after, made these happy times. His Ribbingska neighbors also enjoyed their conversations with our friends and family members. As they left the table, each of them stopped by Peter's chair, touched or held his hand, and offered a greeting and a thank-you for inviting them to the party. These gatherings helped each of them feel more connected to Peter and gave them anecdotes and memories to talk about among themselves and to share with their own families.

A favorite excursion with Peter was a walk to Clemenstorget (Clemens Square) to sit in the shade enjoying the fountain or to have a look at the latest flea market offerings. On one particular day, a small jazz group (guitar, bass, drums, and vocalist) was performing in the square. I asked Peter if he wanted to stop and listen for a while, and he nodded affirmatively. We settled in, and after we had listened for about seven or eight minutes, I looked at Peter and noticed tears falling down his face. I took his hand, leaned over to give him a kiss, and asked him if this brought back memories of the jazz events we had attended together. He nodded, and as he continued listening, the tears kept falling—for both of us. So often I had wondered what he was processing or remembering. At that moment I felt sure that he was comforted by my presence and my engagement with him, and that somewhere inside him he knew of the love and support we had shared.

In subsequent years, our walks to Clemenstorget continued to provide entertainment. We watched each stage of construction as this lovely square was converted into a station for the new light-rail tram system. The tram would ultimately take riders to the MAX IV and ESS developments north of Lund, European Union technology projects that Peter had been very excited about as we had watched the construction on our trips back and forth to the summerhouse. Now this project was another "conversation" piece for us, and in the final months of Peter's life we walked back and forth across the tracks to see how the boarding platforms would look.

By 2012, Peter was comfortable eating his meals in the common area at Ribbingska, but because he needed so much clear space in front of him, he couldn't share a table with four other residents. So it was decided that Peter would share a table with Dagne, a resident who was blind and so talkative that other residents often became stressed when they spent time with her. I found this solution quite endearing—Peter, a person with limited verbal capacity, who had previously been very social and verbal, paired with an elderly woman who was now blind but had become increasingly verbal with the loss of her sight. At one point, even Dagne commented to Peter, in English, that she thought it was great that they shared a table—one person who couldn't see and the other who couldn't talk much! When I pointed this out to Peter privately, he nodded and gave the slightest of smiles. Dagne was touched by this arrangement, and when she left the table before Peter did, she often stopped at his chair, put her hand on his, and said, "See you later, Peter. It was nice to share the meal with you today." She clearly felt the hostility of some of the other residents, so her connection with Peter was increasingly important to her, and it was beneficial to Peter as well.

31

Letting Go and Making New Plans

In the fall of 2012, I was ready to move out of the Washington apartment I had lived in for ten years. Prior to Peter's fall, we had decided to sell that apartment and find one in another neighborhood more connected to the water. We had no buyer prospects, however, and after Peter's fall I took the apartment off the market. Now, two years later, I felt ready to sell, and this time buyers were interested: the apartment sold within days. I decided to pack up everything and put it in storage, and then take my time finding a new place. A generous friend invited me to live in her guest room while I looked for a new home, and within weeks I found an apartment perfect for my needs in a cooperative that Peter and I had looked at previously. The apartment required considerable renovation, though, so I continued to stay in my friend's home while the work was done.

A year later the apartment was ready for occupancy. I was excited to complete this transition despite the sadness of living in a space not in Peter's memory. Whatever capacity he had to "see" things, I shared with him. At the same time, I was creating a new life without him, even as memories of him were in everything that I would be unpacking.

As we continued our telephone conversations two or three times each week while I was in Washington, I sought to connect details of this new life to people and objects that Peter had known. Our friend David Winslow, who designed the kitchen and dining room in my new apartment; my brother Warren, who painted the apartment; friends who helped with the move—I hoped that details of these familiar people would give Peter a sense that I was okay with all this change, and thus reduce any stress he might be feeling about it.

Soon after I moved into the new apartment, I flew to Beijing for a conference of the Chinese Association of International Education. I had attended the annual meetings of this organization a couple of times previously. On one of those trips, Peter had joined me for the conference and some university campus tours, and then we extended our stay to visit the Great Wall and the site of the terracotta soldiers. This time, I reminded him of those shared experiences when I called him from Beijing. I traveled back from Beijing via Copenhagen and worked from Lund for a week before returning to Washington, spending time with Peter every day as usual.

In early 2016, I informed the NAFSA board that I would retire in a year, after serving as CEO for almost nineteen years. It's likely that if Peter's fall had not occurred, I would have retired two or three years earlier, as Peter and I had been considering what we might do in our retirement years. Periodically, during the six years following Peter's fall, I had considered leaving my job, only to conclude that despite the extraordinary demands of traveling back and forth to Sweden every month to care for Peter, the focus that my work required gave me a sense of balance. But now, I was extremely tired, and I was ready for another transition in the coming year.

As I had always done, I talked to Peter about my decision. He stayed alert as I explained my choice to retire and nodded a couple of times, but I felt uncertain whether he was connecting to what I was saying. Then I began the yearlong transition of doing many things for the final time.

By now, Peter couldn't relate to many of the details I shared about my work. First, his cognitive capacities were declining, and second, many of the individuals and programs had changed since Peter had known my board and staff colleagues. Any memories he had were of the few colleagues who had known him and engaged with him many times.

During this final year at my job, I continued the schedule of ten days with Peter in Lund each month, and, as appropriate, did related work in Europe on either end of my Lund weeks, including attending the annual conference of the European Association for International Education in Liverpool. I also had the opportunity to participate in one of the first U.S.–Cuba higher education exchanges following President

Obama's decision to open relations with Cuba. In addition to other representation work, I continued to handle the day-to-day management of NAFSA, and I worked with the management team to produce the annual budget for the year beyond my service.

For me, the ultimate reminder of Peter's inability to connect with current affairs was Hillary Clinton's campaign for U.S. president. Peter loved discussing politics with our friends, and while he often had a hard time understanding and accepting the U.S. obsession with the personal flaws of political candidates and elected officials, he had been excited about the election of President Obama. He had initially planned to be in the United States for Obama's inauguration and had purchased his plane ticket, but as the day approached, a scheduling conflict made it impossible for him to make the trip. SAS allowed him to transfer his airline ticket to our granddaughter, Sara, who joined me for the week of inaugural celebrations. When Obama was reelected in 2012, Peter could still "connect" to his name and once in a while would smile in recognition when he heard it. Four years later, he didn't react at all to news about Hillary Clinton's campaign for president. In the past he would have been excited about it. This was another indication of further decline in Peter's memory. As I transitioned from my job to retirement, I was also noticing other changes in Peter's engagement with me and others.

Retirement was a relief but very unnerving. During our first fifteen years together, Peter and I had managed our personal time within the framework of the transatlantic realities and rhythms of our professional obligations. Since Peter's accident, I had adjusted my schedule so that I could be present for him and oversee his care while still keeping my commitments to NAFSA. The past six and a half years had been intense, and generally successful. Yet, despite how ready I felt for less structure and professional responsibility, I knew that retirement would be a big adjustment.

With the exception of 1997, the year I spent determining my next challenge, I had held leadership roles in each of my professional positions, from my own business to elective public service to a federal government agency role, a corporate senior management position, and finally for nineteen years as CEO of NAFSA. During those years I had also held a variety of board positions at nonprofit organizations, including Landmark Center, the Minnesota Women's Political Caucus, the Minnesota Women's Campaign Fund, the Minnesota Chapter of the National Association of Women Business Owners, Women Executives in State Government, the Communications Consortium Media Center, the Washington Office on Latin America, and Kakenya's Dream. I had enjoyed the challenges and opportunities of each of these roles, and felt that I had made contributions to these organizations' various communities. I would continue to serve on the boards of WOLA and Kakenya's Dream, the US–China Education Trust Advisory Council, and the board of trustees of the Alexandria Trust.

Following my retirement, I changed the amount of time I spent in Sweden and the United States. Because of European Union immigration requirements, I still had to monitor my total time in Sweden, but now I was able to stay in Lund for sixteen days at a time, followed by a month in the United States. This schedule reduced the number of transatlantic flights I had to take and gave me more than a week in Sweden at a time without jet lag. Now that I no longer had to start each day reading and responding to emails and spend my evenings in conference call meetings after being with Peter, I suddenly felt relaxed in a way I couldn't have imagined. I now had flexibility in my time with Peter, I could see friends more often, read, and visit museums—generally have a more normal life in Sweden. Most days I was with Peter twice a day, serving his noon and evening meals and observing the changes in his energy levels.

By 2017, Peter's interaction with me and others was declining—he was generally more quiet, less verbal. Yet he continued to have opinions and make decisions about when he was ready to go to a meal, what he watched on TV, where he wanted to sit in the garden, and which direction he wanted us to take on a walk. Sitting in his studio in front of the French doors overlooking the garden remained a favorite way to spend time. If he seemed particularly quiet and inclined to nap, I would ask him if it was okay with him if I read. He would nod or say "Ja." Later he'd often grab my arm to get my attention. "Do you want to talk?" He'd nod. I'd ask if he wanted to hear family news or offer another idea. Then I'd share a story about someone he knew. Sometimes I'd find a photograph on my iPad of the person we were talking about and show it to him. He would stay with these exchanges for five to ten minutes, and then be ready for a short nap in his chair. I couldn't know how much he understood or recalled when we interacted in this way, but these moments touched my heart.

32

Sweden's System of Care

The cultural and systemic differences between the U.S. and Swedish approaches to institutional caregiving were a significant part of what our American friends absorbed when they observed the details of life at Ribbingska Nursing Home. They asked questions and shared observations consistent with learning a new culture. Because the two societies have much in common and English is widely spoken in Sweden, it would be easy to conclude that the differences between the societies are minor. But without exception, the American friends who spent time with us in Lund during this journey noticed aspects of Peter's situation and care that were unique to Sweden, from the single-room studio apartment for each resident to the dedicated staff for each group of eight to ten residents, and from the common areas for those same eight people to the standard of outdoor time two or three times a week for each resident. Often the staff would bake cakes or cookies to entertain the residents and to fill the ward with the aroma of treats that would be served with afternoon coffee.

Throughout the nearly ten years that I monitored and supported Peter's care in Sweden's health care and elder care systems, I was consistently treated as a valued member of Peter's care team. Except for the brief period in rehab, the medical teams and caregiving staff and administrators responded to my assessments and my proposals with respect and usually with action.

As Peter's primary advocate, I looked for opportunities to support the staff in their work and to recognize the extra efforts they made. On those occasions when I had concerns about staff performance, I always shared my concerns with the administrator rather than directly with the staff. The administrator consistently responded to my feedback with professionalism and appreciation, and took action as appropriate.

Peter was the youngest resident at the nursing home throughout his time there. Sweden's comprehensive system of at-home assistance enables elderly people to remain in their own homes until they are quite advanced in age, with many not moving to nursing homes until they are in their late eighties or early nineties. During the eight and a half years Peter lived at Ribbingska, occupancy of each of the other seven studios in Ward 1B turned over two to four times, giving us considerable practice in getting acquainted with new residents and their families. There were always two or three residents who spoke English quite well and were enthusiastic about engaging with me. They were interested in Peter's story, kind in their conversations with him, and comfortable sitting with him in the garden or the dayroom.

Our dearest friend at Ribbingska in the later years was Erne, a Danish woman who had married a Swede and lived in Sweden since her early twenties. She had the social skills and the compassion of the teacher she had been during her career. Peter relaxed when Erne held his hand as she spoke to him. I always felt that he sensed her sincerity. Later, when she moved to the memory care unit on an upper floor of Ribbingska, Peter and I visited her regularly. She always remembered us and spoke to Peter as well as to me. On her one hundredth birthday, her daughter invited Peter and me to join her family for a celebration that included a reading of the letter from the king of Sweden honoring Erne's centennial.

During the years that Peter lived at Ribbingska, my mother was facing her own vulnerabilities of aging. Since her seventies she had been coping with declining vision due to macular degeneration, which left her legally blind in her early nineties. She treasured the memories of her final trip to Sweden to visit Peter during his first summer at Ribbingska, as she retained visual images of Peter in his wheelchair in his studio apartment as well as the rest of the Ribbingska environment. She loved hearing about Peter and recalling the details of her visit with him there. She lived alone in her own home until 2015 and then moved to an assisted living facility just a few blocks away. From 2012, I visited her for a weekend every month and telephoned her every day. My regular calls with Peter included one on the weekends, so when I was with my mother she had the chance to hear my end of the conversations and often added her own greetings.

As a result of the years I spent observing and interacting with residents and staff at Ribbingska, I became a more careful observer and better listener when visiting my mother. I had come to recognize the importance of being present without talking, fixing something, or creating a new plan.

33

,,,\\\\\\\\\\\|||||||||//////,,.

Our Final Days

In our telephone call just before I left Washington to return to Sweden in December 2019, I assured Peter that I understood he wasn't feeling well and that he missed me, and I told him how much I missed him, too. I reminded him that I would be with him on Friday. Our call ended, as always, with "Jag älskar dig mycket," I love you very much.

Earlier that month, as we concluded our calls, I recognized I was feeling a deeper sadness and exhaustion than I had previously acknowledged. My nine and a half years as Peter's advocate and caretaker had left me feeling depleted, and I had just begun to share these feelings with my sister and a few friends.

My arrival at Kastrup Airport at 6:45 a.m. on December 20, 2019, was routine. At the immigration checkpoint the agent paged through my passport and, noticing the endless entries at Kastrup, asked how long I was staying and why I was coming to Denmark so often. She also asked where I lived. "I'll be in Sweden for two weeks—I have friends and family living in Sweden and Denmark. I live in Washington, D.C." "Welcome to Denmark," she said as she handed back my passport.

I exhaled in relief that I had made it through immigration once again without having to document my days in Europe during the past six months. I kept a detailed record of my days in Sweden, but I was always worried that a close inspection might find a mistake that would put me at risk of being denied entry—an outcome I couldn't have lived with.

I retrieved my luggage and greeted my friend Lisbeth Kolind, who had met my flights all these years. She handed me a parcel of fresh gluten-free Danish pastries, her thanks for the peanut butter I brought her on every trip—an exchange tradition that we both treasured.

Settling in for the thirty-seven-minute ride on the Öresund train to Sweden, a heaviness came over me. The holidays were here, yet I sensed that this time would be different. Antje picked me up at the Lund train station, and we drove to my apartment, where I dropped my bags. We then stopped by her flat for a coffee and a visit. I was feeling more tired than usual and mentioned that I might rest before checking in with Peter. Antje urged me to go see him right away. Her tone and directive got my attention. I left for Ribbingska immediately.

Peter was dozing in his wheelchair in the dayroom when I arrived, and as I touched his arm and leaned over to give him a kiss, he opened his eyes and nodded. Did I just imagine that his look was one of relief or "It's about time"? I had talked to him on the phone twice that week to remind him that I would be with him on Friday, and I knew that the staff had also reminded him. He hadn't eaten or had anything to drink all day.

I sat with him, held his hand, and shared some details about my trip. He squeezed my hand and nodded when I asked if he wanted a drink of water. For the past several months, he had needed a thickener added to his water to help him swallow it. I prepared a glass of water and lifted it to his mouth. He tried to drink, but couldn't take it in. We tried again and again, and eventually over a few minutes he had swallowed half a glass of water. Usually, my initial visits to Peter after coming from the airport were short—just to let him know I had arrived, so he could relax and look forward to having me around for several days or weeks. Then I would go home for a nap and return after he'd had his lunch and nap. Today everything felt different. I didn't want to leave.

We sat quietly together. I stroked his hand, massaged his shoulders, talked to him softly, and watched him doze. He seemed calm—relieved that I was there. When lunch was being served, I asked Peter if he wanted to eat. He nodded. We moved to the table, and I prepared his soup and offered him a taste. With considerable effort, he ate less than half the bowl. This was the only food he'd eaten for two days, and the last food he would eat. Peter, the man with instincts beyond those of anyone else I'd ever known, had waited to eat his final meal until he could share the moment with me. He usually took a nap in his bed after lunch, an important break from the confines of his wheelchair. But for the past few days he had refused to lie down at midday. I concluded that he understood he had limited time and he didn't want it to end until I was with him. He wasn't willing to lie down until I got here. I asked him if he was ready to take a nap in his bed. He nodded. I accompanied the staff in taking him to his room and sat with him as he relaxed in bed. I asked him if it was okay for me to go to the flat and take a rest as well. He nodded. As I left, I assured him I would be there with him when he got up from his nap.

Peter was slipping away—an outcome that had been ever present during the past nine and a half years but was overshadowed by the new "normal" of his life at Ribbingska. That life was now giving way to a final letting go and saying goodbye. I felt grateful to be with Peter at this moment—it was a comfort to both of us. And I was overwhelmed that this journey would soon be over. Tears blurred my vision as I left Ribbingska that afternoon.

I wanted to talk to Antje—to acknowledge all this, and to check in with Peter's children, Jonas and Katarina. But at this moment, I also felt the need for a bit of structure in my life. On the way home from Ribbingska, I stopped to buy a small Christmas tree, which I installed in the apartment before collapsing into a deep sleep for an hour and a half. Later I would conclude that bringing the tree home at that moment was my way of creating order and observing tradition in anticipation of the end of a journey.

The afternoon with Peter was quiet—mostly he slept in his chair. While we sat in the dayroom and watched TV, I talked to him about the family, reminded him about our wonderful life together, told him that Lis would be coming from Denmark to see us tomorrow, and gave him several hugs. When I tried to rub his shoulders, he grabbed my arm to indicate he didn't want that. He took a small amount of water, but ate nothing at supper. I stayed with him until it was time for him to go to bed, sensing that Peter and I were in our final moments together.

Driving through the city on this Friday evening of the weekend before Christmas, I stopped at Saluhallen, the food hall where I'd always bought herring, sausage, gravlax, and beet salad for a Christmas Eve meal. Previously this was an errand I liked to do on a Saturday morning, to experience the long lines and energy of the holiday tradition. Only later would I conclude that I instinctively knew that this year, Friday evening would be the only time I could do this shopping.

At home, holiday music playing and tears flowing, I decorated the small tree with the ornaments Peter and I had collected over the years, remembering that Peter's last time in this apartment was a year ago. I made a cup of tea and a cheese sandwich and relaxed in the ambiance of the tree lights, sensing that once again, everything was about to change.

The next morning, Peter was dozing in his chair in the dayroom when I arrived, and he opened his eyes as he felt me nearby. His nod was short and weak, perhaps a sigh of relief that I was with him. We sat together, and I talked to him quietly, reminding him how much I loved him and assuring him that I'd be with him for the duration. I felt my body settle, perhaps letting go, as I absorbed this latest reality. I stayed until he went to his room for an afternoon nap and was back to greet him when he got up. I reminded him that Lis Frederiksen was coming from Denmark for a visit and asked him if he remembered Lis and Erik. He nodded.

Lis arrived around 4:00 p.m. She told me later that I greeted her with "It's the beginning of the end," but I didn't recall saying those words. The three of us sat in the corner of the dayroom so Peter could see Lis. I had water for him, but he took only a sip or two. He acknowledged Lis with a nod, and for moment took her hand as he had always done, but this time for just a moment.

Later, Peter and I sat at the dinner table, but he didn't eat. He drank a sip or two of water, but his spirit and energy were declining. I stayed with him until the staff took him to bed. I told him that I was going to the flat but I'd be close by all the time and would be back with him tomorrow after Antje and I delivered the Christmas flower to Lennart and Karin, as he and I had done for so many years. To my question "Do you understand, Peter?" he whispered, "Ja."

Lis and I went to my apartment for a light meal and a visit. It was a deep comfort to have her with me as I faced the end of this journey. Lis had been with me from the first day after Peter's fall, and on most weeks that I had been in Sweden during these nine years. The memories flowed as we sat together. She was my first call from the car on my way to the hospital on the morning of August 10, 2010. Later I called from the hospital to tell her about the plan to move Peter to Lund University

Hospital, and she came to stay with me in Lund for a few days to help me. Now here we were more than nine years later. I had learned so much about myself, had become more patient and caring, and had learned to know and love Sweden in a way that Peter had always wished for me but that I hadn't made the time to do until this tragedy happened.

Before Lis and I had finished dinner, the doctor called from Ribbingska to say that we needed to talk. Peter had the flu, and the doctor understood the directive that he should not be transferred to the hospital. He wanted us to discuss the situation in person.

Antje and I drove together to Ribbingska, and I called Jonas and asked him to meet us there. Gathered at Peter's bedside, we agreed that Peter should not be moved to the hospital. The doctor clarified that if Peter stayed at Ribbingska rather than going to the hospital, he would not receive intravenous fluids. He would be kept comfortable, receive morphine for pain, and have a personal care nurse supporting him for the duration. The doctor told us that Peter would live about two to four days without food and water.

We agreed on our respective visiting times with Peter the following day, with Jonas and Katarina taking the morning so that Antje and I could keep our planned visit to Karin and Lennart. Jonas and Antje left, and I stayed with Peter that night until about midnight—holding his hand, talking to him quietly about the decision, and absorbing the reality of the moment.

The next morning, Antje and I drove to Vittsjö to deliver a Christmas flower and visit with Karin and Lennart Johansson, an annual holiday tradition that Peter had started more than twenty years earlier and I had continued with the support of Antje and Fredrik. Lennart and Karin had been our neighbors and caretakers of the summerhouse until they retired and moved into the village a couple of years earlier. Our visit this year was brief and comforting for all of us. Karin and Lennart adored Peter and were heartbroken by the accident and the loss of his energy in their lives. This time we let them know that Peter was declining and we didn't expect him to recover. It was a sad, intimate moment with them.

This morning drive to visit Karin and Lennart was also a welcome quiet time for conversation with Antje, acknowledging the reality of these final days and thinking about the practical details of whom we wanted to contact and what else needed to be done.

Back at Ribbingska at 1:00 p.m., Jonas, his wife, Helena, and the four grandchildren, Sara, Anton, Fabian, and Theo, were at Peter's bedside to say their goodbyes. We shared hugs and the acknowledgment of how much it meant to have shared this time.

For the next two and a half days, I spent twelve to fifteen hours a day at Peter's side. Jonas and Katarina came by for a couple of hours in the mornings, allowing me a slow wake-up each day. Once in Peter's room, I pulled a chair next to his bed and reminded him that I was with him for the duration. The staff brought me food, and I took short breaks for coffee and to visit with others. Soon I was back with Peter, settling into the realization that this journey was coming to an end.

The memory of arriving at my father's hospital room moments after he died in 1970, as my mother stood by his side and raised her hand, softly uttering, "Oh, he's gone," has stayed with me for the fifty years since his death. I'd been in court that day facing a civil disobedience charge for interfering with a city construction project that had no minority workers. I had hurried to the hospital to let Dad know that the case was dismissed. He'd been upset about the charge, trying to understand why I had intentionally allowed myself to be arrested. I had reminded him that he'd always encouraged us to speak up for what we believed, and civil disobedience was an appropriate option. Now, arriving just a few minutes late, I had missed the opportunity for a final goodbye.

I felt content being with Peter on my own during these final hours. Despite the Swedish tradition of gathering on Christmas Eve, I wanted to stay with Peter. I sat holding his hand, watching him breathe, recalling shared memories. I reached out via email and telephone calls to my family in Minnesota and our friends on both continents to let them know the situation and to give them time to absorb this coming reality as well. I was comforted by their knowledge and support.

I recalled a conversation with the physical therapist on the neurology ward nine and a half years earlier. I commented to her that of all the possibilities Peter and I had considered for our final years together, a situation such as this had never occurred to us. She responded, "There is no one on this ward who has ever anticipated being here. If one could anticipate such a tragedy, it would be impossible to live each day. What makes it possible is that we face whatever situation confronts us when we open the door." At this moment I understood even more fully what she meant. This challenge was mine, and each day was a moment to share and to learn.

In the afternoon on Christmas Eve, as the nurse adjusted Peter's position in bed, he opened his eyes. I stood up so he could see me more easily and said, "Hi, Peter. Are you checking to see that I'm still here?" He whispered, "Ja." "I'm here with you until the end Peter. I love you so much. We've had a wonderful life together, and I'm grateful for every moment. I'm sorry you're suffering right now. I want you to know that it's okay to let go." A minute later his eyes closed. Minutes before the end, Peter opened his eyes once more—as if to say goodbye. I held his hand and quietly said, "Goodbye, Peter. I love you." He gave two or three small gasps and was gone.

A few hours earlier I had talked to my mother to give her an update. Now I phoned to let her know that Peter had died. Earlier in the day she had mentioned that my cousin Steve had called her with Christmas greetings, so she'd told him that Peter was in his final hours. I assured her that I would call Steve as well as my sister Marlys and Antje. Marlys would call our brothers and half sister.

Antje arrived at Ribbingska in twenty minutes, joining Jonas and me at Peter's bedside, sharing the sadness and relief. This had been Peter's home, and so much a part of me these past eight and a half years. Although Peter was not the same person I'd married thirty-one years ago, the strength of our bond gave me comfort and purpose to the end.

Jonas, Antje, and I sat together at Peter's bedside for half an hour, speaking little, absorbing the reality of the end. Jonas's wife came to accompany him home, and Antje and I decided to walk home as well. We chose a route past Stefan Holmström's house. Stefan was the first friend Peter had introduced me to in the summer of 1984. He lived in a historic house in central Lund where August Strindberg had lived when he wrote *Inferno*. The lights were on at Stefan's home, so I tapped on the window, and he invited us in. Stefan had visited Peter often during the years, including during these final days. We concluded the day sharing Peter stories and a glass of wine in the comfort of Stefan's kitchen.

The day following Peter's death, December 25, Antje and Fredrik and I shared our modest traditional Christmas Eve meal a day late. It was a quiet evening. We felt sadness and relief, and shared a range of anecdotes from the past nine years as well as our rich life together prior to the accident. I spent the following evening with Peter's children, grand-children, and great-grandchildren, sharing many wonderful memories of time with Peter. Theo, our youngest grandson, now a teenager, re-membered Peter picking him up from day care and sitting on the floor and playing with his friends until their parents arrived. All those young boys loved it when Theo's *farfar* spent time with them. It was classic Peter and a wonderful memory for Theo.

34

.\\\\\\\\\\\\\\\\\////,.

Leaving Sweden

At the time of Peter's death my February trip to Sweden had already been booked, as Peter's birthday celebration had become a tradition for the residents of Ward 1B as well as Peter's family and friends. Now during this period I would begin sorting and distributing art and furniture, determine the steps to be taken to begin the settlement of Peter's estate, plan for selling the apartment, transfer ownership of the summerhouse to Peter's children, and plan a memorial. I intended to maintain the schedule of two weeks in Sweden every five or six weeks for the coming few months, as I'd done for these past several years. The idea of continuing that practice gave me some comfort as I wandered through this process.

Arriving at Kastrup Airport on that early morning in February 2020 felt surreal. The motions were familiar, but for the first time in thirty-six years I was not coming to Sweden to be with Peter. From the winter of 1984, my journeys to Sweden had centered on him: at first I came to be with the man I was falling in love with, and then to share time with my husband, and for the past nine and a half years, to support the care of the person who had been my husband and now relied on me to be his loving guardian.

As she always did, Antje picked me up at the train station. I went through the motions of dropping my bags at my small flat and then joining her in her apartment for a visit and coffee. From then on, my old routines no longer applied. There were no updates about Peter's care, no plans for excursions or medical appointments—only plans to start packing up my things at the flat, as I anticipated putting it on the market in the coming months. After this two-week stay, I wouldn't be back in Sweden until April, as months before I had already booked a trip to New Zealand for March 2020—a trip I had discussed with Antje (who would need to spend more time with Peter) and with Peter (I always sought his support), recognizing my need for a break.

Peter's children and I would meet with the mortician and the attorney to begin the process of settling Peter's estate, review the options for his remains, and plan the memorial gathering. Peter had told me many times prior to 2010 that he wanted to be cremated, and that he wanted his ashes scattered at sea in Öresund (the strait between Sweden and Denmark), between Helsingborg, Sweden (where he'd grown up), and Helsingør, Denmark. He had also shared his wishes with his daughter, Katarina, and she and Jonas were very comfortable with that decision. Because of my previously planned trip to New Zealand, we agreed to wait until April 20 to hold the memorial gathering. An April date also offered the prospect of warmer, sunny weather.

I would sell the flat where I'd been living for eight years later in the spring, which would give me plenty of time to pack and move out when I was back for Peter's memorial. In the meantime, I packed up a few pieces of art and household things that would go to Washington. I would take care of everything else when I returned in April.

We could not have imagined what the world now knows—how everyone's plans for spring 2020 would change. We were making our plans in early February, just a few weeks prior to the world's recognition of Covid-19 and the subsequent disruption of global travel and large group gatherings for more than a year. International travel was curtailed the day I returned from New Zealand, which meant the memorial gathering and the scattering of Peter's ashes were postponed indefinitely. With so much uncertainty, it made no sense to put off the sale of the apartment, so I let go of my plan to sort through the memories it held. In each of my previous moves, I had observed a private ritual acknowledging the joys and sadness experienced in that home. That I would not be able to conduct this ritual upon leaving my Swedish home during such a profound period of my life made me deeply sad. As I had for many other parts of my final journey with Peter, I would look for other ways to fulfill this ritual.

Antje went through the apartment for me and sorted and packed my personal things, while Jonas and Katarina managed the distribution of furnishings, furniture, and artwork and prepared for the sale. I was grateful for the generosity of their efforts. During the nine and a half years I had settled in Lund, I had felt connected to the city in ways that Peter had always wanted for me. That it took such a tragedy and uprooting of our lives to reach this point was sad yet also profoundly uplifting. In this situation, I had developed a capacity for patience, empathy, and compassion that I hadn't known possible.

When I left Sweden in February 2020, I didn't imagine that I was leaving this home for the last time.

Epilogue

Peter's death on December 24, 2019, marked the end of an extraordinary journey, the second ending of our marriage, and a dramatic change in the rhythm of my personal life. For nine and a half years, I had divided my time each month between Washington and Sweden, a schedule I'd adopted as the outcome of Peter's accident became clear.

During our marriage Peter and I had discussed adjusting our lives to work from both countries so that we could spend more time together, but we could not envision a possibility that would not require radically changing our careers. Peter had tried to establish a consulting practice in the United States, but it was not to be. In my case, my skill set revolved around leadership roles, unrealistic in a society where I wasn't fluent in the language.

Expecting to build a relationship within the framework of two continents and two homes was wildly optimistic. Yet our intentionality in making it work resulted in a partnership that nurtured and guided me on many levels. I learned to listen better, to try harder to understand other points of view, to trust my own hesitations, and to effect change by taking action. Throughout my life, I have believed in the inherent value of diverse points of view. The life experiences that people of other cultures bring to conversations are essential to good decision making, and intentionality in ensuring the inclusion of such a range of perspectives has been fundamental to my approach to every leadership role I have assumed. My determination to uphold this belief was strengthened throughout my time with Peter and my immersion in his culture.

Positive relationships with close friends and colleagues have always been essential to my well-being. As a young, single woman engaging in feminist politics, starting a business, and later becoming a politician before Peter was in my life, friends and family provided the support and feedback that kept me grounded. Later, with Peter as my life partner, I found that those longtime friends, as well as friends I made during each new chapter of our journey, continued to enrich my life. Following Peter's injury, my network of friends, family, and work colleagues on both continents surrounded me with love and care that made that chapter bearable.

From my years as an elected official to my time in federal government management to the short period I spent in a corporate role before taking on the position of CEO of a growing nonprofit organization, the challenges and successes of each new experience added to my capacity for leadership. I could not have anticipated the life-changing event of August 12, 2010, or how my subsequent caretaking role would have a leadership component. Nor could I have imagined that by necessity I would create an early model of remote work and become a better leader as a result. I gained greater respect for the art of being patient. I became a better observer and learned to try to understand things beyond my personal bias rather than to judge. I came to recognize the role of advocacy far beyond the political version—in the day-to-day operations of the nursing home, up the chain to the administrator, and at times with the community bureaucracy. I experienced joy in small things, incredible anxiety when I felt Peter wasn't being treated well, and even resignation when my suggestions ultimately weren't accepted as the way forward. I learned to let go and watch—realizing that my perspective was affected by my fears for Peter, an unacknowledged sense of further loss, and my reluctance to recognize and accept the further decline in Peter's condition.

Peter's death required immediate attention to myriad details: clearing out his room at the nursing home, communicating with family and friends, making arrangements for a memorial, beginning the estate-settling process. I was also facing the end of my life in Sweden as it had been for nine and a half years. I had come to feel at home in Sweden on a deep level. Now, without being physically there each month focused on caring for Peter, I would be a visitor. The small apartment where I lived and the car I had driven would be sold. No longer would I need to track my days in Sweden to stay within the European Union's visitor limits.

I had arrived in Sweden just five days before Peter's death, scheduled to be there for an extended period over the Christmas and New Year's holidays. I stayed busy during those final days of 2019, aware that my feelings of sadness and loss were shifting. I had been grieving the loss of my husband for years now, but had also been focused on Peter's care. Ensuring the best care for him had given me strength and purpose. During those years, the changing realities of Peter's abilities and needs defined my own losses as well as my ongoing role. Now I was on my own.

I returned to Sweden in February 2020 on the ticket I purchased months earlier to be present for Peter's birthday. Peter's children and I began planning the memorial and tending to other matters of Peter's estate. However, because of the travel restrictions in force during the first years of the Covid-19 pandemic, a year and a half passed before I could return to Sweden and we could gather for a memorial and the scattering of Peter's ashes in Öresund in August 2021.

During my time in Sweden then, I visited family and friends and spent three weeks at our summerhouse. In the countryside I shared walks in the forest and pontoon evenings on the lake with friends; we picked vegetables and flowers from neighbors' gardens and berries from our garden. I picked flowers for the memorial from one neighbor's bountiful flower garden, then gathered wildflowers to scatter in Öresund with Peter's ashes.

The day of the memorial gathering was sunny and windy—so windy that the boat captain proposed that we take the boat out from a harbor farther south. We stayed with our plan to depart from Helsingborg harbor, and by the time we set out that afternoon, the wind had quieted. After waiting for a year and a half, we had a beautiful day for our final goodbye to Peter.

Four generations of Peter's family and several longtime friends boarded the boat that took us out into Öresund. The boat was idled directly out from the beach that Peter had enjoyed as a child—one of the spots he introduced me to during my first summer in Sweden. We lowered the urn with his ashes, and each of us dropped flowers and said a personal goodbye. Back at the harbor, we gathered at a restaurant where Peter had worked as a young man, where we watched a video montage of photographs produced by our grandsons and shared stories. Friends offered brief remembrances, Jonas and Katarina gave a final toast to their dad, and I shared a few memories and reflections on our life together. It was a modest send-off for a person with an infectious and generous spirit, whose final years were beyond anything we could have imagined. At that moment, several of us shared the deep sense that Peter would have enjoyed the gathering.

Eleven years earlier, I began my journey in Sweden without Peter as my guide but with Peter as my focus. Now I was in Sweden on my own, with no caretaking role and no home base, for a final goodbye to Peter. A visitor, yet feeling infinitely closer to Sweden and my Swedish family and friends, and considerably more comfortable than I had been at the beginning of this journey.

Acknowledgments

I spent much of my adult life believing that I was a poor writer despite having kept a daily journal for more than forty years. At times I did consider writing a book about my years as lieutenant governor of Minnesota, to document that historical experience, but life circumstances interrupted further consideration of such a project. Then after the death of my husband, Peter, my dear friend Pauline Boss encouraged me to write the story of my final years with him. When I shared the first fifty pages with her, her response affected my writing trajectory in a profound way. Her enthusiasm about my writing and her view that I needed to write my whole story so that the final chapter with Peter would have context were instrumental in helping me let go of my self-doubt as a writer and allowed me to thoroughly enjoy the nearly two-year process of writing my story.

I am especially grateful to Betty Soppelsa, my former NAFSA colleague and a consummate editor, and friend, who helped me shape the original manuscript, define and name chapters, and then do it again on the next draft. She was the first to read and reread sections, and for months she showed up regularly with feedback and encouragement. Linda Winslow, an amazing producer of television news, and friend, also read the first draft, then helped me reframe the story before I ventured into writing the second draft. Without their wisdom, enthusiasm, and support, there would not have been a manuscript.

Nan Skelton, a gifted public policy activist who served in the Perpich–Johnson administration in Minnesota, helped me recall details of our efforts to create an administration-wide focus on children.

Karen Desnick, a force of nature, guided me in search of a publisher, researching possibilities and identifying friends who opened doors. For years, Patrick Coleman had encouraged me to write about my years in state government. As I faced the challenge of finding a publisher, he was generous with perspective and encouragement.

I owe many thanks to my family—my sister Marlys and brothers Wayne and Warren, my most special aunt, Ruthie Nelson, and my sister-in-law, Antje Frankel Molt—for their unwavering support through a life of unexpected adventure and unimaginable personal crisis. Their love and support made my journey possible.

To my mom and dad—I wish you both could have shared this moment. The values, guidance, love, and confidence you instilled in me, from arranging those first piano lessons to supporting my education, made so much possible. I am especially grateful to my mother for supporting my entrepreneurial and political journeys in both practical and emotional ways, and, in the past few years, for encouraging me to write my story.

Peter, the spirit and love that you gave me for the years we had made this writing journey possible. Your love, insights, encouragement, and ideas expanded my world and brought me great joy.

I now understand clearly why authors are so grateful to their editors. This book would not exist without Erik Anderson. When Erik first took the time to visit with me about this project, he shared ideas and identified challenges in finding the threads of my patchwork life that would produce a cohesive narrative. Over the next several months, without a commitment to publish, Erik read my manuscript and gave me insightful, challenging, and enthusiastic feedback; he then read and gave me further suggestions on the subsequent versions, until he was ready to recommend the book for publication. I enjoyed every minute of working with Erik, and I am grateful that he saw the potential in that early manuscript and stayed with me. Our work together has enabled me to call myself a writer. And as this project has proceeded through the publishing process, I have been profoundly grateful for the guidance of

Laura Westlund, managing editor at the University of Minnesota Press. Her perspective has strengthened the manuscript and my own confidence. I am also grateful to have experienced copy editor Judy Selhorst's amazing attention to detail, which reduced redundancies and strengthened the message. Finally, Alan Williams, a NAFSA colleague, came to my rescue on several occasions, sharing my screen to ensure that various edited versions of the manuscript were saved appropriately.

Marlene M. Johnson was Minnesota's first woman lieutenant governor, serving in Governor Rudy Perpich's administration from 1983 until 1991. She led a public relations and communications company in St. Paul and was executive director and CEO of NAFSA: Association of International Educators, as well as maintaining leadership roles in the Minnesota Women's Political Caucus, the National Association of Women Business Owners, and the Minnesota Women's Campaign Fund.